anchorbooks

THE BEST OF
ANIMAL ANTICS

As Selected by
Anchor Books Editors

Animal Antics Volume I first published in Great Britain in 2003 by Anchor Books
Animal Antics Volume II first published in Great Britain in 2004 by Anchor Books
Animal Antics Volume III first published in Great Britain in 2004 by Anchor Books
Animal Antics Volume IV first published in Great Britain in 2004 by Anchor Books
This compilation first published in 2005 by Anchor Books

Anchor Books, Remus House, Coltsfoot Drive,
Woodston, Peterborough, PE2 9JX
Tel (01733) 898102
www.forwardpress.co.uk

SB ISBN 1 84418-389-0

Foreword

Picture cute fluffy bunnies haphazardly hopping across lush emerald lawns, leaving a trail of crushed plants manifesting half-eaten leaves in their wake. Picture colourful budgies twittering cheerfully on perches, or exuberantly showering sitting rooms with seed from their cages. Or how about purring kittens rubbing their owner's legs in serene contentment, and excited puppies shredding the mail long before it has been read by the addressees.

Pets come in all shapes and sizes; however dedication, loyalty, love and affection are attributes they all share in abundance. Cosseted and pampered by indulgent owners, they have become welcome additions to our families; enhancing and enriching our everyday lives in the process.

Due to the tremendous response that our *Animal Antics* anthologies always receive, and the vast importance that pets play in our lives, Forward Press have compiled an exquisite collection of poetry to compliment the series. Incorporating the cream of all four anthologies, *The Best of Animal Antics* is crammed with humorous anecdotes, affectionate tributes, and heart-warming versification, giving an insight into their animated and often chaotic lives.

This enjoyable read will entertain and enthral animal lovers time and time again.

A-Z of Authors

Name	No.	Name	No.	Name	No.
Edward B Evans	61	Glenice Siddall	224	Jackie Sutton	177
Eileen C Hersey	194	Glenice Siddall	365	Jacqueline Donnelly	202
Elaine Hicklin	183	Glenys Harris	82	James Rasmusson	270
Elaine Langford	260	Gordon Forbes	313	Jan Ross	367
Elizabeth Arnold	170	Gordon Paul Charkin	147	Jane Earley	124
Elizabeth-Anne Paterson	161	Gordon Paul Charkin	253	Jane Francis	181
Ellen Chambers	61	Gordon Paul Charkin	321	Jane Hill	84
Ellen Chambers	142	Grace Christian	327	Jane Lynch	92
Ellen Chambers	338	Grace Whyte	33	Jane Lynch	205
Elsie Corrigan	75	Graham Dow (11)	60	Jane Margaret Isaac	150
Elyse Lake	261	Graham K A Walker	160	Janet Freeman	219
Emma Bate	192	Graham K A Walker	345	Janet Howden	97
Emma Owen (14)	195	Gwen Gibson	191	Janet Mitchell Treharne	40
Emmanuel Omoro	227	Hannah Elysé	196	Janet Snowsill	183
Enfys Evans	290	Hannah Moore	90	Jayne Walker	21
Eric Ferris	236	Hayley Briant (10)	163	Jean Bailey	300
Estella Reynolds	56	Hayley Jayes	306	Jean Bradbury	351
Ethel Wakeford	171	Heather Dunnfox	253	Jean Mason	49
Evelyn Westwood	243	Heather Dunn-Fox	342	Jean Mason	310
Evelyn Wooffitt	168	Helen Strangwige	272	Jean P McGovern	141
F Fletcher	79	Helen Weedon	62	Jean Stretch	31
F George	203	Helena Henning	285	Jeanette Gaffney	203
F R Smith	239	Helga Dharmpaul	248	Jenny Hitchen	178
F R Smith	366	Hilary Jill Robson	235	Jenny Hitchen	343
Faye Knowles (14)	131	Hilary Tozer	67	Jessica Copland	220
Fergus Condron	351	Hilary Tozer	294	Jill Richards	320
Frances M Gorton	26	Holly Chubb (15)	77	Jo Brookes	37
Frank Murri	130	Ian W Robinson	278	Jo Lodge	228
G Binns	184	Irene Beattie	340	Joan C Igesund	190
G Nutbeem	117	Isobel Laffin	15	Joan Egre	283
G Nutbeem	144	Isobel Laffin	282	Joan Igesund	295
G Semmens	185	Isobel Laffin	298	Joan Jones	76
G Semmens	372	Ivor Emlyn Percival	313	Joan M Jones	201
G White (14)	269	Ivy Lott	256	Joan Prentice	58
Gemini Cherry	226	J A Berisha	76	Joan Prentice	122
Gemma White (14)	354	J A Berisha	355	Joan Prentice	224
Gemmaine Baughurst (15)	78	J Bate	182	Joan Prentice	366
Georgina Biggs	337	J F Grainger	358	Jocqueline Jones	244
Georgina Slape	160	J Grainger	230	Jodie Grant	167
Geraldine Laker	229	J H Russell	343	Joe Coop	129
Geraldine Laker	322	J Howling Smith	289	John Belcher	241
Geraldine McMullan Doherty	278	J L Holden	215	John Worthington	100
Gerry Concah	114	J Lanigan	127	Jonathan Pegg	180
Gerry Concah	143	J Munro	373	Joyce Dobson	97
Gill Smith	25	J Stewart	43	Joyce Haigh	175
Gillian Humphries	234	J Thorpe	128	Joyce M Jones	104
Gillian L Wise	301	J Van Dyk-Harrison	121	Joyce M Woods	277
Gillian McKinley	27	J Waddell	246	Judie Archer	174
Gillian McKinley	335	Jackie Heath	324	Judy Studd	328
Gladys Baillie	330	Jackie Heath (15)	266	Julie Knappett	307
Glenda V Llewellyn	209	Jackie S Brooks	142	Julie Munro	69

Name	No.	Name	No.	Name	No.
Julie Roberts	138	Lisa Pearson	184	Mary Elliott	295
Julie Roberts	286	Liz Gibbons	124	Mary Neill	158
Juliet Marshall	220	Lorna Flint	35	Mary Shovlin	245
Juliet Marshall	293	Lorna G Sim	148	Maureen Morris	223
June F Allum	138	Lorraine Beckham	87	Maureen Morris	335
June Melbourn	242	Louise Farren	177	Maureen Roberts	314
June Toms	163	Louise Holt	240	Maureen Westwood O'Hara	73
K Cooke	25	Lyn Sandford	119	Maurice Gubbins	237
K M Waddington	166	Lyn Sandford	222	May Ward	246
K Titmus	164	Lyn Sandford	323	May Ward	332
K Titmus	329	Lynda Bullock	133	Melika Gumush (13)	272
K Townsley	86	Lynda Peterson	64	Michael D Bedford	239
K Townsley	319	Lynne Walden	312	Michael McNulty	200
Kal George	22	M Carr	339	Michael Ward	208
Karen Grover	48	M Dixon	372	Michele Amos	182
Karen Hodgetts	262	M G Clements	85	Michelle Luetchford	130
Karen Holm	305	M G Scott	149	Mick Gayfer	268
Karen Van Gemeren	51	M Hinton	175	Mick Nash	337
Karin Dyer	133	M J Banasko	18	Mikayla Bruce (14)	297
Kath Barber	192	M J Banasko	355	Moira Jean Clelland	214
Kath Williamson	291	M J Matthews	71	Monica McNamee	364
Kathleen Stokes	375	M Lawson	110	Moya Muldowney (15)	291
Kathryn Newbrook	153	M McNamee	247	Muriel Rosamond Harris	306
Katie Ireson	280	M Sam Dixon	17	N J Brocks	352
Katie-Leanne Findlay	93	Maggie Hickinbotham	347	N Lemel	363
Kaye Townsend	106	Maggie Strong	172	Nancy Elliott	222
Kayleigh Brookes (15)	304	Mandy Jayne Moon	236	Natalie Kennedy	152
Keith L Powell	111	Mandy Jayne Moon	364	Natalie Plows	304
Kirsty Lewis	34	Mandy Keay	49	Nick Butler	149
Kram	169	Mandy Preston	187	Nicky Pitchers	158
Kristian & Victoria Haynes	264	Margaret Doherty	216	Nicole Woollard	132
L Brant	128	Margaret Doherty	341	Nikki Archer (14)	85
L Frost	102	Margaret Gleeson Spanos	165	Nikohl Medley	176
L Haynes	56	Margaret Hibbert	154	Norma Flair Challis	162
L Haynes	293	Margaret Kinshott	107	Norman S Brittain	39
Laura Chaplin	258	Margaret Upson	368	Norman S Brittain	334
Laura Marshall	66	Margaret Webster	11	Oriana	257
Leanne Thompson	101	Marguerite Holloway	70	Owen Edwards	259
Leanne Thompson	326	Maria Ann Cahill	68	P Brewer	169
Lianne Bunn	279	Maria-Christina	189	P Brewer	350
Libi Garner	33	Marion Jones	31	Pablo Rose	162
Libi Garner	274	Marion Jones	332	Pam Newman	180
Linda Ann McConnell	283	Marion Thacker	47	Pam Toth	53
Linda Ann McConnell	347	Marion Thacker	334	Pam Wardlaw	16
Linda Arnold	296	Marjorie Beaven	28	Pamela Hanover	279
Linda Constantatos	243	Marjorie Chapman	131	Pat Hunter	94
Linda Finch	288	Mark Jenkins	252	Pat Hunter	361
Linda Finch	357	Mark Strong	314	Patricia Gittins	55
Linda Roberts	324	Martyn Dickinson	136	Patricia Mackie	300
Linda Spendley	123	Mary A Shovlin	135	Patricia Summers	321
Lisa Booth	98	Mary E Barker	186	Patrick Davies	248

THE BEST OF

ANIMAL ANTICS

The Poems

£1,000 Winner Margaret Webster Shares Her Joy...

How do I feel about winning the £1,000 prize?

Over the moon. I was simply amazed and so flattered that people would consider my poem worth winning. I love writing; poetry, stories - even thank you letters! My inspiration for the poem 'Meal Time Etiquette' came from watching our little cat Nas (no added sugar) playing with the remains of a pork chop. She is all white in colour, but has behaviour patterns of a magpie; hoarding treasures she has 'found', behind the settee. I have four children, now aged 14-20, but an exasperated 'don't' is never far from my lips. It all came together one afternoon when I sat down for a quiet minute, with my pencil and notepad.

How will I spend the money?

Very easily! Some has already gone on a new washing machine, to combat those gravy stains. Food treats seemed appropriate, so while we had pizza and wine, Nas enjoyed a lamb chop of her own. She still ate it on the floor! With the bulk of the money we will probably have a weekend away to see some bigger cats in a Safari Park - we may come back with a lion for a pet.

An Anchor Books Anthology

Meal-Time Etiquette

Don't play with your food, Nas;
you'll make a mess on the floor.
That chop is past redemption -
I've told you twice before.
It might be fun to toss it
and catch it in the air,
but it leaves a nasty gravy stain
on the dining room chair.
I know you like to chew it,
and exercise your teeth,
but not behind the bookcase;
the hoover won't go underneath!
I'll find the bone next weekend
in some secret rendezvous;
like the last piece of burger
that 'escaped' into my shoe.
We love you when you're playful;
having a kitten like you is great,
but don't play with your food, Nas;
just keep it on the plate.

Margaret Webster

Faithful Max

*(In loving memory of Max
For Shirley and Colin)*

Your faithful baby Maxi
Looks down from up above
He gave abiding happiness
And unconditional love
He sees you now from skies ablue
His big brown eyes still gaze at you
He thanks you for the love you gave
He's gone ahead the way to pave.

So in your heart each memory save
He's happy that you were so brave
So when you think of Maxi
He plays in fields of green
He has you there beside him
You're 'heard and you are seen'.

Angela Maria Wilson

The Final Curtain

I see the tears roll down his cheeks,
From sad and loving eyes.
I feel his hands' firm, gentle touch,
I hear his sobs and sighs.

He strokes my soft, brown, furry head
With warm and trembling hands.
He tries to reassure me, but
My legs can barely stand.

I remember past and younger years,
Long walks across the moors.
Resting at my master's feet,
His sleeping grunts and snores.

All through my life I've served him,
I've run to his every call.
I've loved each sharing moment,
His life has been my all.

I cannot bear to leave him,
I know that soon I'll die.
I lick his warm, soft, tender hands,
The vet and he both cry.

How will he manage when I'm gone?
Will he pine and fade away?
Perhaps another dog . . . a puppy?
Would help him fill each day.

I watch my master's loving face,
His tears fall on my paws.
I feel the release of the needle . . .
My heart will beat no more.

Dennis Young

An Anchor Books Anthology

Runner Up

Sausage Dog Serenade

(To my best friends, Sophie and Candy)

We walk together, you and I, in summer's warming sun,
'Cross fields of ripening crops, so much living to be done.
Beside the river, we slowly wander, rabbits scurry from our view,
Bees go about their business upon the flowers of multi-hue.

We stop and sit and wonder at the beauty that we find,
All, it seems, put there for us, to occupy our mind.
I see you both in calm repose, your little eyes shut tight,
Sleeping on that riverbank, in the dazzling summer light.

So happy, filled with innocence, you seem to see me as your guide,
Through the world in which we live, we're together, side by side.
I love you both, you're more than friends, you depend on me so much,
I feel the love that you return, it's in your every touch.

A nudge, a wet nose on my leg, a lick that says it all,
Curling up beside me in a furry canine ball.
You never leave me, always there, no matter what the day may bring,
My little dachshund buddies, how your praises I could sing.

They say that dogs may have no soul, but how can this be true?
For love is surely an expression of emotion, and it's love I feel
from you.
Your love is unconditional, for me you're always there,
You ask so little in return, your love's beyond compare.

At night as I lie sleeping, and the world of dreams may fill my head,
You're both still there, in close company, reposing on my bed!
I think perhaps that in your minds, you're just the same as me,
Not dogs and human, just loving friends, I love you and you love me.

We share so much together, you seem to sense if I'm not well,
But when the tables are reversed, it's sometimes hard for me to tell.
You're sausage dogs extraordinaire, nothing ever could replace,
The simple joys you bring to me, none could take your place.

Brian L Porter

Runner
Up

An Anchor Books Anthology

Lady

The little puppy I carried home,
Wrapped in a blanket warm,
Has now grown into a beautiful dog,
Who is not devoid of charm.
She isn't a pure bred,
She won't win a prize,
But who cares when you look
In her lovely brown eyes.

She brings me her ball
When I'm too tired to play,
'Doing housework is nothing
To what I do all day.'
At least that's what I think
My Lady would say.

She's dug up a bone,
Had words with the cat,
And shaken the stuffing out of her toy rat.
Had a roll in the mud,
And ate a few snails,
And what else besides, my stomach just quails.

She rolls on the floor,
Her legs in the air,
At aerobics she certainly has a fine flair.
I do wish that I was as supple as she,
But I'm over seventy,
And she's only three.

Isobel Laffin

Runner Up

For Bhaji

It's been a while.
I worry that the months between -
so many biscuits crunched, rabbits chased, balls flung by other hands -
may have chased all recollection of me
from that big, daft head of yours.
Not so: your joy, like mine, is immediate and boundless
if tinged, I fancy, by a hint of criticism.
I throw a stick,
you run to fetch
then bark indignantly as I sit down
suddenly weak-kneed with nostalgia.
There are no access rights to dogs.
I take what I can get,
what fits into this gypsy life of mine.
My camera clicks incessantly, racing against time,
clumsy attempts to capture the day's grace
as if a photograph could do you justice.
Later I will play back in my head images of you,
wave-dancer extraordinaire
streaking across the bay at the water's edge.
A last blessing - your head, warm on my lap
reminding me that love and trust
are occasionally unconditional -
then it's time to take you home.
You trot off happily, no backward glance
leaving me, red-eyed, with only the bones of memory
to lick and gnaw,
a stubborn sucking at the last remains of a dream long dead.

Pam Wardlaw

An Anchor Books Anthology

Of Mice And Milk

When cats curl and yawn
To snooze and sleep,
What dreams may come
To tickle feet?

When whiskers twitch
Do they pursue
That squeak of mouse
Yet out of view?

When tails do flick
So swift and fast,
Are they pouncing through
The dewy grass?

Or when snoozing there
As soft as silk,
Do they dream of saucers
Charg'd with milk?

M Sam Dixon

The Model

She walks in a way
Designed to please
Slim and seductive
Her aim is to tease

Sensual and sleek
She models the fur
Posing her limbs
Eyes made to allure

Arrogantly she stretches
A pretence to make
Photographers surround her
Their pictures to take

Awed by her beauty
All men want to touch
She ignores their attentions
It means nothing much

Should we condemn her
As she lays on the mat
Or do we accept
That she's only a cat?

A Mannion

Sad Times

It's funny how my mind went blank, when in his eyes I stared
And only later did I think, on all the times we'd shared
They said he didn't have much time, the tumour's gotten worse
I heard words like 'inoperable' . . . now I'm waiting on the worst.

I remember when he was so young, the day we brought him home
How everyone did make a fuss, all the 'oohs' and 'aahs' intoned
We'd put him in his bed at night and before you closed the door
He'd be dreaming in the 'land of nod' to the tune of a gentle snore

I recalled a summer's garden, when we'd chased a rolling ball
With his little legs and no control, how he'd tumble and he'd fall
With eyes so brown and clear, with sandy hair but short
Made easy friends with everyone, for he was a gentle sort

Who always had a sense of fun, yet I'd never seen him fear
I'd turn around and there he was . . . like magic just appear
He was both true and faithful, and he learned his lessons well
And though he was no Einstein, he was clever you could tell

I thought upon such times we'd shared, times both laughed and cried
And then it was he closed his eyes, just slipped away . . . and died!
My wife and children shed their tears, but I refused to grieve
For the blessing that had been his life and the memories he did leave

We'll miss him and his friendship, those memories will not dim
Of big brown eyes and sorry looks, though gone . . . we still sense him
Only now the times remembered . . . with happiness and joy
Midst the echo of a barking dog and cries of 'Come on, boy'

I believe God waits in paradise, makes a place for me and you
And as He was a carpenter, then maybe . . . maybe kennels too
For the sixteen years we'd loved him, he'd earned this and his keep
It's funny how my mind went blank . . . when they put my dog to sleep!

M J Banasko

An Anchor Books Anthology

A Puppy Called Basil

I rescued a puppy called Basil
He looked all forlorn and thin
My heart ruled my head when I saw him
So I took the poor blighter in.

I gave him my old Whitney blanket
Tried settling down by the hearth
But I could tell Basil was thinking
Yeah mate, you're having a laugh.

He yelped till three in the morning
The noise went right through my head
There was only one thing for it
I took Basil into my bed.

It put an end to his whining
And he slept for and hour or two
Then I woke to his licks and his barking
And a duvet all covered in poo.

It's six o'clock in the morning
My duvet's been thrown in the bin
We're sharing my old Whitney blanket
But I'm not sharing Basil's wry grin.

Now don't get me wrong, I adore him
It really was love at first sight
But I'm gonna sleep by the fire
And Basil can have my room tonight.

Trudy Simpson

Runner Up

The Horse Whisperer

Come closer
bend down
and lend me your ear,
I have
a secret
I want you to hear.
I been a bad pony
just wanted some fun
so I bit the cat
to see if she'd run.
I chased the chickens
all round the yard,
their feathers were flying
I chased them so hard.
I got into the tack room
ate one or two rugs,
kicked over the dustbins
gave the bridles some tugs.
Oh it was heaven
to see the dust rise
as I demolished the straw pile
and helped feed bins capsize.
Come nearer and listen
as I whisper my crimes,
I been a bad pony
    was it your fault,
        or mine?

Dorothy Webb

Poppy's Ping-Pong

Poppy plays ping-pong
all about the house,
upstairs and downstairs
she thinks she's chasing a mouse.

In and out the kitchen,
down a flight of stairs,
Poppy plays ping-pong
under all the chairs.

Peter Morriss

Why Do You Sit Standing On Your Tail, Thomas?

Why do you stand on your tail, Thomas?
Is it a comfort to you, Thomas?
Does it feel warm and safe, Thomas?
Is that why you stand on your tail, Thomas?

This tail that is long, sleek and yours, Thomas
Is it that it makes you feel secure, Thomas?
The tail that no other cat has, Thomas
Is that why you sit standing on your tail, Thomas?

Carole A Cleverdon

My Sandi Crossed Over The Rainbow Bridge

You struggled to make your last journey
You crawled it in your pain
So you could lie down under yonder bush
It was to be the last steps you ever took

But it seemed to be so important
And I now wonder why
Did you need to find infinity with nature
Where you lay down to die?

Though I took you from that spot you chose
I tried to make you live on
But maybe our medical know-how
Will never know, better than you, when the time has come

You will never be forgotten
You touched so many lives and hearts
You were the best friend I ever could wish for
And every day I miss you and hate us being apart

I know that you are waiting for me to join you up above
Sometimes I feel your presence as your spirit sends its love
You are still watching over us my darling and I feel you are close by
Some bonds cannot be broken by death and like me, you cannot say goodbye

Jayne Walker

Green Eyes

Green eyes beam by the flowing stream,
A distant dog does bark,
Aware eyes seek a hunter's prize,
She's a cat that knows her part,
She jumps in the air with a knowing glare,
She knows a trick or two,
She can catch whatever she needs if she has to,
She stands in the torch light,
Fur like gold,
Eyes wild and green,
She has all the mystic a cat should have,
To her name she's true,
She'll disappear in front of your eyes
Then reappear right by your side,
Merlin is small and thin maybe,
Yet in darkness she knows more than me . . .

D May

King Of The Castle

He roams around
In every room,
With a certain inquisitive mind of his own.
Excitement happens
From every new thing,
And does he like everyone?
Well, not quite!
Small he may be,
But king of the castle,
And only the best will do,
What you have he requires too,
Like a child weeping for a toy?
Well, almost!

Kal George

An Anchor Books Anthology

On His Last Legs

When Kipper died I was full of woe,
He left an empty place,
The time had come for him to go,
I missed his doggie face.

Then we spotted Scampy,
Who rather resembled Kip,
No longer the place was empty -
Where Kipper used to sit.

Scampy made himself at home,
Claimed old Kipper's ball.
Playfully tossing his rubber bone,
But the years were to take their toll.

Soft and cuddly, incredibly tame,
Like a tired old man with a pipe -
Rheumaticly slow with the passage of time,
Yet visibly able to cope.

Alas! He got the occasional flea,
So had to be sprayed and bathed -
Which often made him shake or sneeze,
Then everyone would laugh.

He used to bark at hedgehogs,
They weren't his cup of tea,
Even certain other dogs -
Could be an enemy.

But soon he'd have to go to sleep,
It was the kindest thing,
One more cuddle, one last peep,
To say goodbye to him . . .

Wendy Watkin

Goliath The Goldfish

What's reddish-gold and no trouble?
It's Goliath the goldfish blowing his bubble.
He rules the tank night and day,
But he's no bully for he loves to give way.

There's plenty of room for all to swim.
The smaller fish are not afraid of him,
But he's exceedingly big as you can see
And attention-getting is his speciality.

He does all this without a sound
And loves to swim upside down.
He kamikazes into the pebbles below
Then floats upward, strongly so.

He's not overfed, just much fatter,
To be in charge, size does matter.
So Goliath will always be a wonder,
Our princely pet from a world down under.

Christian Moore

Companion

Tender and tranquil, with a queenly grace
Empathy and endearment on such a wise face
Sagacious, but scampish when the need does arise
Sensitive and soft-hearted with angel-like eyes
Idyllically loving, irresistible, sublime
Charismatic, comely, heavenly, divine,
Adoringly affectionate, and *Tessica* is mine.

Angela Jones

An Anchor Books Anthology

Terrierific Walk

A twitch of the nose,
Ears suddenly drawn,
An exciting new smell,
On the wind is borne.

Tail's now erect,
And nose in the air,
They start to move off,
And hunt as a pair.

The movement more urgent,
Now nose to the ground,
They're both in the bushes,
Searching around.

Now in the thicket,
And well out of view,
Just a movement of branches,
To give us a clue.

They suddenly emerge,
And back they run,
Both with tails wagging,
You can see they had fun.

K Cooke

Sonnet For Angus

Our Angus is a robot toy,
he's made of electronic bits
and brings us lots and lots of joy.
We ask him for our favourites;
when we shout out 'karate chop'
he sits right back and waves his
arms.
He walks off until we shout 'stop'!
He'll dance (among his many
charms).
He kicks his pink and shiny ball,
and keeps an eye on where it goes.
While if by chance he takes a fall
he gets back up and shakes his
nose.
Yes, Angus is the perfect pet.
He needs no taking to the vet.

Gill Smith

My Four-Legged Friend

Who gives me such love
Never reproach
My constant companion
Fast asleep on the couch?

Who sits by my side
Watching TV
But when she gets bored
Climbs onto my knee?

Who runs to the door
When I turn the key?
'Where have you been?'
She questions me.

Who creeps out in the night
Only a shadow in view
Hunting for a mouse
Or a tiny shrew?

Who finds it great fun
High up in the trees
Stalking a bird
Whom she loves to tease?

Who never answers me back
As I am the boss!
But a flick of her tail
Lets me know she's quite cross.

Who is this creature
So precious to me?
My four-legged fried
Who drapes over my knee.

Her name - *Jemima, my puss*.

Frances M Gorton

An Anchor Books Anthology

Always There, Always True

You're always there,
in my life. When
I have a tear coming
from my eye, you lay
your head upon my knee,
and you put a great
big smile on my face.

And all you ask for
from me is warmth,
love and care, so
thank you for the
years so far, and the
many years ahead
of love and care we share.

I know I can always
count on you, my
faithful friend,
always there, always true.

Gillian McKinley

Harry Potter

A little ball of fluff
White and palest grey
Watching him at night-time
Just brightens up my day

He swings along the bars
And runs around his wheel
He looks at me with trusting eyes
And my love for him is real

I worried when I got him
Thought the cats might try to bite
But I didn't need to be concerned
They gave in without a fight

I called him Harry Potter
I thought it had a real nice ring
His antics make me happy
And he's such a magic little thing!

Bernadette Mottram

Rescue Dog

Coat of liver brown burnished
With bronze and copper
Adorned with white splashes,
White freckled ankle socks.

Round amber eyes
Reflect a soul of curiosity,
Humour, endless affection,
Spirit of adventure.

Half-tail, half-feathered,
Rarely rests from wagging,
Displays your love for life,
Excitement, pleasure.

The darker side -
A past best forgotten,
Legacy of nervousness
Slowly wearing away.

Rescue dog, see you blossom,
Return our love a thousand-fold.

Rosamund McCullain

Lines For Charlie

Carefree walks along a Dutch canal
by the Nunnery - where Frisians stand.
Past mansions of a lost golden age,
boats net-curtained, flower pots in rows.

Beside the dark Seine, we glimpsed the Pope.
You ran in bright meadows in the Alps.
In Vareggio we gazed out to sea
my thoughts were of Shelley, not of you!

In Bellagio you flirted and charmed.
Then in Baden Baden you slept on silk.
Remember Rheims - the chill champagne cave,
and Nice where we shared bouillabaisse?

Cruel September is still the saddest month,
faded rose petals on a sunburnt lawn.
Herbaceous border stabbed with a drunken
stake where memory and love lie intertwined.

Marjorie Beaven

An Anchor Books Anthology

Star

Hand in paw
As we nestle into dreamland
Amidst plump pillows.
Your sea lion eyes
Growing heavy with sleep,
Your contented sighs
Coming from deep
Within that white, furry belly
Covered in whorls of fluff,
That endless stroking
Has twisted into tufts,
Your fox-like tail drums me
A goodnight upon the bed,
Upon my chest
You rest your sleepy head,
Your tail beats slower,
A soothing metronome,
Guiding us into slumber
In this happy human/canine home.
Amidst plump pillows
We snore into dreamland
Paw in hand.

Stephen McMurray

Does He Know?

Woken up by a sweet lick
on the face, it's Baloo.
It's snowing outside,
so I take him out to play.
It's freezing on the snowy hills
but Baloo wants to play.
First I was shivering cold,
until I looked at Baloo's face,
my heart warmed, he lit up my day,
but does he know how he lights my life?
I walk him home, his tail swishes from side to side,
I don't need sun on a summer's day
cos I've got Baloo by my side.

Tara Harris (13)

Buster

He's daft, he's dizzy; dopey too,
Just like a monkey in a cage.
Wilful, and very loveable.
He's a big, strong dog,
Incredibly soft!

He gallops around like a horse,
Bounding in and out of the trees,
He leaps about, he's full of fun.
Then: laid on the rug,
Tired out, fast asleep!

He came to us when I was sad,
So I had to look after him.
I walked with him for many miles.
He'd be at my side.
My true, faithful pet.

He has his faults, so do we all.
He's been known to be in trouble.
Then he gives you that doleful look
That says, 'Aren't I good?'
Oh, those sad brown eyes!

But he is a good, loyal friend,
Who will always be there for me.
His head resting upon my knees,
Hair on my carpet.
Muddy paw prints too!

Sarah Robinson

An Anchor Books Anthology

Jake

Not just a dog, my special friend,
You're always by my side.
Your presence brings me so much joy,
Through life's uncertain times.

What would I do without you,
Your head upon my knee?
I love you Jake, so very much,
And I'm so glad you love me.

When I'm sad and feeling down,
And cannot find my way,
Your laughing eyes, your smiley face,
Bring sunshine to my day.

We share no greater pleasure,
Than a walk, a game or three.
As long as we're together,
Me with you and you with me.

Jean Stretch

Muffin

My boy Muffin's a lovely boy
When we go walking he jumps for joy
Over the fields freedom is found
What's more pleasing for any hound
Drinking from the river, slowing when he tires
Rolling in the cows' muck, dashing under wires
Making friends with all he meets
Be they human or canine
My boy Muffin loves his walks
And I'm so glad he's mine

Marion Jones

Dear Shep

What a tiny scrap you were dear Shep, when I first set eyes on you.
Head tilted to one side looking up at me as if to say,
'please take me home and love me'.

Those soulful eyes of deepest brown, seemed to plead
'don't leave me here, for I am all alone, the others have
found a good and loving home'.

That's how it all began, my dear and faithful friend who
became my shadow, always by my side, making me laugh,
bringing joy to a sad and lonely life.

Our outings to the park, both fleet of paws and feet, as we ran
side by side. Your joyous bark as you would chase after a much-loved
ball, scampering amongst the leaves of green, and brown and gold.

Walking along a sun-drenched beach on golden shifting sand.
Playing at the water's edge, shaking the water from your coat,
the droplets shining in the sun.

The first time that you saw the snow falling down from a leaden sky,
how you made us laugh, dear Shep, as you rolled over and over
in sheer delight. The warmth of the fire as we sat reliving the events
of yet another perfect day.

But the years have passed my beloved pet, we have seen the seasons
come and go, and know so well the joy, that love can bring.
Your black silky coat, my golden hair now threaded with grey.

Back from our walk, slow and sedate, no longer fleet of paws and feet.
It's time to rest, and yes, to dream of when we were young,
your faithful head resting upon my slippered feet.

Carole Chignell

An Anchor Books Anthology

Tale Of Courting

'Off my patch,' said Puss to Alex,
'this territory is mine,
your presence causes vex.'
Intruder arched his creamy
back with cold blue stare, sat stiff,
proud, gazed around, ignored Black's glare.
She is not a bad-looking puss,
ran through his mind, *could be a nice mate*
if so inclined. He eyed sleek, black fur,
green eyes glow, *I know*
I will be alright if I go slow,
of course she has a split in her left ear,
this marrs her beauty quite a lot I fear.
'*Get off my land!*' Tabby hissed,
not in the least to be kissed.
'I only came to say hello, now you're
asking me to go?'
'Yes, off you go, you chocolate cream,
your symmetrical perfection makes me scream.
Whoever heard of a blue-eyed cat?
You are Siamese, I want none of that.'
Her hackles up, she pounced towards the male,
quick as lightning, sparks flying, she bit him on his tail,
he howled with pain and spun towards the dear,
she took the chance and bit his beautiful right ear.

Grace Whyte

Zeusless

Zeus, you are our baby.
We can't wait for your return.
We miss you when you are away.
Without you we simply yearn.

For you to bound thru' the cat flap,
And run around the house.
For you to demand food then nap,
Dreaming of a mouse

Fighting with your toilet roll.
And attacking the DVD.
Lying on the table,
And eating fish food for your tea

The cats all seem lost without you,
You're the leader of the pack.
Please hurry home, Zeus, we miss you,
We all just want our little man back

Libi Garner

Dog

Jump, jump, spring, spring
You'll know what breed they are
They're always happy to see you
Even if you'd just walked out of the room
They're happy and exciting
And love to have a chew
They'll leave their food
But do anything for treats
They're really fussy madams
They'll run for miles and fight all day
But never come back crying
When they sleep, they really sleep
A deep sleep like in Sleeping Beauty
When their big brown eyes look up at you
It's enough to send you flying
They'll bark all day
And will be a real pain
But our life will never be the same
Or as plain without them.

Kirsty Lewis

Smithlan Just William

Erect.
He stands transfixed.
Eyes scan the horizon.
Nostrils flare,
Ears a-flicker,
He tastes the air.
Blind to lush railed paddocks,
Returned to ancestral plains.
Wild thing,
Bursts out, unfettered,
Takes flight,
Pursued by imaginary foes.
In self-controlled panic,
Jinks right, left, right.
Bucks, kicks, squeals,
Head down;
Charge!
White, wild-eyed,
He hurtles to
Halt.

Diane Humphreys

An Anchor Books Anthology

As Sweet As Honey!

Honey, Honey, Honey!
You really are so scrummy!
Those pointed ears
That tail so curvy
Those paws that carry you in crazy fervour
But when you climb upon the sofa
Girl! You are such a loafer!

(Springtime is here so you I'll pardon!)
Spending your hours in the garden
Sniffing out those toads and frogs
Nosing them from under logs!
Those poor mice and slow-worm too
Hiding, terrified, in the grass
Wishing and hoping that you would pass!

Oh! Honey, you are so full of life
Sometimes bordering on strife
Playing, loving, barking, sleeping
Often keeping one eye open, peeping!
Looking regal, acting wicked
You're a very good friend to me
Such great fun and company!

Sheila Lewis

Suki

A beautiful cat, so full of fun,
she loved to play skip and run,
in the garden she would not stay,
a dreadful fear that she would stray.
Of dogs and humans she had no fear,
the time would come to shed a tear,
a car or stolen would be her fate,
or so I thought until that date.
Over the wall just one more time,
up the steps and follow the line.
The line my dogs had walked ahead,
but now my beloved Suki's dead.
A greyhound and another dog,
along the path they did plod.
They chased and killed my lovely cat,
as though she were some hated rat.
I shall never forget the love she brought.
Right now I'm feeling very fraught.
But time will mend my broken heart,
in my life she played a part.

Lorna Flint

Cat Lives

Too young once
to be the mistress
of my eyes
in my palm I held
an unbroken happiness
we may recognise

As first love.
I should have married:
a silence runs too deep.
Your sleeping brother hides,
taunts the window, carried
into its own sleep

The new day.
Teaser, warrior, the lion's friend
in the tall grass,
a dancer in Amazon leaves:
the summers never end.
The days shall pass

A prophecy of love.
You shall grow old
in the wind,
against the sky
your tail will unfold,
a question.

All your days will be kind.

Simon Richardson

An Anchor Books Anthology

My Little Jimmy

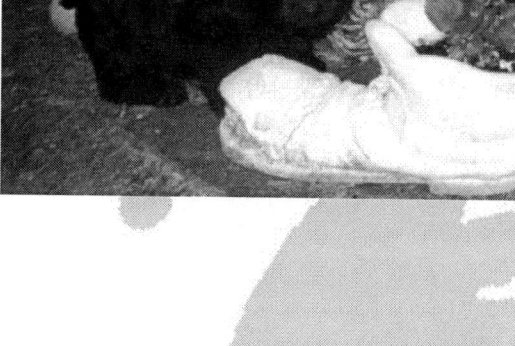

Here's a picture of *my* little treasure
He brings me such a lot of pleasure!
Should there be a prize for fun
My little pup would surely win No 1!

I've never seen him sitting still
Except to gobble down his meals
He loves to help around the garden
Digging up all I've planted!

He's got a taste for slippers too
And nibbles at socks and shoes
Just ten weeks old, he won't be told
This little Scottie's rather bold!

He has his naughty little ways
But loves a tickle and some praise
Each day my Jimmy learns new tricks
And then he gives my hand a lick

He looks at me with big, brown eyes
And never wants to leave my side
A friend for life, I do agree
Forever may he stay with me!

Ros Heller

Bilton's Carol

(To be sung to the tune of 'Away In A Manger')

Shut up in a stable, no comfy warm bed,
The little dog, Bilton, lay down his wool' head.
The swallows were nesting, but now they have flown,
And little dog, Bilton, is all on his own.

The 'satians are barking, and Bilton next door,
That little dog, Bilton, can't sleep on the floor.
I love you, dear Bilton, forgive me I pray,
If I have to leave you th' occasional day.

Jo Brookes

My Striker

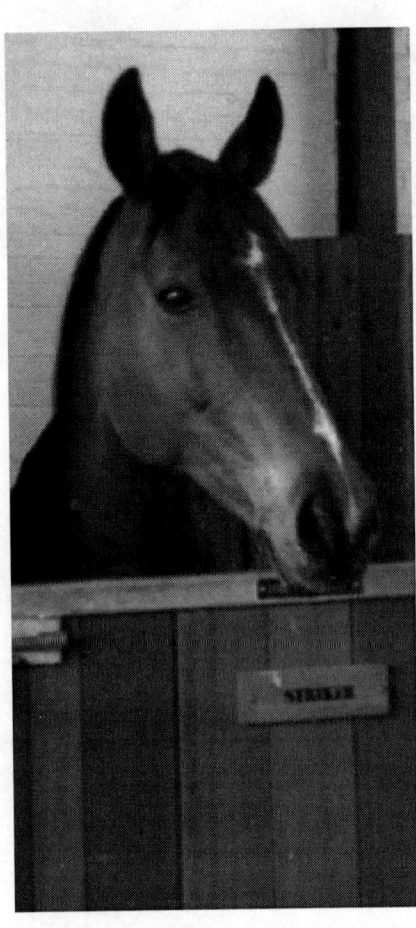

My Striker, you are so fine,
My darling, dear, sweet equine.

Being a thoroughbred, so elegant and sleek,
I love you right down to your feet.

Your bright bay coat glistens in the summer sun,
It shines so bright as you run.

Mane and tail, silky black, free and flowing,
There's no stopping you when you get going.

In your paddock through the sunny haze,
I love to watch you roll and graze.

Through fields of pretty fragrant flowers,
We wander together for hours and hours.

Then, when it's cold and starts to snow,
It's into your snug warm stable you go.

All rugged up, safe, just right,
I give you a carrot and a kiss goodnight.

My Striker, you do not know what you mean to me,
For you are my living sanctuary.

Sharon Hudson

Jester

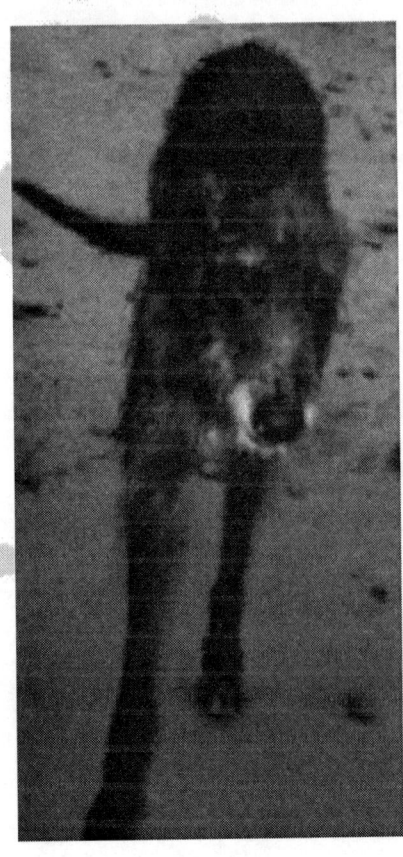

I crumbled when he died,
After taking one last look into his pained eyes.
The last year had been an agony of waiting and hoping,
Operation followed operation,
But still his weakness became overwhelming.
It started with fits, spasms racking his whole body,
When it passed, he'd stumble around in a daze,
Lost in the home he'd always known.
A Scottish deer hound, proud and tall,
Long grey hair, gentle to all,
From elegant, loping strides,
To a puppy-like crawl.

I held him all that long last night,
Tried to deny the existence of dawn's first light.
I'll never have another, didn't keep the lead or bowl,
Didn't even keep the photos, they were too painful to behold.
But in my mind I see him,
And on the wind I hear him howl,
And I imagine the rabbit's scattering
As through Heaven's fields he prowls.

S Wellings

Lost And Found

The dog was hungry and scraggy when found
Starved of affection, he just wandered around
The bins and tips, the only food he could find
Alone in a world where no one was kind

One day it happened, a warden came by
Caught in his net before he could fly
Down to the pound, he took him away
There a place where he could stay

They cared for him, fed and tended him well
But time was short for him there to dwell
Too many dogs like him were all about
Only a reprieve, but fast running out

However a rescue bid was on the way
A young man came along to save the day
He fell in love at the very first sight
The dog responded with eyes shining bright

Into the car, he was then driven away
The young man named him Rory that day
New home awaiting with love and affection
A master to serve with loyalty and protection

Norman S Brittain

Two Balls Of Fluff

See him lying very still,
Watching, waiting, ready to pounce,
With eyes wide he creeps along,
To pounce upon his brother,
He's not watching to see him pounce,
Got you . . . now they play.

Rough and tumble through the grass they go,
Just two large balls of fluff,
Playing in the sun,
All their legs in the air,
Rolling round and round,
Jumping higher than the last time,
Knocking each other to the ground,
Just two cats having fun,
With play over, here they lie, exhausted now,
Sleeping in the sun.

S Hutchings

Snitch

(6 July 1993 - 15 September 2001)

In the July of ninety-three
A little ball of fluff was given to me
She came from a litter of seven
And she surely was a gift from Heaven.

With her in our lives we felt so rich
Our little puppy, Snitch
Although she did not bite or bark
She was truly a bright spark

She used to hide in boxes and a bowl
She really was a funny soul
She would make me smile every day
She had such an endearing way

Everyone who saw her will never forget
Our very special little pet
Great pets are very rare in any lifetime
I'm just so proud that she was mine

She had the sweetest temperament and the sweetest face
That's something time could never erase
No matter how ill she was she did not fail
Wagging her little bushy tail

We lost her nearly two years ago
The pain I feel no one will ever know
We had to have her put to sleep
The sweetest little soul you could ever meet

That little puppy from a litter of seven
Truly was a gift from Heaven
She was so brave until the end
Rest in peace my little friend

Janet Mitchell Treharne

A Message From 'Chance'

I have had my share of problems,
Never loved, I had no home,
Head bowed, sat in the corner,
I thought, destined for a life alone.
I have one ear up and one ear down,
And don't hear too good these days,
My one shoulder had been broken,
So front paws face different ways.
My pads were sore and bleeding,
I was 5 kilos underweight,
Though the rescue centre helped me,
I was in a bit of a state.
I remember my family stroking me,
Their eyes and voices as they'd talk,
And that really wonderful feeling,
When we went up the lane for a walk.
The warm blanket Mum wrapped around me,
My head tucked under her chin,
As I lay on her lap, I knew I'd got a good home,
And that I'd never feel lonely again.
I needed medicine and two operations,
And now my weight is as it should be,
A warm bed, toys and all the love in the world,
A big garden and fields to run free.
I'm cared for and know that I'm lucky
I have a home to live out my days,
But there are so many more like me you know
That could be helped in all kinds of ways.

A Corfield

Those Skinny Greek Cats

We had everything packed the previous night for our holiday in Greece,
The suitcases were by the front door, ready for the cab to turn up on time,
All that remained in the lounge was a red 'Lonsdale' bowling bag ready to zip,
It only contained a camera, a shower cap and a pack of playing cards,
We had conserved enough space for the alcohol and cut-price cigarettes,
Which we intended to return from our holiday in the sun with.

It's always difficult to say goodbye to our pampered feline friends,
Especially Jester who loves to give you a kiss on the lips,
He always knows when we are going away on holiday due to that sports back,
He usually climbs inside, hoping we'd feel sorry for that sad look on his wee face,
Then take him along for the ride.

However, this morning was different, as he was nowhere to be seen,
Maybe he was in the garden chasing squirrels and had fallen out on us,
Sure we'd send him a postcard written in cat speak with all our love,
Mandy had the tickets and I carried the bag, a little heavier than I thought,
The taxi was waiting for us and we loaded the luggage in and off we went.

We had the feeling that my gym bag moved ever so slightly,
Must've been the vibrations of the cab on roadwork city.

We approached the check-in and airport personnel put our suitcase through,
I decided to take my bowling bag onto the plane with us as hand luggage.
'Mandy, I could've swore my bag moved again.'
She thought I was losing it.

Security told me to put personal items on the conveyor belt for the X-ray,
As my bag went through, I watched the screen and all these black and white images,
That was when Jester's cover was blown by airline staff,
who saw his shadow move around,
I couldn't believe what I was seeing, as the bloke unzipped my
bowling bag,
There, inside, was Jester, who was clutching a photo in his mouth,
It was a colour snapshot of a skinny Greek cat sitting under an olive tree.

Ben E Corado

An Anchor Books Anthology

Bonnie

Some years ago, when we were sad,
and life had little meaning,
we sought for something to fill our days
to combat the gloomy feeling.

A friend who knew of our sad state
said she'd had a happy thought.
A few days later she entered our gate
and what do you think she brought?

Not flowers, not books, not something sweet,
but a greyhound pup with four white feet.
It was golden and white, very sleek and slim,
we didn't know if it was *her or him*.

'Take her, she's yours,' said this generous lady,
'I have others at home - this one's the baby.'
She turned away to hide a tear,
'You'll treat her well, I have no fear.'

We named her 'Bonnie' and now, years later,
we have a pet with a lovely nature.
On morning walks she romps and plays,
making us smile at her frisky ways.

At home she is quiet and loves to lie
with head on paws, while keeping an eye
on both of us to make quite sure
we haven't dropped any food on the floor.

Like many dogs she loves only one,
in Bonnie's case, this is Duncan, my son,
he is her lord, her master and friend,
forever, whatever fate may send.

J Stewart

Elsa

You were abandoned to fend for yourself.
Just six months old, I took you in.
A beautiful puppy with big, sad eyes.
And I loved you so.

Hungry and tired - you slept for days,
but you suddenly came to life.
Though gentle, just a bundle of fun.
And I loved you so.

You quickly learned all there was to know.
Intelligent beyond your years.
Your confidence grew as time went by.
And I loved you so.

You loved your ball, sticks and toys.
Ne'er a dull moment, living life to the full.
A wonderful friend with so much to give.
And I loved you so.

We walked for miles in the sun, rain and snow.
You were always by my side.
Never a problem, always so good.
And I loved you so.

Two years have passed and I miss you so
You were my life, but I had to let go.
Though it was hard, the time was right, but Elsa,
I still love you so.

Cynthia Richards

An Anchor Books Anthology

Mangy Mutt

Whisky Clarke they call him when I take him to the vet
'He's not my child,' I want to say, 'he's not my child,' and yet
I feed him and I brush him and I keep his bedding clean
Hoover up the dog hairs and walk him in between.
There is no *love* between us, no warmth or repartee
He looks to me for daily needs so I am never free
He's smelly and he's scruffy and he always follows me
He's underneath my feet, especially when I get the tea

I walk him by the river
I walk him up the lane
And when I get him home
He wants to go again

His mournful eyes look up at me as if to say, 'I'm here'
He'll bark at almost anything when nothing's really near
And yet at night when Father says, 'Whisky, come on boy,'
He's curled up fast asleep; I think it's just a ploy
For if *I* dare to open the fridge door or the cupboard
He leaps up from his reverie as if I'm Mother Hubbard

Curry, cake and shepherd's pie
Spaghetti, beans and bread
Whisky eats the lot of them
I think he's overfed

He'll finish off the Sunday roast, chocolate, nuts and jelly
He'll eat and eat the whole day long, filling up his belly
And then when he has had a rest he still expects his dinner
Is it any wonder the vet says he should be *thinner!*
So this is Whisky, family pet, there's little more to say
He's part of everything we do, in all - and every way.

Ruth Clarke

Freckle

Freckle is my faithful dog
Scared of cats, the silly sod
Always there when I need him
'Cause he's scared I might leave him.

Black and white with spots as well
A waggly bum with a tail to tell
Big brown eyes that beg you to love
A spaniel look that pleads a hug.

Bouncy, fun and full of joy
Puppy-like with every game or toy
But brains and beauty sure don't mix
Freckle's always in a fix!

When I'm low or feel upset
Freckle is a wonderful pet
Head on my lap or paw on my knee
Understanding and patient is he.

A dog like him is just unique
Not brave or courageous, but rather sweet
Friends for life, it's plain to see
I love him and he loves me.

Freckle is my faithful dog
Throw him a stick, he'll fetch a log
True companions in life's long walk
What a pity dogs can't talk!

S J I Sutton

Monty

Monty is a Persian, an aristocrat of cats;
He may be five, but he is lithe,
He abseils down net curtains,
Leaving shreds hanging from the rails.
He is a veritable ball of fur, adored by one and all;
He will curl beside you on the couch then catch you unawares,
With one swift push of his strong foot, he'll push you to the floor;
He's partial to home baking, but it's tuna he likes best,
He knows the can before it's opened and demands to be fed first!

R E Sturdy

An Anchor Books Anthology

Rusty

It's raining cats and dogs, and I
Bored: nothing better to do
I sit by the window dreaming
Of sunny lands like Africa and Peru

My eyes catches a movement. Outside
The ground is moving, heaping up
A pointed head, two furry paws
Slowly poke through the grass.

I stand still, fascinated
Such a laborious deed!
Boldly mole goes on digging
Fast, increasing its speed.

Suddenly a flurry of black
Sweeps across my eyes. A pounce.
Rusty the hunter! I think horrified
Mole will not stand a chance!

In a flash I rush out into the rain
Filled with hope. Surely I might
Save the creature from slaughter?
Mole would get over its fright!

Sadly, as I looked into the hole
I had to accept the hard fact
No sign of mole, and there, proudly
Licking its chops stood . . . my lovely cat!

V Malavolta

My Precious Friend

They locked him out in rain and snow
When we first rescued him
He was so hopeless and forlorn
His life was cold and grim
I fed him, loved him, gave him hope
We walked, we ran, we played
And I believe with all my heart
That he was Heaven made
And when my days are over
And I'm in my place of rest
I hope I see my precious friend
Cos he was just the best.

Marion Thacker

Jack The Lad

He came from a dogs' home, he'd had a bad time
But I was determined and called him mine
I went out shopping and bought him a bone
Couldn't wait to get it home
He ran to the room and jumped on the chair
Thinks, *do I dare?*
I must be barmy
It's worse than fighting a ruddy army
My friends all say he's handsome
And his spirit is worth a king's ransom
But they don't know till he bares his fangs
And in a flash they up and go
The solidness of my love will win one day
He'll curb his din - see it my way
It will come to him out of the blue
I'll look forward to that, in the meantime - phew.

S F Mellor

Mandy

Mandy, what would we do without you,
around the house you stick to me like glue.

Your hearing and sight are no longer good,
to live forever I wish you could.

When you have your clip you look as beautiful as ever,
I am glad you are always the same, you don't change like the weather.

Your little black nose is still as bright as can be,
when I look at you my heart just fills with glee.

Mandy, my sweet little poodle, I love you so much,
you're a little curly girl and so soft to touch.

You still get excited when I reach for that lead,
with those big brown eyes you stand there and plead.

When we get to the curb you remember your training,
we even go out walking when it is raining.

Mandy, I love to look at you when you're asleep,
I really can't bear to think about the day I shall weep.

Mandy, Mandy, you're the greatest dog in the world to me,
and that also goes for the rest of the family.

Karen Grover

    An Anchor Books Anthology

Gemma's Trophies

Hello everybody, please don't think I'm a bore
My name is Gemma Mason, and you've seen me once before
I'm really not one of those big-headed kind o' pups
I've just popped back to show you my trophies 'n' my cups

Jean Mason

My Little Friend

Each morning as I wake,
Your little face is there,
A curly tail begins to wag,
To show me that you care.

A little game of hide and seek,
You always want to play,
Peeping from under blankets,
That's how we begin our day.

You race me to the kitchen,
Then sit beside my chair,
You race me to the bedroom,
Whizzing past me on the stair.

Our evenings spent together,
Cuddled up upon a chair,
A nudge from your wet nose,
To remind me you're still there.

Constantly by my side,
With you I can depend,
Never to feel lonely,
With my devoted little friend.

Mandy Keay

My Friend Brandy

(For Olwen, with love)

My friend Brandy
Sleeps peacefully on my knee
Every evening when she's had her tea

She purrs contentedly
Her tummy's rather full
With delicious chicken and fish -
Her favourite dish!

Her fur is ginger, brown, black and white
Eyes gleam and shine
In the dead of night

She hunts mice and rabbits -
Wild birds too!
Just like a lion in London zoo

My friend Brandy
Is really very sweet
I love her dearly
And she makes my life complete

Christine Hardemon

Bugsy And Poops

You'd think it was Tom and Jerry
Not Bugsy and Poops
Is it a cat eat cat world
At our house? Well, oops!

You see, Bugsy is bold, a biting type
And Poops, quite reserved and refined
Not in name though, but in character
And to endure Bugsy's ways, she's resigned.

They've been together now for seventeen years
Poops has learned to live, love and bear
Bugsy's bored with no response to his dares
They're a sweet odd couple, yet equally dear.

Dianne Adams

An Anchor Books Anthology

Texas

I wanted you as soon as I saw you,
you came straight over to me.
I was only visiting the breeder,
ended up bringing Texas home for some tea.
Tasmin thought you were great,
she never let you out of her sight.
We wanted you to sleep in a crate,
but you cuddled up to her every night.
I remember redecorating the bedroom,
a baby gate to keep you downstairs.
Being little, you crept right under,
and was soon asleep on the chair.
Playing in the snow one winter,
you both looked so happy and well.
My garden would never be perfect,
but hey, what the hell!
I wonder where it started to go wrong?
The arguments and fights you had.
Two Staffies snarling and snapping,
your injuries would make me so sad.
In the end I could stand it no longer,
four years I tried. Oh, the stress.
Tasmin attacked you quite badly,
your leg was a horrible mess.
We re-homed her to a family in Kent,
the hardest thing I've ever had to do.
Guilt and relief mixed together,
but at least I still had you.
We enrolled at agility classes,
I worried that you would attack.
You had to be restrained and muzzled,
was surprised when we were asked back!
Three years have passed since that happened,
at training you're doing really great.

You're happy and settled at last,
and you've even got a playmate.
Texas - I just want to say that I love you,
my soulmate, my very best friend.
Our relationship grows stronger and stronger,
one that will never end.

Karen Van Gemeren

My Labrador

My dog is called a Labrador
So black and shiny and sleek
And underneath is a temperament
So warm and loving and meek

She comes and goes wherever I go
So happy, so loving and faithful

In days long gone
Other dogs passed by
They looked so proud and prim
You preferred to stay by my side
As we would go for a swim

Now we're both old
We both feel the cold
And you're no longer such a floozy
You're just my own, my faithful dog
My own and lovely Suzy

Trevor Lewis

To Sam

(Written on behalf of Richard Milner)

Such special hours I spend with you
Oh! Sam, my gundog, tried and true.
Quiet at my side when I felt pain
But joyous the 'woofs' with walks again -
Along the shore ere break of day.
How your coat gleams in sun's first ray!
To you, my voice I never raise
For all your actions command praise.
At the trials it is your quest
That you are going to beat the rest!
I lift the trophy - triumph high -
I know I dare not catch your eye -
This bond between us will ne'er end
My Sam - incomparable friend.

Beryl Mapperley

An Anchor Books Anthology

Prize Boxer

You wanna know about me?
I'll let you know
I'm Jake the prize boxer
I'm running the show.

This is my turf
So don't come too close
Till I say so
Because I'm the host.

My owners depend on me
To watch the house and provide safety.
So here I am sunbathing, as you can see
Life's a beach even without sand and sea.

I learned to swim when I was just four
When I want to wee, I head for the door.
I keep the house clean but hog the couch
If you dare try to move me, I'll make you say 'ouch'.

I'm eight years old, I know I don't look it
Walking three times a day keeps me physically fit.
My passion? Okay - it's squeaky toys!
Don't laugh at me - I love the noise.

I also enjoy running after sticks
I reward my owners with jumps and licks.
I'm an excitable type, majestic they say
Yeah, they're right. That's all for today.

Pam Toth

Tribute To Devotion

Why do I feel such pain?
I ask myself time and again
For Gina, some people said, was just a pet
A dog hardly deserving the sorrowing regret
But I believed she came from above
To me with so much love
Affectionately she would bring her lead
As a means to simply plead
To go with me wherever
As long as we were together
But now sadly she is no longer here
I walk alone and often shed a tear.

Doris Duncan

Best Friends

To my little scruffy pal who shares my heart and home
I know you'll never give up on me even when I moan
If only people could be like you and understand my cranky ways
Your eyes shower me with forgiveness
Emanating through a love-struck haze

You always seem to know what's wrong and offer good advice
Instantly you are there for me with a wet kiss
And never do I have to ask twice
In times of upset you help my heart to mend
Which makes me know, without a doubt
You are my closest, most treasured friend

At night you keep me safe and sound and guard my bedroom door
When morning breaks and I stir
You're there to offer a 'Woody' wake-up paw
What have I done to deserve this love?
Please tell me because I am unsure
I think I am the luckiest girl to have a best friend like you to adore

C J Fulton

My Dog, Benjie

Four short legs and big floppy ears
a soft wet nose and a tail,
two large brown eyes with a pleading look
then he lets out a wail!

I take his lead within my hands
and his eyes light up in delight.
He starts to bark and leap around
and tugs with all his might!

We have this ritual every day
and then we saunter out.
He starts to sniff around and then . . .
well, he's a male without a doubt!

Round and round the park we go
only stopping now and then.
Well, he has to greet all of his friends
before we go home again!

S J Roberts

Thomasina - Cat Burglar

At an animal shelter, a small black and white cat captured my heart
Her name was Thomasina and I knew without her I could not depart.
A timid little cat I thought, not one who would be inclined to roam,
Little did I know I was inviting a little 'cat burglar' into my home.

From the moment she settled down into her new garden and house,
She seemed quite uninterested in all the birds or occasional mouse.
No - I discovered that Thomasina had much bigger prey on her mind,
And it certainly was not of the ordinary rodent or feathered kind!

Saplings from the local park began arriving each day by the door,
And even my neighbour found several on their conservatory floor.
The mystery was soon solved when eventually Thomasina was seen
With a sapling clutched in her mouth, racing away from the scene.

She then turned her attention to the laundry just up the road,
Because soon small hand towels were brought daily to my abode.
Together with a football shirt, assorted underwear, and various socks,
A child's dressing gown, T-shirt and even some pretty dolls' frocks.

Greenhouses were raided of gardening gloves and packets of seeds,
Neighbours soon realised who was responsible for the dirty deeds.
Of course all the stolen items are quickly returned to everyone,
And Thomasina's antics are regarded by the neighbours as great fun.

Even the local laundry has come to regard her as 'one of us',
So now when she visits them each day she receives a lot of fuss.
They even have a photograph displayed on their notice board,
And greet me in a jovial way when I return her latest hoard.

Thomasina has continued her daily thieving for the last six years,
Scaling 6ft fences and gardens patrolled by dogs - she has no fears.
Nothing seems to deter her, not even pouring rain, snow or ice,
Life would certainly be so much simpler if she just caught mice!

Patricia Gittins

Sooty

Black as jet, all soft and furry,
Slow and precise, with no hurry.
But watch him pounce at a mouse,
When it runs around my house.

Sleeping, a long cat nap, on my bed,
Making me wonder what is in his head.
Dreams, in colour or black or white?
What just made him jump with fright?

Curled up in a tight little ball,
His purr of love is worth it all.
All his affection, and warmth and love,
Squeeze him tight if only I could.

A two-way street, all caring and kind,
He gives all, and I give mine.
If feeling down and low,
I know just where to go.

A cuddle, a stroke, a purr or two,
I feel much better loving you.
You do not scorn or pass judgement,
Love you give without harassment.

Sooty, Sooty, pussy cat,
You are the best and all that.
Love you offer, love you give,
You are the best cat ever to live.

Estella Reynolds

Gloria

Gloria is my 15.2
Known to pop a buck or two
She trots and canters to the rear
Watch the twitching of her ears
She doesn't like to stand still long
Trotting to that rocking song
Sitting trot and hover too
Now she knows just what to do
Her browband sparkles like a queen
She's sometimes fast, she's real keen
She jumps the jumps, her legs are flying
She makes me feel like sometimes crying
She's a good girl now, she does her job
I love her lots and she's my cob.

L Haynes

An Anchor Books Anthology

Oh, I Do Like To Be . . .

Can we go to the seaside please?
I really like it there,
I can run off all my energy,
Race around without a care

I love the cliffs, I love the beach,
I like to tease the sea,
I run in and bark and snap at it,
And it comes out after me.

The 'land drain's' best, it cools me off,
And I can have a drink,
The sea is good, but not for long,
It makes my tummy pink.

I want to go and run some more,
Down on that yellow sand,
And push my face down bunny holes,
Why do they smell so grand?

Chase up the rocks and down again,
I never want to stop.
You see, when I've raced down the cliff,
The gulls land back on top.

Oh, how I long for coastal days
To come around once more,
So I can chase and bark and dig,
After all, that's what I'm for!

Sara Marlow

Canine Revelation

I fell beside your door quite late one night
So hungry, wet and cold from winter's sting.
At once you understood my helpless plight,
And I soon realised to you I'd cling.
A puppy then, abandoned in the snow
By heartless human with no thought or care
In doing what he did, he'll never know
The constant love and loyalty I'd share.

You taught me right from wrong and I obeyed;
I learnt to guard our home and all within.
Because I am a bitch, you had me spayed,
To cancel out unwanted puppy sin.
Devotion in my life to you untold;
Together we face life and growing old.

Pearl M Burdock

Tess When She Was Young

'Where is my ball?' she said
As she rushed around
'I have looked everywhere,
It must be found.
You cannot use the hoover
Or take up a mat
Or go for a walk
So don't put on your hat!
I've had lots of balls, this one was red
Or was it blue?
You must know where it is?' she said
'Well let's go down the avenue
And I will find a stick
But the ball is better
Cos you can just give it a kick
I shall have to find something
What! A squirrel in a tree?
Well anyway we'll have a walk
Just you and me

Dorothy Bloomfield

Tigger

A handsome cat, my friend Tigger
With ginger fur, got bigger and bigger
One day he woke me in my bed
A dead pigeon lay on my breast.
Some other days he'd bring a mouse
After all it was his house!
One day he brought his lady friend
The Siamese ones he did defend
Well he had to bring a bird or two
Brought in alive, then away they flew
He only liked to play with them
And saw me counting one to ten.
One time he was away three weeks
I searched around in all the streets
Until I found him in a mess
Coils of wire around his chest
A snare or some kind of horrible trap
And no one seemed to care a rap
But he survived that awful day
One of his lives was whisked away.
For nineteen years I had my cat
In dreams I see him, still quite fat.

Joan Prentice

An Anchor Books Anthology

Our Cat

Our cat is crazy, our cat is mad
But she's a loveable creature, best we ever had
She comes in of a morning ready for something to eat
When she acts out her performance
She comes to us for her treat

When we are out in our garden she's always somewhere about
She watches us plant the soil in and she pulls it back out
She comes up to our bedroom and scratches on the door
She much prefers to sleep on the bed, she doesn't like the floor

Grace has beautiful colours in her fur
She's soft and cuddly like a teddy bear
Always playful, so much fun
She loves to stretch out in the sun

Cassandra Evans

My Cat And The Fish

She spies the goldfish that swims around
And leaps to the table from the ground
Crouching down on the table top
She watches it swim and wants it to stop

She sits there waiting patiently
The fish is swimming so happily
She is so quiet, she's so shrewd
Waiting there to make her move

All of a sudden she sees her chance
She licks her lips, she's in a trance
She taps the bowl with her paws
Exposing her very long sharp claws

She dips her paw into the hole
On the top of the goldfish bowl
Her paw ends up soaking wet
And the fish begins to get upset

She hears a key turn in the door
And jumps from the table to the floor
Maybe one day she'll get her wish
And catch and eat that damn goldfish

Tina Davis

A Man And His Cat

(For Graham and Oscar)

You sit on the couch, your eyes slowly closing
Your body relaxes, you are ready for dozing
You really could do with a nap.

You gladly drift off - and don't hear the sneaking
Four paws coming closer, two green eyes are peeking
And soon they are fixed on your lap.

You're halfway in dreamland - *he's* ready for jumping
A jolt brings you back, all you feel is a thumping
And then there's his loud, happy purr.

He turns round and round, and soon he is nestling
Your hands stroke his warmth - at last you'll be resting
And with you this soft ball of fur.

Brigitte Hale

My Sly Cat

My cat's name is Zara
And he is a sly cat
Because when I went
To watch football on TV
Zara went to the cupboard door
That was open and he went in
And he took the cat biscuit box, then
He pushed the box and
The box fell and lots of biscuits
Spread around the kitchen floor
And he ate them all.
I went in and I was
Shocked and angry and
Sent him to bed!

Graham Dow (11)

Holly

I well remember that day you
first came into my life
a small, lively bundle,
all tail and ears
ever to cause such laughter and tears
chewing the furniture
soaking the floors
a mini menace on four little paws
such a terror come to stay
I would not have had it any other way
chasing cats across the park
greeting guests with the loudest bark
being mad for all to see
but always giving love to me
and when in your later years
protecting me from many fears
as often walking in the dark
you would ever leave your mark
and your close protection lend
a brave and ever faithful friend
I thought we would always be strong together
but came the day your bright eyes dimmed
and so though I could not bear the parting
I knew it was time for you to go
and as I held you one last time
trying to hold back the tears
I held on to the memories
of all the love you gave me
through so many happy years

Edward B Evans

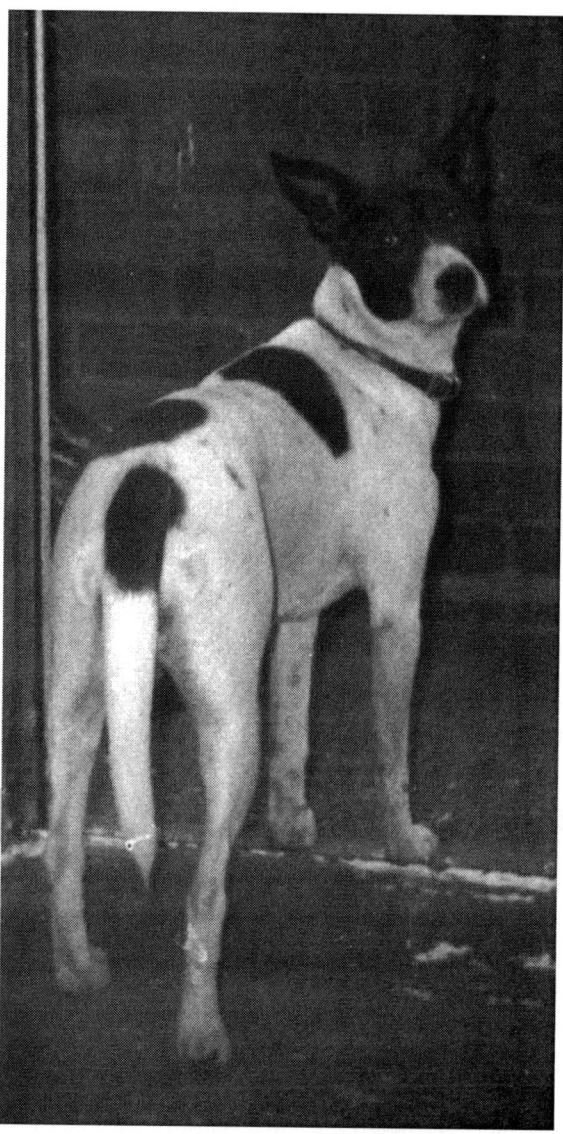

My Dog, Annie

Annie is my soulmate, my best and truest friend,
She will follow me round until it's her end,
She is loyal and loving, what more can I say,
I know she won't leave me 'til her dying day,
She will jump on my knee when I shed a tear,
She will lick my face, she knows no fear,
If I had an option and I had to choose,
I know this for certain, the human would lose.

Ellen Chambers

Red Alert

(Inspired by Cara)

I admit it, my horse is a nutter.
A speed-freak, maniac, loon.
Nought to sixty in seven,
it ought to be Heaven,
but who wants to go there so soon?

She's mad, crazy, a fool.
Show her some grass and it's *'go!'*
Charging along, no thought for poor me
watching us coming up fast to a tree.
Why can't she be normal and slow?

She's a hooligan, fruit cake, plain batty.
Lord knows what goes on in her brain.
She's addicted to hills, attacks them with verve,
up and then down (to test out my nerve).
It's like riding The Runaway Train!

Chestnut mares! Who'd have one? I ask.
Red-headed temper as well.
Tantrums ensue if I put on the brakes,
leaps in the air as umbrage she takes.
No novice ride you can tell.

At shows, God help me, she's worse,
pursuing the horses ahead.
The judges all laugh as they know what she's like,
zooming about like a mad motorbike.
It's the whole-class canters I dread.

But I love her, her mind is so sharp,
she keeps me well on my toes.
Anticipates all I'm planning to do,
shows off like mad, loves an audience too
- and gets one wherever she goes.

Finally back in her stable, she sleeps;
relaxed now, hanging over the door.
All her energy spent, head drooping low,
snoring a bit, but planning I know
to go out and gallop some more!

Helen Weedon

An Anchor Books Anthology

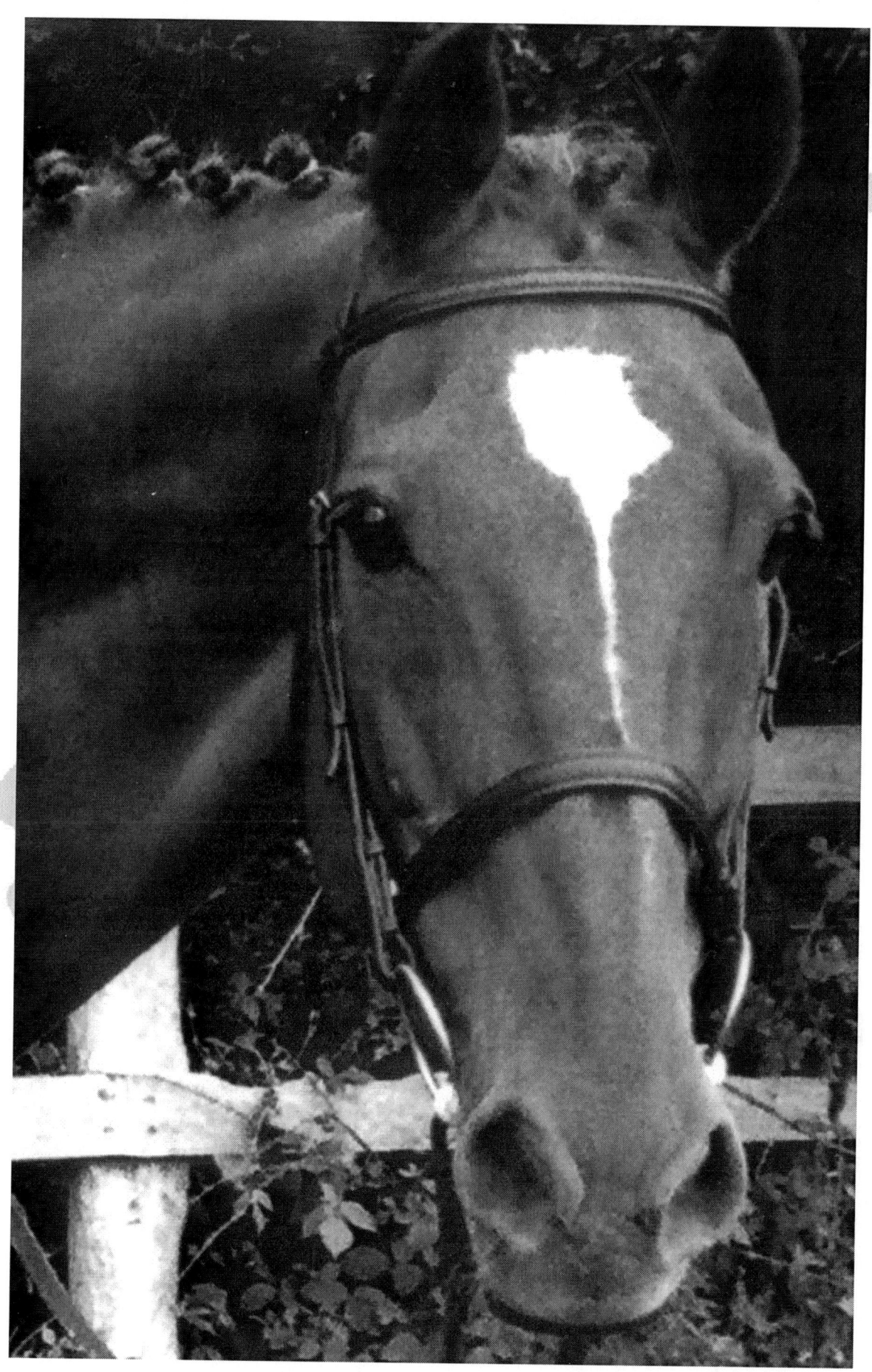

Oreo - 11 Month Old Chocolate Point Siamese

(Dedicated to Oreo, love your mummy)

With his chocolate points
and his cream, smooth coat,
he's wilful, he's royal
and yes, I must gloat,
he's stunning,
he's handsome and pretty unique,
twenty-four-seven
he's under my feet
devoted I am
as he is to me
together forever
that's how it will be!

Lynda Peterson

Polly

A mischievous dog was thee,
A King Charles named Polly,
The sort who dug underground,
And turned the house upside down.

You had never seen a more adventurous creature,
The type that come bounding just to meet ya,
A dog that would get showered with hugs and treats,
Who would walk in from a walk with dirty feet!

Late at night she would lay on her owner's lap,
After a tiring day she began to nap,
And wake up early next day,
She'll bound outside and begin to play.

But one thing was for sure that she would miss,
A delicious meal in her dish,
Full to the brim with her favourite food,
Would be sure to put her in a different mood!

And in this picture as she dreamt,
She was sure to know what 'this way up' meant!
So now I hope that you see,
How boisterous a dog can really be!

Sarah Carrington (12)

I Could Have Danced All Night

I could have danced all night
my partner's just my height,
we look so good together.
If only he'd kiss me
I'd be so glad that we
are going out together.
The music's slow and sweet
he's knocked me off my feet
our love will last forever.
But what is that you say
I only want his hay
cupboard love, who me? No never!
A horse has got to eat
he brings a tasty treat
to sit and munch together.
We know our love is right
we'll really dance all night
to seal our love forever.

Dianne Lapworth

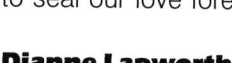

Not So Lucky

Lucky the dog must think he's a cat
And that he has nine lives
For he keeps running off to have some fun
But he will find it just isn't wise
For one of these days he won't find his way home
And he will find it's no fun in the dark on his own
There are all sorts of things out there in the night
That can suddenly jump out and give him a fright
It's creepy, it's scary and he will have the desire
To wish he'd stayed home in front of the fire
All snugly and warm where he likes to be
Until the next time when he wants to run free
You can't keep him locked up
You can't keep him tied down
So I think you'll agree, although with a frown
The next time he runs away from home
He will just have to find his way home on his own
And if he decides that he's not coming back
He will just have to stay out there all on his Jack (Russell).

Alan Wilcox

The Dog Who Would Be King

I'm always getting into mischief
For why I do not know
But it's good fun and I can't stop
And that's all they need to know

I run across the fields of green
And down the rabbit runs
And you should see me go stone deaf
When my master calls me to 'come'!

My bowl is always brimming
With my favourite yummy snack
And then I get more treats
When I roll over on my back

It's a dog's life, I know, and you can bet
I wouldn't trade it for a thing
For the way my master treats me,
You would think I were a *king*.

Laura Marshall

Abbey

Oh Abbey, you're so naughty
What will I do with you?
Some days you drive me crazy
The naughty things you do

You run around barking
Pull washing off the line
Bring mud in from the garden
You sulk, you snore, you whine

But every coin has two sides
And the other side of you
Is a lovely Border collie
Gentle, loving and true

You love to have a cuddle
You're loyal and full of fun
You're always there when I need you
I'm proud to be your mum

Carole Phillips

An Anchor Books Anthology

Timmy

Timmy in the garden, my beady-eyed cat,
He points his toes, all elegant, there he goes.
On a hot summer's day, stashed away, under the mastershum leaves.
In the shade, asleep like a babe.
The early evening, in he comes, on my lap he sits.
I feed him his favourite cheese and onion crisps. Not to be missed.
He purrs and patiently watches the telly with me.
He paws his claws into me, all happy and content.
I don't mind, he's my faithful friend.

Timmy in a box,
We made him a small vertical box,
He sits in his box all proud and tall.
It's another cosy world, for Timmy, once more.
Timmy jumps on the bed at night,
Pushing his nose into my head,
He curls up in a ball, dreaming of adventures,
And pussy cats for evermore.

Stella Robinson

My Dog

(Dedicated to my 'Purdy')

My days with her were so full of fun,
Running, playing, shooting the gun,
But now that she is old and grey,
And cannot run, skip or play,
We'll sit together in the sun,
And sit so close we are as one,
Deep in thoughts of those yesterdays,
My furry friend those were the days,
But now we sit, then we walk,
Take a drink and have a talk,
And take things slow and easy,
For time is getting short for you,
And I want it bright and breezy.

Hilary Tozer

Cinderella

Cinderella, small and white
Cinderella's eyes so bright
Watching, waiting, anticipating
Will Prince Charming call tonight?
Is that what makes your eyes so bright?

Cinderella, soft and small
With a coat of cotton wool
Whiskers a-quiver, small tail twitching
Waiting patiently in the hall
Waiting for your prince to call

Cinderella by the fire
Busy cleaning face and paw
At last a knock upon the door
And you can't wait a moment more
But this prince isn't what I visualised
It's that ginger tom from number five

Edith Malkison

Little White Dog

A sense of loss,
an emptiness all around,
there was hardly a sound.

A book drops to the floor,
a little ajar my door,
my little white dog appears,
gone are my fears!

A cuddle close,
a brown eye looks into mine,
a conversation takes place,
a bond is created.

A walk, a cuddle, a feed,
is all this little dog does need.
Yet he gives so much love and feeling.
He seems oddly enough, more capable
than most human beings.

Maria Ann Cahill

Puppy's Holiday Plans

I know, Mum, where we'll go on vacation:
The Lake District must be our destination.
The Derwentwater in Keswick sounds a smashing hotel
Where well-mannered pets are welcome as well!

I promise to mind my Ps and Qs
When we sit in the bar and admire those views.
We'll scoop my poop and wipe my paws
When we return from the great outdoors.

They've sixteen acres to explore you know,
With lakeside walks - I can't wait to go!
Our trekking kit's ready, with my folding bowl -
Those fells and mountains will be so good for the soul.

Will there be squirrels and rabbits to chase?
Don't forget my toys when you pack my case.
A first-aid kid with sun block might seem absurd,
But a sunburnt nose sounds too painful for words!

What fun we'll have, Mum, when can we go?
With so much to explore, I'll love it so.
You won't have to worry, while you dine out late -
I'll be curled up, exhausted, in my cosy crate!

Julie Munro

His Royalness, Samuel Lord Tiverton, Emperor Of Hargrave

He came as a present for Thomas, one of a litter of three
And we couldn't have known as we chose him what a magical cat he would be.
Now dogs learn a thing if you teach them, follow rules if they're properly shown
But don't come on strong with a cat chum unless you like living alone.
Sam made it clear from the kick off, began as he meant to go on
We'd be the waiting on lackeys and he'd be the waited upon.
To be fair he worked for a living, renowned for his tally of mice
And the rats that stole from the horse feed? Well they never stole from it twice.
Dogs in his presence were wary and a fox that was up to no good
Took fright when Sam flexed his muscles, decided to leave while he could.
Sam wore the trousers in this house, none of us argued with that
But we're all broken-hearted without him, our Sam was a helluva cat . . .

Marguerite Holloway

A Dog's Life!

I sleep all night, most of the day,
You're off to school, why can't you stay?
I'll see you off, I'll watch you go,
I can't wait 'til you come home!
I'll play with my ball, that's on the string,
You know that it's my favourite thing!
My nan will throw it down the path,
I trot along, I make her laugh!
I'm worn out now, it's time for lunch,
I wolf it down, crunch! Crunch! Crunch!
I'll sleep now until you get back,
Then we can play after my nap!
We'll play for the whole afternoon,
I'll listen for the van, Gramp will be home soon!
Then I'll sleep and eat my tea,
Then you and Gramp can play with me!
I'll curl up on your lap tonight,
Then we can turn out the light!
'Night, night, Lizzie,' I hear you say,
But tomorrow is another day!

Sinead Carter (13)

Barney And The Moon Fairy

Last night, when the moon was shining bright
A fairy came to stay.
She tickled Barney on the nose
And said, 'Come out to play.'
'Alright,' said Barney, 'let us fly
Up through the clouds
To the deep blue sky.'
So up they flew with their wings agleam
And then they slid down a silver moonbeam.
Barney said, 'I wish we'd brought Buzz.'
But the fairy said, 'He's not a fairy like us.'
'Then I'll take him a present from the skies,'
Said Barney in delight.
Oh what a lovely, exciting night.
So he found the tiniest baby star
And tied it to his paw.
'Come on,' said the fairy, 'just one more game
Then homewards we must soar.'
'Goodbye little friend,' said the big round moon.
'Bye-bye,' whispered the fairy, 'I'll see you soon.'
When Buzz woke up this morning
The first thing that he saw
Was a little twinkly diamond shining on the floor.
'Hey Barney!' he said. 'Just look at this
Do come and have a peep.'
But Barney smiled and closed his eyes
Rolled over and went to sleep.

M J Matthews

Cool Cat

In the garden one afternoon,
there was suddenly
a great caterwauling.
I saw our Annie,
beloved tortoiseshell
suddenly aroused
hurtling up the side
of the tool shed,
jaws back - and
canine teeth exposed,
hissing, snarling
like an angry tigress,
'How dare - dare you
come into my domain?'
she spat at the quiet creature,
calmly reposing on the roof,
who looked down with great disdain,
paws folded
one across the other,
staring nonchalantly ahead,
as if to say,
'You needn't fuss -
I was going anyway!'

Rosemary Jacobs

An Anchor Books Anthology

Love A-Bounding!

My dog, he loves me, he's like a teddy bear
I love him so much, he doesn't have a care
We walk out each day, and spend time to play
He runs all around, and enjoys every day.

He wants to be the leader, that I can tell
I try to make him understand that we two are to gel
That none of us are the boss, but he doesn't understand
He's only quite young, and not long on this land.

He's learning to tell me things, like when he wants out
And knows to return to me, when his name I do shout
He knows when it's teatime and hears his biscuits fall
Into his tin dish, with meat; I don't need to call!

He likes when it's bedtime, he's 'floppy' and soft
And sits on my knee, whilst his head rests aloft
He's lovely, he's happy, and love is the key
So warm and so cuddly, his eyes have 'that plea'.

He's growing, he's learning, to listen and watch
His bark, shrill and excited, it raises a notch
But look at that face, so sweet and so kind
That's how I'll remember him, with love in my mind.

He's growing up now, and he has his own ways
Like standing beside me, and watching, in gaze
At the signal I give him, to stay or to walk
His eyes are so pleading, they almost can talk.

His life is more settled now, he has his own space
A quiet little corner to think, sleep, and just laze
To look forward to 'walkies', his play and his food
When he looks with 'those eyes' it just changes my mood!

So here is God's creature, so knowing and fine
And here by my side, till the end of all time.

Maureen Westwood O'Hara

Mitten's Smiles

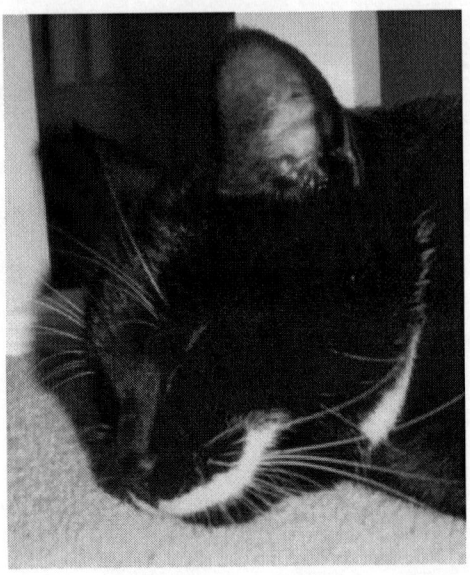

I wake up in the morning
With a smile on my face,
Born to be happy,
I smile away the days.
God maybe painted me
To help me on life's way,
I know I needed rescuing,
I feel lucky every day.
I know I am very spoilt
In every single way,
I show them my gratitude
With a smile every day.

Beverley Dales

The English Setter Poem

6.30am
T ime to wake up my owners
H ey, I'm hungry and I need some nosh!
E veryone's up now (loud barking's the trick)

E ven though they tell me to shush!
N ow it's time to go for a walk,
G ot to get to the fields in a hurry.
L ead's on ready, has *she* got my treats?
I f not, she'll soon be quite sorry!
S niffing around she calls out my name -
'H ush woman, this could take all day'

'S elective hearing' *she* says I've got,
'E xplorative' that's what I say.
T o tease her I start to make my way back
T hen something else needs my attention,
E ventually *she* has to bribe me with food,
R esult! I win again!

P ut on my lead and wander back home
O ur village church clock strikes ten.
E xcited by lunch around one o'clock but
M y bed will do nicely till then!

Goodnight!

Sarah Patterson

An Anchor Books Anthology

Dudley Dreamer Of Devlin

(Written in 1989 when Dudley's mum and dad were away and he stayed with his grandee)

What is a good boy? I would like to know
Grandee calls, 'Get your lead' and off we go.
But I don't do my duty out on the grass,
I come home and do it, and then, bang! Crash!
Grandee chases me round and smacks my bot.
She doesn't hit hard. It doesn't hurt a lot.

I chew up the rose leaves that are there for décor.
Then I go to the next bowl looking for more.
I then rush around the room, swinging my slipper.
Grandee gets in my way and I land her a clipper!
I've hurt her poor ankle and she yells out in pain.
But I lick it all better and all's well again.

I chewed up some paper and it was really quite pleasant!
How was I to know it was for wrapping a present!
I slipped through Gran's legs and went out in the rain.
She was really quite vexed when I came in again.
I was all wet and muddy and things weren't quite right,
Because when I went out I was fluffy and white.
A little while later after a shampoo in Daz,
I was fluffy and white as ever I was!

I'm not really naughty, just so full of joy,
So tell me, please, what is a good boy?
But Grandee still loves me, she tells me so
And she'll miss me so much when I have to go.

We often sit down and have coffee and bics.
Then I tell her I'm sorry and give her some licks.
I put my head on one side and lift up my paw,
And that really gets her and she hugs me some more!

Elsie Corrigan

Emmy

My Emmy is so special, she's tortoiseshell and white.
Her fur is soft, her purr is deep, her friendship's a delight.
She has black ears with ginger tips, her white bib's just like lace.
She has two pairs of the whitest socks, and a pretty ginger face.
I'm sure she thinks she owns me and I believe she owns me too.
I know full well she loves me and I love her through and through.
When work and people irk me and no one seems to care,
I go home to precious Emmy whose love is always there.

J A Berisha

A Few Of My Best Mates

Cats, hamsters, rabbits, budgies, hens
Over the years I've had many friends
My Sealyham 'beaut' loved chasing cats
And was very good at killing rats
She loved watching 'Lassie' on TV
And begged very nicely for her tea

Next came my Chihuahua, 'Dooley' was his name
Folk took him for a fox cub because he looked the same
He was a mischievous little cuss
Who used to like a lot of fuss
He'd curl up on my knee to sleep
And when he died, I had a good weep

My present dog is a rescue one
Goes by the name of 'Roy'
He's a Border collie
A very handsome boy
I've had him since the age of 2
And he is simply great
I wouldn't be without him
For he is my best mate
He loves playing cricket, footie and such
A bit slower now, but not that much
His eyesight now is not so good
He's also deaf as a lump of wood
Still I'm 76 years, he's 105,
So I guess we're both lucky to still be alive

Joan Jones

Moo's News

One Saturday afternoon
Whilst having a drink
Moo started contracting
And made my mum think

She shut the lounge door
Shooed Moo into her pen
She then started howling
And heaving and then . . .

Out came the first one
A perfect lil pup
She heaved a bit more
But she didn't give up

Out came the second
No sign of the third
And for many an hour
No howling we heard

But then hours later
She had the third one
And a long line of births
Had just then begun

Mum rushed to the vet
With the pups in a box
While I stayed at home
My eyes glued to the clocks

Then later that night
We heard keys in the door
And Mum had come home
With puppies galore

Six little babies
All tiny, with spots
And from that moment on
I shall love them all lots!

Holly Chubb (15)

Sandy

He came to us, dear Sandy
A poor, unwanted stray,
And when we went to pet him
He'd cringe and cower away.
Such was his fright
That he'd wet upon the floor
But that made me love him
A thousand times more.

As the days passed slowly
I taught him how to play.
His confidence was growing
He ceased to shy away.
A sparkle now shone in his eyes,
A smile upon his face,
His tail it wagged constantly
Back and forth in space.

He was still only a puppy
For he was only one,
He'd already had six homes
And was wanted by no one.
He was beaten and battered,
Forgotten and left alone,
He didn't know the joy of love,
Nor the contentment of a bone.

But now he lives with me
A part of the family.
We even got him a best friend
Whose name is Buddy.
They play about together
Two friends right from the start,
My two bundles of joy
That stole away my heart.

Gemmaine Baughurst (15)

An Anchor Books Anthology

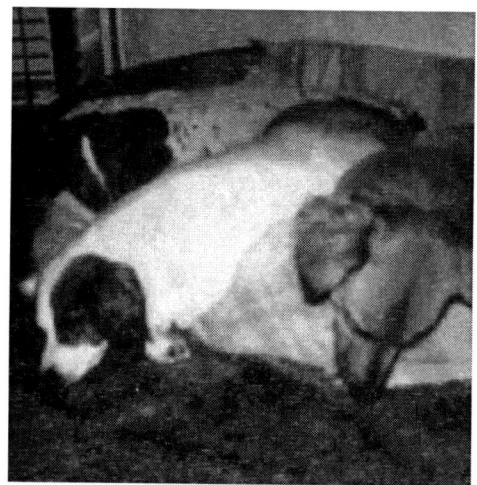

Here They Are

Here they are, my three sleepyheads,
All huddled together, didn't like separate beds,
It's Lucky, Lucy, Minky and all,
They might have woken up if you threw them a ball.

But now they're in Heaven and I miss them so much,
All I have left is their picture to touch.
They were mother and daughters,
All full of fun, we have fifteen great years,
Then they left, one by one.

F Fletcher

The Lost Kitten

I have lost my little kitten
And have hunted high and low
I wish that I could find her
Because I love her so

She ran to me every morning
When I got out of bed
I knew she wanted feeding
And her little dish is red

I've put the meat into her dish
Hoping she will appear
But when she doesn't come
I can't help but shed a tear

Perhaps if I were to look around
Maybe just once more
I might find my little kitten
For it is she I really adore

Her colour is grey and ginger
With a little pinch of white
What's that asleep in the mop bucket?
She must have slept there all night

Violetta Jean Ferguson

An Anchor Books Anthology

Who's In My Garden?

Who's in my garden? Who can I see?
Something just moved there, under that tree

Though I'm soft and docile and greet friends with glee
Patrolling the garden is my job you see

But I've been a-snoozing in the heat of the day
To conserve all my energy for after tea play

How could they have got in? And right past my nose
It's an unfair advantage when I'm having a doze

It might be a burglar, I'd better get Mum
Oh where has she gone to? Come quickly, come, come!

I look in the kitchen, and right down the hall
Checking just briefly they've not stolen my ball

But no sign of Mum yet, where can she be?
I must warn her of danger under that tree

I'll check in her bedroom, she's up there I'm sure
But no sounds emit from behind the closed door

Let's face it - she's gone out and left me in charge
So I'll have to deal with the intruder at large

Outside again now and approaching the tree
Wary of course I creep silently

Now although I'm a big dog, I'm not very brave
Especially when left to protect and to save

Oh no! It's just moved and is making a sound
But wait - it's my mum! Just messing around

I rush up to greet her - she gives me a hug
So I roll on the ground just where she has dug

She says I'm a softy for a big girl of three
But I'm glad I've got her - to protect and save me!

Cherry Vincent

Loyalty

Poppy, Willow and Beau, a delightful trio to know
Monarchs of all they survey and show
How they welcome all who pass by and glow
With that special pride and enjoyment to grow

Willow, a lady of beauty and a superior air
Not easy for her, she is deaf, not a care
Poppy, her friend, so helpful for her needs
Such a soft tongue and a kiss to show pleased

Beau, a gent, so sturdy and keeping in touch
With his beautiful lady friends he cares so much
Always aware of strangers who enter his domain
A true gentleman and friend to his charges will remain.

C King

Tribute To Jock

He was a funny little thing but he captured my heart
I knew we would choose him right from the start
A bundle of fluff, looking sad and forlorn
Didn't know he could act it, just did not dawn
Aha, he thought, *here comes some more*
Put on my sad face, show them my paw
They've stopped and looked, but there's more to see
My goodness, they're coming back for me.

With an excited yelp and a wag of his tail
Couldn't help but love him, just could not fail
On the long journey home he would not behave
As good as he got he certainly gave
Asserted himself, he was in charge
He was the boss, his ego was large.

But over the years, discipline and direction
Given with much love and affection
Gave us a dog we cherished until the end
A very dear, loyal and faithful friend
A wonderful character, he loved to run amok
But how we all loved and adored our naughty Jock.

Glenys Harris

An Anchor Books Anthology

My Friend Basil

My friend Basil, he's a fluffy little chap,
He likes his belly rubbed when he's on his back,
He doesn't like baths, he can't stand the soap,
But he likes muddy puddles which is a joke,
He likes chasing balls and wooden sticks,
From Southfield golf course he finds and he nicks.

Basil is our puppy dog, he's nearly sixteen years young,
This poem's about him, it's a song to be sung,
My friend Basil, he's my best mate,
Even at Christmas on the ice he skates,
My friend Basil, he's true, brave and strong,
My friend Basil, can't do anything wrong.

My friend Basil likes it in our car,
My friend Basil, he's a real star,
He sits on his seat with his head in the air,
My friend Basil, he hasn't got a care,
My friend Basil, he's our puppy dog,
My friend Basil likes to run and jog.

Basil likes sweets, just like me,
When we're playing we're both free,
My friend Basil lives in Oxford with us,
My dog Basil never swears or cusses,
My friend Basil, he's my best friend,
He loves me and I'll love him till the end.

The Warrior Poet - Eamon John Healy

An Ode To Izzie

She came from Cats Protection,
Small and scrawny, black and white.
We saw that cheeky little face,
And adopted her on sight.

But what they failed to mention,
(Because they didn't want her back),
We were taking home a villain,
She's a kleptomani-cat.

To strangers she's all innocence,
And kittenish surprise,
But behind the cute and cuddly,
Lies a mistress of disguise.

If it's not nailed down she'll nick it,
We discovered to our dismay,
Turn your back for just two seconds,
And your biro's gone astray.

You've just read another chapter,
Go to mark the page you're at,
But the bookmark's done a runner,
With some help from Klepto-Cat.

Clothes pegs, toys and bits of twig,
Add daily to her prizes,
We think she may have Gallic blood,
In snails she specialises.

Five minutes in the bedroom,
And my make-up brush is gone,
And cotton buds are whisked away
Covertly, one by one.

She jumps up on the office desk
To see what can be snatched,
Those paper clips look easy but
That mouse's tail's attached.

Although she's such a little thief
Her actions are not the norm,
These antics give her hours of fun
We won't demand reform.

Yes, she came from Cats Protection,
But there's no denying that
Now it's us that need protecting,
From the kleptomani-cat.

Jane Hill

Aldazi

(For my yearling Arab gelding, Aldazi)

His legs so long and twiggy
His mane so soft yet frizzy.
Large, kind eyes and a tender touch
He looks like he wouldn't ask for much.
With a small dished face
He is full of grace.
His head so high
As if touching the sky.
Slender legs floating across the floor
You just want to watch him all the more.
A little stringy tail being carried behind him
Whisking gently as friends run beside him.
His red roan coat gleams in the sun
As he runs and bucks for fun.
When being led
He is strong with his head.
His tail's held high
And his spindly legs get in a tie.
People say I must be mad
To handle such a high-spirited lad.
They say at my age I should have a plodder
But the Arabian is far more hotter!

Nikki Archer (14)

My Budgie

He's a funny-coloured yellow that is trying to be green,
And he's the scruffiest little bird that I have ever seen.
He cannot make his feathers flat, though that he tries to do,
And those on his head often stand up just like a cockatoo.
It's sad to say he cannot fly, his wings are not quite right,
He can flop down to the floor, but never can take flight.
He's a very busy bird with his mirrors and his toys,
And the antics he gets up to gives me lots of joy!
He likes to go and stay with the lady who lives next door,
She has a budgie named Pippa that I think he has fallen for.
He can talk a bit, his favourite piece is asking, 'What you doing?'
And visitors often get a surprise when they hear the question coming.
He's only a little tiny thing, but he fills a space so big,
He's been the nicest present that anyone could give.

M G Clements

Gemma And Lucy

Home from work, sat in my chair, the afternoon ahead,
Chores to do from morning's flight, including my own bed,
'No chance,' said my little dogs, 'it's time for us to play,
You may have had a busy morn, but we've wasted half the day.'

On again with hat and coat, leads held in my hand,
Time to go out for their walk, though I could hardly stand,
Been on my feet since early light, not their fault after all,
Slipping the leads around their necks, I picked up their football.

They ran and ran through all the woods, delight upon each face,
I soon forgot my weary legs, and matched their frenzied pace,
The wind blew gently through their fur, they barked with pure delight,
I'm glad I came out on this walk, would not have missed this sight.

We played for over two whole hours; they did not want to leave,
And as I had enjoyed it too, I could not them displease,
So after a quick coffee break, so eager for their run,
Off we set for one last time, a final burst of fun.

Who am I to fool myself, we stayed till darkness fell,
For they had met some friends of theirs, I had too as well,
Two more hours went whizzing by, at last back home, all fed,
Two happy dogs, one weary mum, heading for my unmade bed.

K Townsley

An Anchor Books Anthology

Unconditional Love

A King Charles spaniel we bought from Skegness
Having triplets, we thought it best
He fitted in like hand in glove
And gives us all lots of love
I let the children pick his name
They said 'Scooby' to his shame
Chasing, chewing, biting all in sight
For such a small pup he has a big bite
Now he is learning his bite is in doubt
For all his first teeth have fallen out!
The joy he's bought into our house
Is wonderful and true
To have a dog we love so much
Scooby Dooby Doo!

Caroline Hasan

Untitled

We're a brown marbled Bengal,
and a British shorthair cross.
If you do not know us,
then that is your loss!
We're cheeky and funny,
and very naughty too.
With our own sleeping quarters,
and a portable loo!
With a cat-pen outside,
for fresh air and fun.
Then back in the house,
when the warm day is done.
With lots of nice logs,
and catnip-filled toys,
we think we're very lucky,
and two very happy boys!

Lorraine Beckham

Dear Ria

You were five months old when you entered our lives,
With your big brown nervous and sorrowful eyes.
A cigarette burn scarred your right ear,
And any loud noise made you tremble with fear.

You didn't know how to run after a ball,
How to play and have fun or respond to a call.
Your tail didn't wag, you were a sorry sight,
But slowly you blossomed, your eyes became bright.

With patience and love you began to adjust,
Until at last we had won your trust.
Unconditional love was our reward,
For making you happy, safe and secure.

But the love and the laughter you gave us each day,
We knew to you we could never repay.
Then when you were ten it all went wrong,
And we knew somehow we would have to be strong.

One awful day we were told you had cancer,
And this time, Ria, we hadn't the answer.
We made a call and the vet came again,
And gently he took away your pain.

We held you as we said goodbye,
It broke our hearts to watch you die.
We laid you to rest and planted some flowers,
It was an honour, Ria, that you were ours.

You left us nearly two years ago,
We still think about you, we loved you so.
You were unique, our hearts won't mend,
We miss you Ria, our very best friend.

Rosemary Allkin

An Anchor Books Anthology

Max And Moe

Meet our guinea pigs, Max and Moe,
A friendly pair who love to go
Playing tig around the toilet
A funny duo are our pets.

Intelligent too, good at spelling
Great at maths and story-telling
Or so we would like to think
Saying that with a smile and a wink.

They love to sleep on a bed of hay
And run around when it's time to play
They took Dad's advice to stop messing on the floor
They're the smartest guinea pigs you ever saw.

Well sad to say Moe passed away
Max was lonely and we mourned each day
But now he's got another hairy friend
We hope this friendship will never end.

Hannah Moore

Ginger Cats

Ginger cats,
Ginger cats,
How I love ginger cats,
Purring gently on my bed,
Tiger stripes on soft svelte head.

Cindy chirps like baby bird,
Felix's voice so loudly heard,
'Want my tea Mum, want my tea,
Anything will do for me.'

TV time, all work is done,
Tired out with all that fun,
Catching slow-worms, chasing mice.
Now a cuddle, oh, that's nice.

Here comes Cindy, pad, pad, pad,
Eyes are pleading, why so sad?
Felix pushing, 'My turn please.'
'Stop that digging in my knees.'

Ginger cats,
Ginger cats,
What a bother - ginger cats.
All cat lovers will agree
That they mean the world to me.

Stephanie Stone

An Anchor Books Anthology

Toby

You fill our lives with so much fun
When you bark, prance around and run
You're full of life, excitement and cheer
It's jolly good, Toby, to have you near.

You're well mannered too, properly trained
A good reputation you've certainly gained
You patiently wait whenever we're out
And jubilantly greet us as you jump about.

You sense our presence from afar
With barks of joy you come to the car
You detect the movement on our grounds
And alert us to any unfamiliar sounds.

Whenever you want us to show you the door
You entreatingly approach us with uplifted paw
And your special bark that's face to face
Is a clear signal that you want some space.

If we forget to fill your tray
You never fail to have your say
You're sensible, lovely, faithful too
Life would be duller for sure without you.

Every day you come with great affection
For our love, embrace and attention
You're part of the family, Toby our pet
Do you matter to us? You bet!

Carol Small

Sam

Our faithful friend, our trusting Sam
Our loyal and loving 'little man'
You've shared our lives for many years
Through laughter, sadness, joy and tears

We brought you home when you were small
A cute and cuddly furry ball
One look and we could not resist
The sweetest pup to ever exist

You settled in and soon became
An essential part of our family frame
Life before Sam we soon forgot
As you quickly took the 'top dog' slot

From tiny tot to adult male
With silky coat and flowing tail
Feathered ears and eyes so bright
You really were a handsome sight

Walks to the park, then running wild
Jumping and playing like a child
Fetching sticks or chasing a ball
And hounding cats, you loved it all

But time won't stand still, it flew by fast
Long walks are now a thing of the past
Weak heart, and hearing no longer supreme
Running days over, except when you dream

As twilight of your life draws near
You're just as precious, still as dear
Forever you'll be our 'little man'
Our faithful friend, our trusting Sam

Jane Lynch

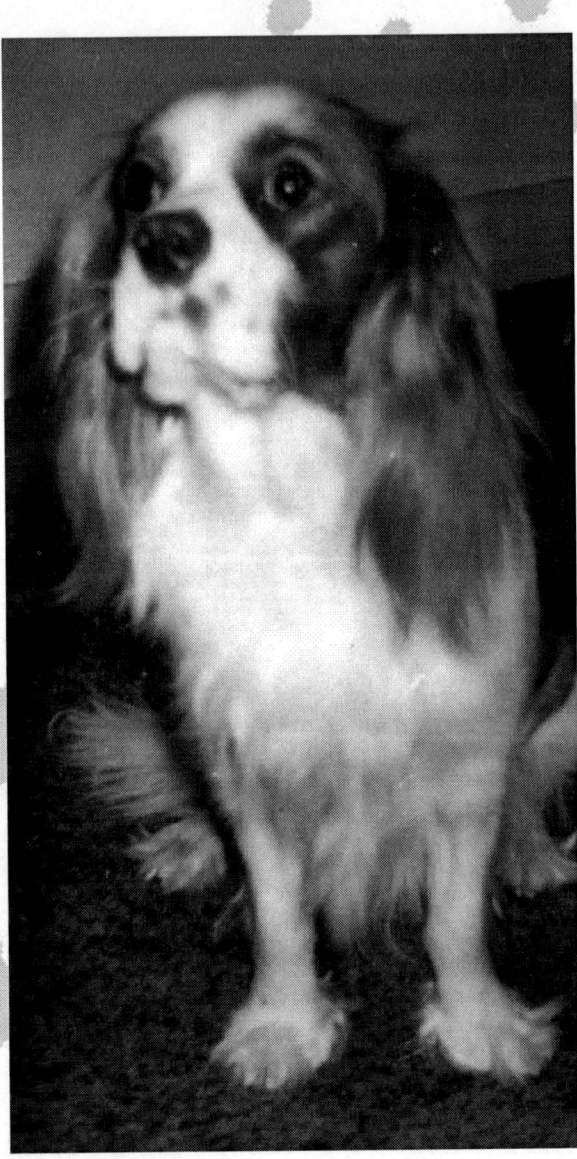

Skye

Running and jumping all over the place,
With her tennis balls she has a race,
Vases break and flowers fly,
But that's not enough to stop little Skye,
Cushions and pillows are nibbled to shreds,
Digging up roses from flower beds,
Outing visits into the greenhouse,
Stealing cucumbers and chasing a mouse,
Running in circles like a rodeo bull,
Pulling up carpet threads in the hall,
Curling up in someone's arms,
She impresses people with her puppyish charms,
Her love and kisses are full of emotion,
She offers her heart and devotion.

Katie-Leanne Findlay

Labrador

Nanna, you say that Ben has eaten five penguins
I find that so hard to believe
I thought that penguins had beaks and things?
Tell me what bit did he leave?

A Labrador dog has an appetite
He loves to be cuddled and stroked
He will eat anything from cabbage to string
But what would we do if he choked?

You never said that you meant chocolate biscuits
Me being only six thought the worst
The Antarctic has not lost any penguins
But I hope that our Ben doesn't burst.

Diane Stead

Our Dog Rusty

Rusty is our dog and he likes a jog
He's always getting away and we have to pay
He gives us such fun and likes a run
Also the sun when he eats a bun

Rusty can get dusty and becomes musty
He likes to be cool so he jumps in a pool
He was born in May, wanted to stay
He got his way, it made his day

He likes to doze but has a good nose
We love him loads even though he eats our clothes
Take Rusty down the garden path
So he can have a good crap

He likes to sniff the ground
As well as a good look round
Ho is now eleven
Sometimes he is in Heaven

He does have fits
When we need our wits
He's a good dog
He sleeps like a log

Likes sunning himself on the grass
Which some would think brash
He is a lovely friend, loyal and true
We will tend if he is feeling blue

He is always there
He does care
We hope he lives forever
Because he is very clever

Pat Hunter

An Anchor Books Anthology

An Ode To My Dogs

From left to right are my four lovely doggies,
Rosie, the King Charles, simply hates the moggies!
She's eight years old,
Is boisterous an bold,
She came from a neighbour
Who said I was doing a favour . . .

Next is Daisy who's sweet and lazy,
Being a few months old,
She rarely does as she is told!
She lays in the sun,
Always playing and having fun,
She has a collar that is pearled,
I wouldn't change her for the world . . .

Trixie-Belle is a right little tinker,
She's full of life and loves anyone who'll meet her.
Although sweet-natured, loving and fun,
If you came near her mum, she'd soon bite your bum!

Patsy-Jane was never a pain,
She used to believe that she was a Great Dane.
Being a gift from my mum when I was just four,
She was lively and kind and was never a bore.
She is in that place called Doggy Heaven now,
I'd like her as a guardian angel if God will allow . . .

Donna Townsend

The Joys Of Malik

A tiny ball of fur we chose,
Oh what fun we have in store.
From that tiny ball of fur,
Grows a big Persian cat
In all his adult glory.
Sure of foot and oh so elegant,
Not Malik, he can not jump without falling flat.
Elegantly walking among prized possessions,
Not this cat, he would rather send them flying.
A mouser he would never be,
He only has two speeds, dead slow and stop.
From that tiny ball of fur has grown
A cat who knows he is the boss, not us.
But for all his faults, and he has many,
We are still so proud to call him ours.

Zandra Collisson

Bess And Her Babies

Eyes tight closed they begin to breathe,
That safe and cosy place they don't want to leave,
It is time now to come into this world,
Their fur is damp, their whiskers uncurled,
Purring loudly their mum lays proud,
To have given birth to a furry crowd,
Snuggling up to their mum's coat of silk,
They all settle down to some lovely milk,
When they are full they have a nap,
While Mum goes out through the cat flap,
Later on they have a play,
As Mum tries to teach them to use the tray,
Cleanliness comes first with a cat,
Then food and how to catch a rat,
Plenty of rough and tumble to make them tough,
A scratch and miaow when they've had enough,
More independent, they start to wander,
And reach great climes on the bookcase yonder,
Up the curtains, along the pelmet,
We've got to go round wearing a helmet,
Protecting ourselves from falling cats,
Who are supposed to be pretty sitting on mats,
Not running around wrecking the house,
Clawing and shredding a poor toy mouse,
Sitting by the window catching some sun,
Watching the others having some fun,
Sleeping while rocking to and fro,
Dreaming of the day when it's time to go,
Eyes wide open they begin to breathe,
That safe and cosy place they begin to leave.

Dianne Leeming

An Anchor Books Anthology

Cat-A-Walling

Tosh - the handsome, coal-black cat,
Sharpened his claws on the kitchen mat,
While dreaming of Alice, sleek and trim,
Would she, he wondered, go out with him?
The 'Fe-line Good Food Guide' he bought.
'Cat's Cradle' - four stars: *That's it*, he thought.
A fine front dustbin, lights down low,
And afterwards, 'The Fence Top Show'
Where lots of clever cats there'll be
Strutting their stuff for Alice and me.
I'll offer salmon and kitty kibble,
That's bound to be a tempting nibble.
Saucers of cream to finish the meal,
Then off - exploring, with great zeal!
Tail a'swinging, whiskers combed,
Claws extended and properly honed.
Along the alley - across the yards,
An exciting evening on the cards.
Chase the mice across the field
See what the garden pond may yield.
Sitting close with tails entwined -
A good cat's lick, then wined and dined,
The alley cats' chorus will sound divine,
As I ask Alice to be mine!

Joyce Dobson

Jet's Farewell

We knew the day was coming
It was plain for all to see
You did your best to save me
Regardless of the fee
I couldn't climb the stairs no more
Or jump up in the car
My walks were getting shorter
I couldn't manage very far
And so that fateful day arrived
Away to the vet's we went
He shook his head and held my paw
A very kindly gent
And so we said our last goodbyes
Now please don't cry for me
I'm free from pain and happy now
Because my dad's taking care of me!

Janet Howden

Poppy Dog

Silly, poopy, big and bold
Growing from young to old
You look so mean and scary too
I guess that's why I love you
Your bark, so loud, can wake the dead
A wagging tail, a droopy head
A big bull mastiff, a big friend
Constantly driving me around the bend
Although fierce in looks I know the truth
You're gentle and soft from claw to tooth
You're crazy and mad, you must get it from me!
You fill our hearts with happiness and glee
Your big mouth is full of drool
You're a slobber dog, a real fool
You're my little poppy dog friend
You love your food, you make me spend
I love the way you prance about
You'll be my friend no matter how much I shout
You don't care how good I look
But when I first saw you my heart you took
You looked so cute, so sweet, so small
Now you're big, cuddly and tall
Your soft fawn fur, your black mask face
You follow me around from place to place
You're always loving and always there
You always seem to care
You love your long walks in the sun
Filled with laughter, filled with fun
I know that I really need you
And I know you need and love me too!

Lisa Booth

An Anchor Books Anthology

Basil

He came to us a kitten in November ninety-eight,
A rescue cat from Steventon, smaller than a tea plate.
His tabby stripes were uniform, a handsome ball of fluff,
He was into everything, more trouble than enough.

Basil grew quite quickly, a friendly little chap,
It soon became apparent he was a scaredy cat.
He did not like the dustmen or the recycling lorry,
And would hide on top of kitchen units, looking very worried.

We all loved him dearly, he was the centre of attention,
Never would a day go by without Basil getting a mention.
Sunday was his favourite day, he would sit right by my feet,
As I used the electric carving knife to cut our Sunday meat.

Daytimes were spent warm and comfortable, mostly fast asleep.
Night-times he was in the garden, patrolling his favourite beat.
He brought us presents of birds, frogs and once even a rat,
Did he kill it or find it? Was he really a scaredy cat?

He became ill in the summer of two thousand and two,
And was diagnosed with heart disease, which made us all feel blue.
Six months of visits to the vet with tablets morning and night,
Wrapped in ham and cream cheese, this treatment he quite liked.

Two weeks before Christmas, Basil passed away,
The suddenness of it all made it a very sad day.
He is buried in our garden, in his favourite place,
A stone with his name on marks the very space.

I don't think any animal could have been loved any more,
He never knew any cruelty or was ever locked outdoors.
Our lives were all the better for having him as our pet,
Basil the tabby we will never forget.

Steve Cannon

Our Friend Lucky

*(Dedicated to our best friend, our dog.
Spelt in reverse you will find God)*

Jet-black fluff, a smudge of white,
A muffled whimper in the night.
I creep downstairs not to alarm,
Just to check he's in no harm.

'Yes things are new and strange my dear
Let's get some sleep, dawn is near.'
Again a murmur of sadness deep,
I check once more, I cannot sleep.

Near his bed I crouch down low,
Giving comfort and assurance now.
My presence seems to ease his pain,
The silence shows I must remain.

The memories of those early days,
The smudge of white went very grey.
Unconditional love in silence given,
The kind we feel; we receive from Heaven.

The sound of excitement and love abound
Screeching and pounding on the ground.
Sparkling eyes and moister-soaked nose
Laying upturned in a familiar pose.

To enter a home knowing this awaits,
Even before one enters the gates,
But alas, now, just memories to save,
We thank God above for this blessing he gave.

I know in my heart, this love cannot die,
Especially divine love from up high.
A knowledge that can heal the pain,
To know we'll see our Lucky again.

John Worthington

Untitled

You've heard of Santa Claus,
But have you heard of Daisy Claws.
She gets on her doggy sleigh
And makes all the doggies happy on Christmas day.
She's a real good girl and gets spoilt in every single way.

Daisy May

Charlie

There in the pet shop, waiting to be chose,
Two dark eyes and a shiny, wet nose.

A shaggy coat, four legs and a tail,
A cute little puppy up for sale.

Ears pricked up, sitting *so* tall,
He was the smallest one of all.

Two hundred pounds for a pedigree breed,
Was an excellent price, we all agreed.

There was a chance that couldn't be missed,
His sweet little face we couldn't resist.

We paid the price and took him away,
He was a present for my birthday.

What would we call him? Charlie, it would be,
His mischievous character soon we did see.

Chewing a shoe, table leg or a chair,
Whatever he could find, he really didn't care.

Chasing around, running in a race,
Licking your arms, feet and face.

Out in the garden, digging up a bone,
Covered in mud, bringing it in the home.

Sleeping in our bed, what a cheeky fellow,
Barking in the morning, his way of saying hello.

And now he looks so scruffy, fur black, tan and grey,
He often needs a bath, but he always runs away.

Playing in the garden, he chases all the frogs,
Take him for a walk and he barks at great big dogs.

He has grown *so* fast, he is a puppy no more,
Our dog Charlie, who we simply do adore.

Leanne Thompson

I'm Very New

How do you do!
I'm very new
But I would love to play with you

Please don't growl or be rough
I know you're the boss and want to be tough
We could have fun and play lots of games
I could tug your ears and be a right pain

This is strange for a puppy like me
To be on my own with no family
I have no mum or a cuddly ted
All I have is this big bed

I can't help crying because I'm sad
Don't bark at me and get so mad
Please love me a little and keep me warm
I'm very frightened and so forlorn

I want to sleep but not on my own
Please! Please! Please don't moan
If I could share your bed with you
Perhaps tomorrow I won't feel so new

L Frost

An Anchor Books Anthology

Paw Prints In The Snow

One day, I followed your paw prints through
The snow, until I found you;
Why does that day of long ago,
Persist in my memory more so
Than all the other joyous moments you gave?

Dear pet of yesteryear, a tabby, grey
Striped tom, your green eyes shone;
They were playful, mischievous, and yet sad,
All in one; Rainface was the name
Often called, and it gave you fame.

My favourite time with you was when
Curled on my bed you slept; you would
Keep my feet so warm; the moonlight then
Lit up the room, such a comfort to see,
In the wee small hours, my friend with me.

It was wintertime, white all around;
Glistening snow lay on the ground;
I looked for you, but could not see,
For sometimes for days you'd missing be;
I put on my coat, my hat, my gloves.

Jaunty, anticipating, as if on a spree,
And wondering if perchance you I would see:
But what are those prints, yes, a clue!
So, I followed your paw prints through
The snow, until I found you.

Valerie Hall

Blade

They say he's just a cat and has no feelings;
That he doesn't understand that his brother's dead
And that the food bowl for
Twins has only food put
In one side,
Because his brother died;
But still he seems alone;
And afraid;
My cat: 'Blade'.

Alex L Jones

'Our' Cat

We don't take 'cuddly' pussies,
We take the ones that most need a home.
The ones you can't handle, who spit in your face
As across the flower beds they roam!

It's the tiny progress that pleases.
'She came and sat down like a friend,
As if she was happy to be companionable,
Perhaps she will come to love us in the end.'

The next time you step towards her
She flees, with every appearance of fear.
That is the sum of your achievement,
She's been living here over a year.

She sleeps in our conservatory,
With the freedom to rove far and wide.
She sunbathes in a great big flowerpot,
Hunts from her own bushy hide.

She's black and white, called Berry,
With a princess' haughty disdain,
Tempered with circumspection
For the humans she has to maintain.

We get pleasure from watching her lifestyle,
But I fear the day is very far
When we can stroke her, fuss her, play with her -
So, we'll soldier on as we are!

Joyce M Jones

Bess

Wag my tail with gusto when visitors arrive,
No one notices me.
Always loudly bark when strangers stroll past my home,
No one notices me.
Fetch mail from letter box, place it at owner's feet,
He does not notice me.
But when I leave a puddle on the kitchen floor,
Then they all notice me!

S Mullinger

Smokey

I have a dog called Smokey, his pedigree I'm not sure,
For his mother went away once, we think she was on a tour,
His coat, it is a brown one, with little spots of white,
But no matter how you tease him, he would never bite.

Now car tyres are a target, or even stony walls,
He can lift his leg so easily and lubricate them all,
'Cats', he cannot have them, he thinks they should not be,
For once they come in vision, he will chase them up a tree.

But once it comes to football, he thinks it is great fun,
He can hit the ball so hard, you would swear he had a gun,
His skills, they are amazing, he can go from left to right,
And with a glancing header, he can put it out of sight.

Now that is my dog Smokey, with bushy tail and all,
He is a grand old servant, that will obey my call,
With lappy lugs and big brown eyes, he is a sight to see,
A true and trusty partner, and a loyal friend to me.

Catherine McCracken

Little Ones

Watching them grow so gradually
Little spirit, wild and free
Beady eyes wandering around
Listening quietly to every sound

Watching eyes a-glaze and more
Jumping until the paper's tore
Their small faces searching openly
What's in here? Let me see

Something moving, so I can play
To tire me out 'til the end of the day

I like to purr when I am glad
Sometimes I may even seem sad
I have a brother, 'Dillion' by name
Whom often likes to play a game

But Dillion has a little pink nose
And jumps the covers between your toes
My name's Tom and I am black
I have long hair upon my back

I sometimes smell although I'm clean
A problem that is seldom seen
I have a daddy whom doesn't like me
He just likes to roam and be free

Nelson's his name but he isn't tame
He's a wild striped tiger all the same
A mother too who's adopted me
She licks, washes and lets me be

She holds me down with her paw
And even opens any door
Tiny nose and weenie eyes
It's time to say our last goodbyes

V J Haynes

Teddy

Fluffy bichon couldn't see
The sun was bright and so was he
He found some shades and wore a 'T'
So summer was quite funny for me.

Kaye Townsend

An Anchor Books Anthology

My Pony Sweet Pea

Faster than a bullet,
Blacker than the night,
Jumps higher than a deer
And always gets it right!

Shinier than a new van,
Even cuter than me,
Friendlier than an old gran,
My pony Sweet Pea.

Sophie Punteney

Big-Little Poodle

My miniature poodle, Rupert, of 14 years,
So full of mischief he has me in tears.
His expressive ways to let me know his needs,
Big brown eyes that say 'please'.

The different barks I have got to know,
One for the postman as he fetches the post,
One says welcome home, I like the most.
His presence makes a house a home,
Down on the rug with his bone.

Mischievous moments I call happy hour,
Who would believe such a small dog's power?
Digging up the lawn, shrub or flower,
I could watch him for many an hour.

At quieter times when I watch TV,
He curls up on the settee.
Occasionally he will open one eye
As good as to say, 'Any tea and biscuits going today?'

Margaret Kinshott

My Pet Hahns Macaw Called 'Benny'

Hello, I am Benny and look, I am waving at you
And I can do tricks too,
I roll on my back and play ball on my belly,
I can do this even whilst watching telly.

I love my new mum and dad,
They love to play with me and I am glad,
Without all this attention I would be sad,
When I call Mum she comes running, that can't be bad.

I have a lovely home with two cockatiels for company,
I am not so sure that they understand me,
I play most of the day on my play frame with glee,
It's great fun and I'll never want to flee.

I like Mum's shoulder as I like to talk into her ear,
We dance together without much fear,
I will do any trick for a treat,
Mum thinks that's pretty neat.

Toys are my favourite things,
I even like to swing on my rings,
My cage is a fun place to be,
I love it here as you can see.

So with that I will wave goodbye,
Bye-bye from Benny, a much-loved Hahns Macaw.

A Heath

An Anchor Books Anthology

Heatherbell

I was once a poor but angry wild cat,
What had I done to deserve such a fate?
My undercarriage was hairless,
The chest skin had turned brown.

My mother couldn't care for me,
But lucky for me I was befriended,
This kind lady (Betty) took me under her wing,
Nursing me back to health as you can see.

After a year of her ministrations,
I decided I wanted to be in a single pet household,
My mind was made up, Jan lived in the upstairs flat,
She had no pets, she needed me, a cat!

I still visited just to annoy Misty the collie,
It was very pleasurable to fling everything on the table,
Down on him, his only reaction was to stare at me,
To get under his skin I just wasn't able.

When tiring with Jan, to get away from it all,
I discovered that a leap from the bed,
Would enable me to reach the wardrobe,
On top of which I could be hidden from all sight.

But, there was a social side to me too,
When Jan watered the garden, I was out there, like a bolt from the blue.
It was there that I met up with Goldie,
As her name suggests, she was a golden retriever.

She became a very good friend of mine,
We spent many happy hours together in the garden,
Where an assortment of neighbouring cats and dogs
Would meet to catch up on the local news.
If I needed some medical help, it was there,
So it was sensible to be passive and quiet like me!

M Lawson

The Night Shift

The animals look after us or so it would appear
Our two King Charles' just love a fuss
And yet they hate to hear
The black cat that preceded them
In house and our affection
Who didn't welcome them one bit
In fact displayed rejection.

She rounds them up and takes their chair
They really feel that life's unfair

Charlie likes a cuddle and we rub Dolly's belly
While Purdey cat avoids all that and jumps up on the telly

The morning comes and they want fed
Purdey jumps upon the bed
Charlie follows close behind
While Dolly very often finds
Her little legs won't let her join the other two
So we get up and help her - what else can we do?

The animals are sleeping all cosy on our bed
Which makes it very difficult for us to lay our heads

We think they must be tired and suppose it's only right
That they should have their rest . . .
After guarding us all night.

Dawn Sansum

Christmas Or Birthday?

I would like a cat for Christmas Dad
Or maybe a little dog
How about a goldfish then, we already have a tank
With the one left it can snog.

I would like a snake for my birthday Mum
You say you cannot stand the sight
Yet you look at my stepfather quite a lot
And he seems to you quite all right.

I would like a pony for my eighteenth birthday
So in the night I can ride away
Away from this place where
No pet ever is allowed to stay.

Keith L Powell

Bramble Lady

Our little Border terrier has a mind all of her own,
And if she doesn't get her way she'll quietly moan and groan.
She fixes us with soulful eyes and stares with great intent,
Just willing us, 'please play with me', or 'a walk, it's time we went'.

Officially 'Bramble Lady' but often 'Brammie' is her name,
But whatever she's called and whatever she does, we love her
Just the same.
Say words like 'biccies' or 'walkies' and her head cocks to one side,
She loves to seek for a favourite toy which under the cushions we hide.

She's quite a little 'piggy' and she likes to chomp and chomp,
Then chase a ball around the stool and on the lawn to romp.
She loves her tasty titbits and often sits and begs,
Then runs very fast, though six years ago she lost one of her back legs.

Brammie likes her teeth cleaned, which we try to do each night,
When brushing her coat she stretches out with obvious delight.
When we tickle her ears she often makes little noises of pleasure,
And licks and nibbles our fingers and face - she really is a treasure.

Though so nice to us, with other dogs, it's really a different story,
All bitches and Westies she hates the most -
It really could get rather gory!
But we keep her in check, hold tight on the lead,
And we limit to barking, so avoid the dark deed!

When bedtime comes she chooses her place, taking the greatest care,
Sometimes deciding to sleep downstairs curled up in a deep armchair.
But more often than not it's upstairs with us, either on, or in, our bed,
Ignoring her basket for most of the time, on our pillow
She lays her head!

Yes, this is our little doggie, who is loved by all of us,
(Though when she catches 'froggies' we're inclined to make a fuss!)
Some things are good, some things are bad, she covers the full range,
But when we sit to consider - *there's nothing that we'd change*.

E Marcia Higgins

An Anchor Books Anthology

Amelia

Today I lost a friend.
A friend of sixteen years.
A faithful companion.
Do you wonder at my tears?

She used to walk by my side,
as we went out for a walk.
She was full of love and tenderness,
in her own way she could talk.

She was never any trouble,
though she was old, she seemed so young,
and we'd tell each other stories,
as the years slipped along.

I thank God for giving her to me.
She will be always in my prayers,
and we buried her with dignity,
to let her know that someone still cares.

In a world that's full of bitterness
and hatred and all that,
she was one of God's great gifts to me.
Amelia my cat.

Gerry Concah

Doggy's Doo

Sally went do-lally causing such a ballyhoo
Miss O'Mally's doggy crossed her lawn and did a poo
A poo on her new patio - it was her joy and pride
So Sally went do-lally and she tanned the dog's backside
O'Mally spotted Sally tan the hide of doggy Sue
Unaware her spotty treasure had deposited a poo
Didn't dilly-dally, filled with righteous indignation
With violent remonstrations went to rescue her Dalmatian
Do-lally Sally pointed out the poop upon her flags
O'Mally now deflated said, 'She's such a scallywag
Pooping on your patio, a place I know you prize
But doggies do do doggy doo, I do apologise.'

Bill Goulden

An Anchor Books Anthology

Joey

I have a little budgie, she is a little dear,
She climbs upon the wind-chimes and rings them very clear;
She talks her little legs off and sings most of the day,
It's 'Pretty Joey, pretty Joey' on her merry way.

When she wants her food, she goes into her cage,
But if you try to shut her in, she goes into a rage;
She seems to say 'no way' as she darts out and flies away,
Back into the window, and then she's on display.

She loves it in the window, watching wild birds come and go,
I think she'd like to join them, but you know that can't be so;
They'd be jealous of her colours, and kill her in no time,
So she has to stay at home with me, and realise that she's mine.

She stays in the window or on the chimes until the end of day,
And someone draws the curtains, there's no more time to play;
Then she'll fly back to her cage, and on top of it she'll sit,
Until next morning curtains are drawn, then she starts to flit.

Thelma Cook

Parsley Cat

Big fat body, tiny head,
always mewing to be fed.
Loves a brush, and lots of fuss,
Parsley cat is one of us.
He likes to snuggle on your lap,
and drag wildlife through his flap!
Tuna is his favourite fish,
if you can get it in his dish.
Black and shiny, eyes of green,
to other cats he can be mean,
but we love Parsley, and his purr
shows he's a happy lump of fur!

Diane Bowen

So Long My Friend

(Dedicated to Roxy)

Sorry you had to go this way
i wish you didn't have to
i wish you could stay
i'm gonna miss you that's for sure
what more can i give you
wish i could give you more
i have done all that i can to try to understand
but i know it's nearly time for you to go
hey baby i'm gonna really miss you so

so my friend please don't cry
in my heart you will be by my side
we get once chance in this meaning of life
do not know why you had to die

it's three in the morning i didn't get any sleep last night
kept stroking your face and wondering why
you look so good cannot believe it's true
you've only just left me tell me what am i going to do
i held your paw i wish you could have let me know
before the angels took you
how did they know?
We get one chance in this cruel, cruel life
promised i'd care for you right through your life
just put your collar and tag on your bed
thought of the nice memories and the good times we had

goodbye my friend you don't mind if i cry
sitting here with your toys i have tears in my eyes
you look so peaceful a relieved look on your face
the pain has gone
have fun in your new place

Stephen A Owen

An Anchor Books Anthology

My Dog Milo

Milo's small
Milo's strong
Milo keeps going all day long

His nose is wet
His tail is short
When he sleeps he often snores

My bed he sleeps on
All the room he takes
I'm sure he's eaten all my cakes

He's my best friend
I love him so
My life without him
Would never glow

Milo to welcome me home
A positive paw when I'm alone
Cheerful terrier, happy chap
He always greets me with a yap.

Amy Sedgwick

The Cat

Aloof and alone the black cat stalks the darkening streets.
Pushing aside rubbish in its search for a meal,
it finds what it wants in packaging real.

'Hark now' a new sound is heard in the street.
The black cat ventures to cautiously meet,
the meanest of adversaries.
With hackles rising and claws intent
on inflicting punishment on the intruder.

As the black cat coils to spring
the stranger too prepares, and swings,
in a dangerous manner to oppose the king.

As the howls of the sparring two meet, a hush falls over
the neighbourhood, waiting with baited breath
the outcome of the fight to the death.

Suddenly the intruder, punished enough
slinks away into the night to lick his wounds and think he's tough.
The black cat also licks his wounds and wanders away along the street.
He's lived through the danger he had to beat,
and gave of himself like a soldier brave
who will live to fight another day.

G Nutbeem

Spotty

There's a long thing behind me
And try as I may
By chasing it in circles
I will catch it some day

I cannot imagine
What this long thing can be
I only know it's there
And following me

Is he a friend?
Does he want to play?
I yapped at him loudly
Not a thing does he say

When I get excited
The long thing I will tell
He wags from side to side
Taking me with him as well

He gets me into trouble
Knocking things on the floor
He even hurt me
When he got trapped in the door

That's when I discovered
That long thing behind I see
Isn't a friend come to play at all
It's really a part of me

Well I am a baby dog
And named as Spotty
Even my owners laugh at me
Because I act so dotty

Christine Cyster

An Anchor Books Anthology

Social Climbers

Prunes for tea
For Pansy
And me
'Cause we're a couple
Of swells.
We like to keep regular
Hours each day,
As all the best girls do,
We dine from our bowls
Of best china clay,
Don't bother with spoons
Or a fork,
'Proones,' we say,
With plums in our mouths,
And chatter the best
Doggie 'talk'!

Lyn Sandford

My New Rabbit

We brought him home, I was so pleased,
We made a rabbit hutch.
I gave him oats and talked to him,
I loved him oh so much.

Now when I talk to Rover the dog,
He answers me, 'Bow-bow.'
And when I speak to pussy cat,
She purrs and says, 'Miaow.'

But bunny never says a word,
Just twinkles with his nose.
And what that rabbit thinks about,
Why no one will ever know.

So bunny sits there looking wise,
And twinkling with his nose.
And never, never, *never* tells
A single thing he knows.

My mum says that the fairies
Must have put him in a spell,
They told him all their secrets then
They whispered, 'Pray don't tell'.

David Sheasby

Pearl

Sneaky and stubborn, born to rule
She's a doll and nobody's fool
Obedient, yes up to a point
An ideal doorstop in her joint.
So laid back in fact she's cool
Unless she's hot, then she'll drool
Accepting love and food of course
Walking ladylike, taking her choice
Of sniffs and smells along the way
Laughing gently come what may
She's so precious, a gentle babe,
Guarding her gate in the wind or rain.

Angela Allen

Our Dog Sam

His coat is shining and his nose is cold
He's our baby, he's only six months old
Sometimes he's good other times bad
But he's the best dog we ever had.

He gives a loud bark whenever he hears a sound
We are never afraid when he's around
When he is naughty he runs away
We couldn't be mad at him
Not even for a day.

He loves to fetch us things
Anyone watching would think he has wings
Unconditional love is what he gives
We'll give him love for as long as he lives.

Now our Sam has passed away
We think about him every day
For such a little dog he gave so much love
Now he fetches things for the angels above.

Cassandra Evans

An Anchor Books Anthology

Finicky Eaters

Open up another tin Mum
Open one that's tasty
Be sure you read the label
Please don't be too hasty
Yesterday you gave me duck
I wasn't very keen
The day before was rabbit
God knows where that had been
Now if you give me sardines
Then a plate of trout
And in between some nice rare beef
I'd have nothing to moan about
Open up another tin Mum
I don't like this one very much
The gravy's just like water
And the meat resembles slush
Yesterday was plaice and shrimp
The day before was cod
I'm afraid I didn't eat it
Because it looked so odd
The tin of heart, that wasn't bad
The lamb was tough and tasteless
Go by some nice fresh salmon
I'm sure that wouldn't be wasted
Look for some nice new flavours
Water buffalo, squirrel or dog
Visit Coop, Marks and Tesco
You may even find some frog
So open up another tin Mum
Open one I really like
Oh no! Forget about it
I'll go and catch some mice

J Van Dyk-Harrison

A Walk On The Wild Side

A winter's day a wild wind blowing
My dog knows just where I'm going
He skids on the lino on the way to the door.
We're off to the park. I must be mad, that's for sure!
But hey . . . it's OK, I'll wrap up warm,
Together we will weather the storm.
Once out of the door, he's off like a rocket
Nearly wrenching my arm from its socket.
The lead stretched out to its fullest extent
As I lean into the wind, my back is bent
Unclip the leash, there, off he goes
To investigate scents of what . . . heaven knows.
My sock has slipped down inside my wellie,
My dog comes back wet and smelly,
So I throw a large stick into the lake
Out he climbs - oh for goodness sake!
Both covered in twigs, we don't give two figs
As we track back to the dry and the warm
Away from the wind, the wet and the storm.
The two of us take it all in our stride
We've enjoyed *a walk on the wild side.*

Audrey Lucas

Friendship

You can never be lonely if you have a good friend
Either she or a he, well the sex just depends.
Someone you rely on, when the going gets tough
Someone who loves you from morning till dusk
Seeing you at your best or even your worst
They still give you comfort, when left in the lurch.
When you have a worry, they will worry with you
Whatever the circumstance, they remain true.
Years make no difference when you're growing old
They know all your secrets, to others untold.
I'm writing you know about my best friend the cat
Nineteen years I've watched him play on the mat.
One day too weary, to go out of the door
The following day, sadly lay still on the floor
I stroked him, and cuddled, sensing his fear
I dreaded this time when he would not be near
Our Tigger, passed on maybe five years ago
How much I miss him? You'll never know.
But I'm sure he's in Heaven waiting for me
My ginger haired buddy, I so long to see.

Joan Prentice

An Anchor Books Anthology

A Big Dog Called Blue

I'll tell you the tale of a big dog called Blue,
When he was a puppy he chewed up my shoe.

He chewed up my sofa, he chewed my armchairs,
He chewed at the carpet that went up the stairs.

He chewed up the car if he got shut inside,
He chewed even more when we went for a ride.

He chewed at his lead when we went for a walk,
He chewed at the phone while I tried hard to talk.

He chewed at my feet and the legs of my chairs,
He even chewed lumps from the bottom two stairs.

I was outside one day, just for minutes, not hours,
He chewed my new slippers, and even my flowers.

My flowers were the last straw, for him, not for me.
The look on his face was a picture to see.

The carpet was tasty, and so was the wood,
But the flavour of flowers was not quite so good.

Now Blue is a grown-up, a puppy no more.
He doesn't chew carpets or gnaw at the door.

I think of those flowers with a smile on my face,
So glad there was something not quite to Blue's taste.

Linda Spendley

A Just Reward

There are drawbacks to being a poodle!
One occurs every night of the year;
My brush and comb come out of hiding,
And my human says, 'Jacob, come here!'

She says that this brushing and combing
Shows that she really cares,
And that if she didn't do it each evening,
I'd have sore ears and matted hairs.

I have to lie down on the carpet
While my human starts work with the brush;
If any small tangles get pulled by the comb,
She ignores my protest, and tells me to hush!

I hate having my eyes and my ears done!
It's not just the undignified pose,
But to make sure she can do the job properly,
She holds me still by the nose!

But I get my reward when it's over,
And the brushing and combing stops,
Because I must admit I feel better,
And I get four doggy chocolate drops!

Jane Earley

My Name's Tinky

My name's Tinky, and I'm in charge
Everybody knows it, when I'm at large
I don't fear the cat - I try and pull her tail
She runs away with flattened ears, letting out a wail!

My name's Tinky, and I'm here to stay
I'll tell you off and nip you
If I don't get my own way.
I'll scream and scream until I'm definitely heard
And then I'll come and bite you - oh what a naughty bird!

My name's Tinky, and I'm the 'big cheese'
I can be cute and cuddly - but only when I please
I'll love you when I want to
And ignore you sometimes too
I'm changeable and cheeky
And irresistible to you!

Liz Gibbons

Kits

This is a poem about our cat Kits
On the window sill he sits,
Watching the birds on the lawn
Stretching and giving a lazy yawn,
Thinking I'd like to get you in my paws
And torment you with my claws,
Then he moves off to his own space
Curls up with his paw over his face,
Dreaming of the mouse that got away
Hoping to catch it another day,
That's the poem about our cat Kits
He's a horror but we love him to bits.

Richard Trowbridge

Lucky

She stretched her sleek black body,
as back and forth she paced,
perched upon the worktop -
whiskers in your face.

A cat of great importance,
pampered as can be . . .
'I want my dinner, woman -
it's dinner time! I say.'

'Is that my tin you're opening?
Come on, I need that food;
hurry up - stop dithering
I'm in a hungry mood.'

'I think I'll go and chase a mouse,
well maybe perhaps a bird,
I simply must get out of the house,
I'm feeling rather bored.'

When we got another puss,
it didn't bring much joy,
for Lucky, thought that she was boss,
ignored him like the plague.

'That Timmy Tab, that's joined us,
is not my cup of tea,
at night he mews and makes a fuss
he really gets to me.'

She looked at him, as if to say -
you're not quite in my class.
Push off, you Tom, do go and play
you're sitting in my place.

She'd give him lots of dirty looks
because he'd stole her space.
'You'll never be in my good books,
push off, you're just a waste!'

Wendy Watkin

An Anchor Books Anthology

Torment

I adore the ground you walk on
I adore the floor too
I adore any transport
That'll take me away from you.

Oh for peace and quiet
Oh for the beauty it brings you
For you've made my life a living hell
All the years we've been through.

I curse the day I met you
I curse the day I brought you in
You've been nothing but trouble
To answer for my sin.

Don't look at me with those dark eyes
Don't you see it's too late
Why aren't you going
I'll open up the gate.

Don't wag your tail or lick my face
You'll bring a tear to me
Oh all right, just one more night
And tomorrow we will see.

J Lanigan

Sophie Pup

Coat dark as night with nutty brown patches
all rumpled and tangled
from where she constantly scratches
fast as lightning
that streaks through the sky
she's here in a flash
and certainly not shy
her life is a playtime
and we are her toys
she's happy and funny
full of such joys
nutty as a fruit cake she bounces around
so full of herself she hardly touches the ground

Yet when she's asleep
all cuddly and soft
and our world is at peace
we know without her we'd be lost.

Daphne E Cornell

Untitled

Vegas, my four-legged friend,
He's got a heart of gold
He's clever, sweet and funny
And he's only three years old.

He stands at fifteen hands
And his coat is shiny bay
He knows it's time for dinner
And he gives a cheery neigh

He didn't take to racing
It's not his cup of tea
But I'm so glad I found him
And brought him home with me

His ears are always forward
I still can't believe he's mine
To own him is an honour
He's my superstar equine.

I treasure every minute
With my horse that I can spend
And I wonder what I've done
To deserve my horse, my friend.

J Thorpe

Paddington's Poem

My name is Paddington Bear,
You see I really don't have a care

Sometimes I might have a run around,
Catching imaginary things on the ground.

Mum and Dad think I'm a bit of a fool,
But us cats know we're really cool.

Do you know they made me a house?
It's got tunnels, a slide and even a mouse.

And at the end of all this playing
I know exactly where I'm staying.

Curled up in front of the fire
Just perfect when I need to retire.

L Brant

An Anchor Books Anthology

Pony Tales

Cantering over the hills on my horse,
Enjoying the freedom to ride without thought,
Over the hills and over the dales
Where Reynard has shown other horsemen his tale.

My horse is a thunderbolt riding to war.
Those trees in the distance hide foreign gun corps,
And those hedges are hiding brave soldiers of old,
But my William and me jump ever so bold.

I draw my sharp sabre and hold it on high.
I hear bullets and missiles and my battle cry!
As Bill moves to the gallop, his heart is so large,
Behind us are soldiers I lead in the charge.

The enemy fire is now very strong
But the drumming of hooves are driving us on,
For we're on them in seconds and galloping on.
My horse guards have followed, so nothing went wrong.

But, then I see Father waving at me,
And Mother is standing upset as can be.
William is trotting and coming to the walk
As we prepare to face fire from a 'fatherly talk!'

Joe Coop

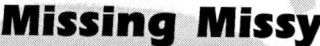

Missing Missy

You are an angel,
Your silver, silky coat is like a handmade pearl dress,
Your eyes fill up the sky,
Your feet are fluffy,
Like the clouds you stand on,
As the wind blows,
I can hear you speaking to me,
As the rain falls,
I can feel your comfort,
As the sun shines,
I can feel you playing with me,
When I'm upset,
I can feel you drying my tears and giving me all your love,
I know wherever I go, whatever I do,
I know you will always be there.

Rachael Wilson (15)

A Platonic Marriage

(For Patch, with love from Ginger)

Oh Patch! You know I do admire
Your fluffy, soft white coat
Just the way you wriggle your cotton tail
Makes my heart feel quite afloat
With your dark eyes twinkling
From underneath that velveteen brown patch
And that mischievous glint in those sad beautiful eyes
I wish it was possible that we could make a match!
You elegantly laze in the sun
Sprawled out longways, blocking the door
So I have to climb up when I want to drink
Using you as a stool, because you leave no room for floor!
Every day you beat me to the food
We always seem to have that race
Eventually, when you've had your fill
You let me feed my face!
I don't mind your dominance -
I'm used to all your ways
Just because you are the best rabbit friend
That a guinea pig could wish for, to spend out all his days
You wash me, groom me
Help me to scratch any itch
The feel of your tongue is so soothing
Relaxing me every inch
I often think about what it'd be like
If we were animals of kind the same
We could have a family together
But that would spoil our games
So I am settled to be content
Just to be with you everyday
In our platonic marriage, seeing out the future
Being together, we will be able to face come what may.

Michelle Luetchford

Friend

Is the word
'pet'
appropriate for
you?
A 'friend',
a 'companion',
is more suitable
and true.

Frank Murri

An Anchor Books Anthology

I Miss You

(In memory of Katie Knowles 2002-3)

Katie Loo I miss you
I miss your black spots
Your soft white skin
Those brown eyes
That made you win
Your thin ears
Your cold tears
That ran down your face

Katie Loo I miss you
That cold wet nose
Those black and white toes
Those sharp claws
Those big paws
Those long legs
Those white pegs
That dug into my skin
That made you win
Our game

That joy that filled up inside me
Was something not to hide
And I'll never forget you,
As you're still by my side.

Faye Knowles (14)

An Acrobatic Moment

The pear tree in my garden acts as host to many things,
Creatures that can crawl and climb, as well as those with wings.
The blossom looks so beautiful on branches gnarled and grey,
Springtime brings those visual treats that change with every day.

The latest is a flock of very acrobatic birds,
Starlings, tits and sparrows, and a woodpecker I've heard.
But this morning, on the peanuts, I saw a lovely sight,
Two squirrels swinging upside down, which put the birds to flight!

They scampered through the foliage, and had a tasty snack,
Up and down the pear tree trunk, they just kept coming back.
My kitchen window vantage point shows views, the best of all,
And it never seems to matter if the crop of pears is small!

Marjorie Chapman

Pixie

P ixie's a cat.
I rritating,
'X -tremely mischievous!
I n the garden at every opportunity,
E very other cat, *watch out!*

Nicole Woollard

In Memory Of Scott

Our hamster was a rascal,
He played the fool and had a ball.

Ran up and down the ladder,
Spun the wheel,
His beautiful colouring had hamster appeal.

Apricot and white,
Soft and smooth,
Intelligent and bright, you had to approve.

Impressions of Houdini,
Planned in advance.
Waiting till it's late at night,
Escaping at every chance.

All packed up,
The boxes full,
Scott's in his cage kept in the hall.

I heard a rattle,
Movement in the night,
I screamed and ran out in a terrible fright.

Scurrying around the house he went,
He sensed we were moving and then repents.
We saw the sadness in his eyes,
One look around to say goodbye.

Today he died at nearly two,
My little friend what will I do?
A happy life with love galore,
My confidant who came and saw.

Angela A Shaw

An Anchor Books Anthology

Early Morning Wake-Up Call

They spied you from the start and
alarm calls rouse the whole block.
We turn from the open window,
bring in focus the neon clock

while you sit there, you silly thing,
black and white against the green.
You think to get away with it,
but your body cries out 'mean!'

Such a hue and cry you've begun,
as they seek only to protect.
Oh no, your fluffy presence
will not force them to neglect.

For weeks the two have laboured
in shifts both day and night.
They've dive-bombed you before.
It's you who'll have the fright.

So come on in, you silly thing.
Let them stop that infernal racket.
If you want a meal of blackbird
you'll need a camouflage jacket.

Lynda Bullock

Indie

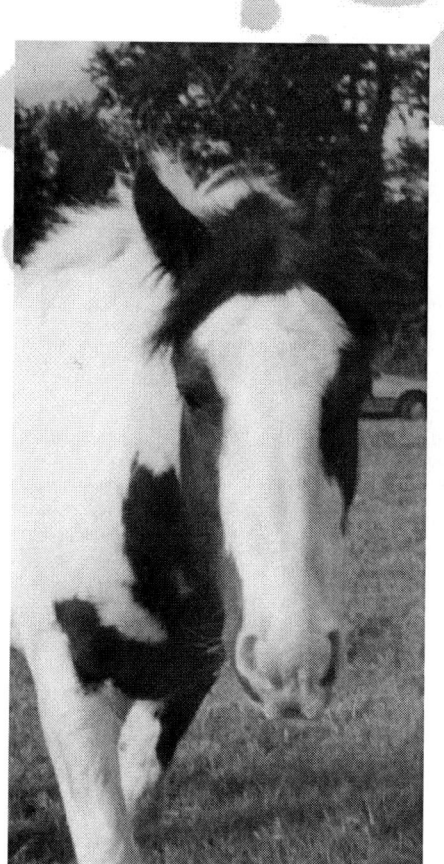

I'm a coloured cob called Indie
In a paddock on my own
I have lots of friends
but they've left me all alone
I ran at them and bit them hard
to let them know who's in charge
I watch them playing happily
I would like to play as well
maybe they'll forgive me when they know I mean no harm
after all, I'm rather nice with lots and lots of charm.

Karin Dyer

A Busy Dog Called Sally

Come on, it's getting up time, I'm licking your face,
You're slow at moving - but I'll match your pace.

Where are you going? I'm coming too
And bringing my ball while you go to the loo.

Well throw it then, or nudge it with your toe,
I'll catch it anyway - I'm very fast you know.

I'm up the stairs before you and waiting at the top,
You really are slow you know - why do you have to stop?

Can I have the empty loo roll? I love to rip it up
And hear you rant that I really am a mucky pup.

Are we going down the garden and watering the plants?
I'll follow you around and try and catch the ants.

Are we going for a walk? Where's my lead and ball?
What do you mean if I don't stop screaming we'll never leave the hall?

Which is it today? The field, the country or the park?
Why should I shut up - you know I always bark.

There goes a rabbit, I'm nearly on its tail,
Down the hole it went - why do I always fail?

Back in the car, head for home without a single shout,
No point barking now, I really am worn out.

Feeding time and then a little nap,
I wish you'd move your knitting - I can't fit on your lap.

Dad's home, yippee, *now* it's time to play,
Let me find my teddy - I always get my way!

Evening time and while you two have a little chat,
I'll check the garden for any signs of that darn cat.

Now it's bedtime, I'll snuggle under your chin.
Please put your arm around me - I really am done in.

Barbara Morris

An Anchor Books Anthology

Smokie

My cat kisses my bare toes
Why she does it, nobody knows
Is it because I feed her turkey breast?
Or for all else I do, all the rest?

She comes yamming at my door at midnight
She feels lonely and 'out of sight,
Out of mind', she wants my attention
So I let her in to decrease the tension

She regally stalks around in all her majesty
If something happened to her, it would be a travesty
She's out all night and I worry no end
Till in the dawning morning comes my friend

I am very fond of her, though she's only mine on loan
I watch her for my neighbours when they are away from home
I am the resident pet-watcher of the street
Though it takes some effort, it makes me replete

To get to know furry friends not my own
Is a joy, adds spice to life, I would never have known
Although it means early mornings,
When I'd rather have a lie
Smokie is worth it,
She's the apple of my eye.

Mary A Shovlin

Louis

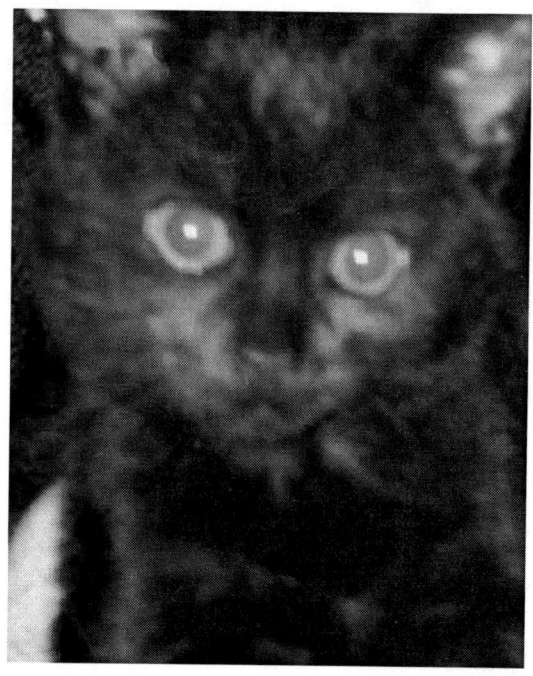

If you live with us
You'll obey our rules.
So what do you say
To that pussy cat?
There will be no catching
Of birds or mice,
You'll have to cope without that.
So Louis became an indoor cat
At the age of nine weeks old,
And we wondered if he'd take to us
With all his heart and soul.
As the months flew hurriedly by
And Louis grew from kitten to cat
Our love grew for each other
And *yes folks, that's a fact.*

David Ashley Reddish

Once I Was A Lonely Dog

Once I was a lonely dog, just looking for a home,
I had no place to go, no one to call my own,
I wandered up and down the streets, in rain, in heat and snow,
I ate whatever I could find, I was always on the go,
My skin would itch, my feet were sore, my body ached with pain,
And no one stopped to give a pat, or gently say my name,
I never saw a loving glance, I was always on the run,
For people thought that hurting me was really lots of fun,
And then one day I heard a voice, so gentle, kind and sweet,
And arms so soft reached down to me, and took me off my feet,
'No one again will hurt you,' was whispered in my ear,
'You'll have a home to call your own, where you will know no fear.'
'You will be dry, you will be warm, you'll have enough to eat,
And rest assured that when you sleep, your dreams will all be sweet.'
I was afraid I must admit, I've lived so long in fear,
I can't remember when I let a human come so near
And as she tended to my wounds, and bathed and brushed my fur,
She told me about the rescue group, and what it meant to her,
She said, 'We are a circle, a line that never ends,
And in the centre there is you, protected by my friends,
And all around you are the ones that check the pounds,
And these that share their home, after you've been found,
And all the other folk, are searching near and far,
To find the perfect home for you, where you can be a star.'
She said, 'There is a family that's waiting patiently,
And pretty soon we'll find them, just them, just you wait and see,
And then they'll join our circle, they'll help to make it grow,
So there'll be room for more like you, who have no place to go.'
I waited very patiently, the dogs came and went,
Today's the day I thought, my family will be sent.
Then just when I began to think, it wasn't meant to be,
There were people standing there, just gazing down at me,
I knew them in a heartbeat, I could tell they felt it too,
They said, 'We have been waiting for a special dog like you.'

Now every night I say a prayer, to all the gods to be,
'Thank you for the one life, and all you've given me,
But most of all, protect the dogs in the pound and on the street,
And sent a rescue person to lift them off their feet.'

Martyn Dickinson

Brandy

Sit still my friend, and take a pew,
For a shaggy story I will lend to you.
Of a gun dog who became my favourite pet.
No weary smile, or small regret
I do perceive when her bounding little body I receive
Her energy seems endless, almost beyond the bounds of love
But as I scratch her ear; I know, in the warm of my heart -
She can never get enough.
I stroke the tricolour standard, the flaxen fur that is her coat
I think of when I've lost her, and get a lump within my throat.
She is the best companion, she is the only one
And I know for sure, I will miss her
When her wagging tail is finally gone.

Damian Davies

He's A Scruff

I've never liked dogs that dribble and drool,
At the slightest whiff of food.
Dogs that even when 'seen to' by vets
Have behaviour extremely rude.

Or dogs that dig up beautiful lawns
And pull up plants, for fun.
That roll in all the muck they can find
Before stretching out in the sun.

Some dogs bring home slugs and snails
And pass gases that turn you blue.
Some dogs don't just smell their friends
But sniff at humans too.

Well, my dog, he does all these things.
He's a filthy little beast.
And just because I love him so,
I don't care in the least.

One look at his face, just melts my heart.
He's loving, he's loyal and more.
I wouldn't change the slightest thing.
He's Scruff the dog I adore.

Christine Ash-Smith

My Best Friend

He has eyes to see danger well before I do,
He has ears to hear things I don't know are there.
He has a bay glossy coat that shines with radiance,
He has a long silky tail that glides through the air.
He has a mind that somehow can tell how I'm feeling,
He has the strength to carry me without a care.
He has the magic to calm me, which I find healing,
He will give all he's got which nowadays is rare.
He has the power of flight over fences,
He has the stamina to go all the way,
He keeps us safe with all his senses,
He will always be with me, forever and a day.

Julie Roberts

Our Special Friend

One of our pets, is black and tan,
A truly good friend to *any* man.
Very rarely does he whine,
Our Tibetan terrier, pet dog Shine.

With Dad he goes walkies every day,
From us he *never* goes astray.
When the days work is done, he is full of glee,
Together, with me, he watches TV.

At times he feels, things are not right,
When one of us goes out, he is in a plight.
His loving ways makes him, a little cutie,
Shine really *is*, our very own beauty.

His name, really is no surprise,
He has such *bright* and *shining* eyes.
When it's time to go for a walk, he is like a child,
With joy, and happiness, he goes quite wild.

More sincere friend than *any* human being,
His love, and affection, really *is* worth seeing.
Shine gives to us, *such* pleasurable hours,
We truly are *so* glad, that *he* is ours.

June F Allum

Perspective

(For Poppy)

Working all the hours God sends?
No time for family or friends?
Broken promises every day -
Job demands get in the way?
Chasing targets, building teams?
Empowering staff, suppressing screams?
Ruining Saturday by dreading Sunday
Because on Sunday tomorrow's Monday?

Get a Labrador!

You'll be late for work for the first time ever,
With your watch and car keys gone forever:
Crunched to bits, just like your mobile,
Along with your latest client profile.
Forget the laptop: she's had the charger,
And the scanner. And the enlarger.
You left them for her, as she knows,
On the side, right under her nose -
Next to that fabulous sticky toffee,
Beside that jar of revolting coffee;
She won't blame you for making her sick -
She'll roll on her back, give you a lick.
With her beautiful head and innocent eyes
She'll restore your perspective, tell you no lies.
She'll take you for walks, praise your every endeavour,
She'll trust you completely and love you forever.

Clare Baldock

Remembering Libby

She was given to us, one summer's day
Wagging her tail, she just wanted to play
Running up and down the garden, feeling so free
Our lovely nine month old Labrador, Libby

With her head on one side, her paw, aloft
Our approval grew then, so very soft
We loved her so much, right from the start
As she nuzzled our hands, she melted our heart

She ran away once, which was a disaster
Perhaps, to look for her very first master
We caught her at last, as we looked high, and low
By then, she appeared limping, very much so

I bathed her sore paws, with ointment and lint
With kindness she was treated, she could tell, at a glimpse
She never attempted to run away, like that again
She knew her new mistress, was here all the same

She picked up a stray bone, one clear night
I took it out of her mouth, out of sight
She sulked no end, when taking her back home
I gave her a biscuit, but still she dreamt, of that bone

Next day, I brought her bones, from the local butcher's
Making up for the loss, that she did suffer
Through her antics, she was our dear friend
Our golden Labrador, we loved, right to the end

When we own pets, we should be firm, but kind
Be gentle, with them all, then you will find
A good friend to love, right from the start
Till, they grow old, and sadly time to depart.

Jean P McGovern

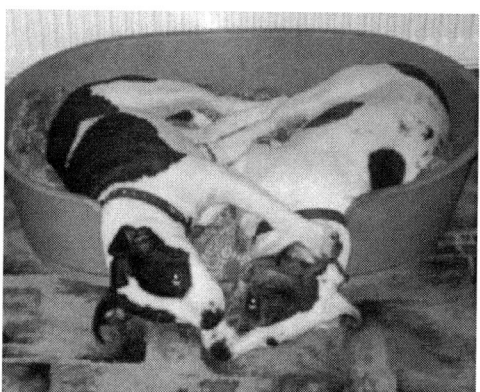

My Poem

Boycie, that's his name,
My dog who is so very good.
At three he is so lacy,
More like six,
But best of all,
He's my two-year-old's best friend,
That's Boycie White.

Charmain White

Calli

Calli my poppet, my cute little mugwump
Sweet little calico cat, all furry and cuddly plump.
She was born in the wild, to a young feral mother,
Might not have survived, like her poor little brother.
A pretty patch coat, with long silky fur,
A thick fluffy tail and a quiet soft purr,
Big yellow-green eyes and a beautiful face,
She follows our Sammy all over the place.
She sleeps on our bed, curled up by my knee,
Warm and contented, a safe place to be,
A good little hunter and willing to share,
She's left me a present at the foot of the stair!
Calli has an admirer, Tosh, the cat from next door,
She leads him a dance, has him wrapped round her paw,
Our cute little rascal gives him a bad time.
She hisses and spits, a saucy feminine feline.

Jackie S Brooks

The Wood Pigeon

I was walking round my garden last Thursday afternoon,
I love to see the flowers that have come into bloom,
Must go inside to get the clothes to hang upon the line
It won't take long to dry them with all this sunshine,
When all at once my breath was took as I looked on the ground,
A tiny little baby bird, no mum or dad around,
I gently picked the baby up cupped in both my hands,
Oh Lord, I cannot save this bird, it's such a tiny thing,
Then all at once I remembered I had a small syringe,
The small syringe held just 5mls of baby food when mixed,
I had such a fight to get this syringe inside its beak,
But it was the only way to feed it, it would die if it got too weak,
So each feed time we struggled, I knew I had to win,
I couldn't let it have its way, that food had to go in,
I had to buy another syringe, I am so glad to say,
As I'm writing this poem it's on 20mls, four times a day,
As it keeps on growing more food will go his way,
And I can see that it will be a wood pigeon soon some day,
It has dark grey feet and a dark grey beak and grey feathers too,
And I'm so in love with this baby bird, I think you would be too.

Ellen Chambers

True Love

Their pictures hang upon our bedroom wall,
with stories that have to be told.
Five marvellous, loving, caring friends,
each one with a heart of gold.

Turbo was our Labrador
and since he was a puppy,
he thought that he was human,
and fancied himself as a yuppie.

Bossy was Turbo's lifelong friend.
He was strong and jet-black as coal,
and the love that bonded between these two,
came definitely from the soul.

Amelia was our grey streaked tabby cat,
who followed us wherever we went.
She was playful, loyal and loving,
certainly heaven-sent.

Pilly Willy was our Siamese cat,
not quite like the rest of his breed,
who would always respond when he was called,
a good example, who would always take heed.

Ming too was a Siamese cat,
the first one to cause us to grieve.
He was quite young when he left us,
and we still find it hard to believe.

Believe us when we say how much they are missed.
Seven times a thousand times seven,
and we know they'll be happy in their place of rest,
up there in the animals' Heaven.

Gerry Concah

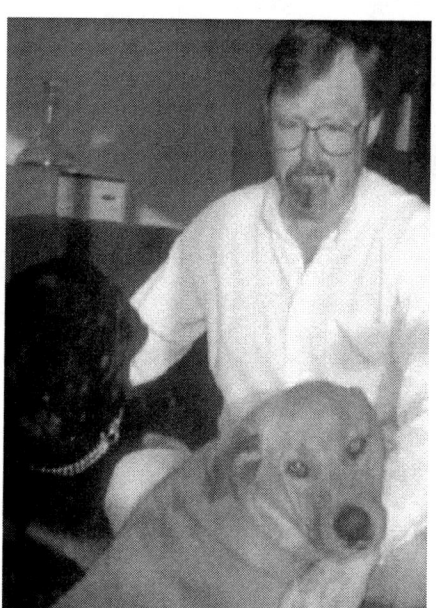

Pepe

I have a cat called Pepe, she really is a dear.
She leaps from branch to fence, with never any fear.
Her exploits vary and are very many
How she manages the games she invents,
Are really quite uncanny.

Something large descends on my chest, while I am asleep
It's only Pepe come to play a game of hide and seek.
She settles down beside me, with a very gentle mew,
And pretty soon we're both asleep, until the morning dew.

It's fun having Pepe, as a live in guest.
She's taken over my life, and now I never rest,
From playing games with Pepe who always gives her best.
She rushes around the furniture so nothing's sacred anymore.
Papers to skid on are not a chore,
As Pepe spreads them all over the floor.

She loves to play with her many toys,
And amuses my grandchildren, three boys.
An elasticised spider is her main delight
As we watch bemused at her paws so slight.

G Nutbeem

An Anchor Books Anthology

Sheffy's Way

My name's Sheffy, a Ragdoll cat
who used to live in Hayes.
Two humans chose me 'bove the rest,
which proves that greasing pays.

Cos they had really come to see
my sister who's a lynx,
who ran around to try an' impress;
the dimwit little minx!

Our brother wasn't much better,
and he's a darker hue,
too dim to see what they saw in me,
a lovely pointed blue.

These humans were enamoured.
They'd been shown far too much.
So I had to make it easy
and apply the creeping touch.

I kept well out the way at first
then flopped into their arms;
by this time they were taken so,
with my wondrous little charms.

Now we're all glad but I must say
I hope they both can see
I'm not much bothered what else they do,
just come and play with me!

Tony Ball

An Anchor Books Anthology

Druids Incantation

Druids incantation,
A somewhat magical name,
Witchcraft not his occupation,
But a wizard all the same,

A warlock, a druid,
An ancient Celtic priest,
So many interpretations,
A mustang at the very least,

His power lies in his beauty,
An allure, which casts a spell,
How priceless is his elegance,
I'm too bewitched to tell,

His coat so sleek and smooth,
The dapples so beautiful and bay,
One white sock remains missing,
His trademark, some might say,

The star, the stripe, and the blaze,
They make a majestic mixture,
In among them a whorl,
It looks to be a permanent fixture,

Druids incantation,
A somewhat magical name,
His body and soul full of enchantment,
His spirit can never be tame.

Rhona Scott

Dog Almighty

On this cold ground; there he'll sleep
Where wintry winds and fierce snow drive
That he may lie by his master's side.
He'll kiss the hand that no food brings,
Then guard his rags and master's things
He guards the sleep of pauper master
As if he was a prince hereafter.

Gordon Paul Charkin

Simba

Simba, oh Simba
Although you're laid to rest
You've left some wonderful memories
With the ones you loved the best
Your green eyes glistening
Your whiskers bristling
Your paw pads, black as night
Though meetings with the Misk
Usually ended in a fight
We'll miss the love you gave us
Your cries of Mam, Mam, Mam,
We'll miss the feel of stroking you
And your muzzle in our hands
Simba, oh Simba
Although you're now asleep
We'll treasure all our memories
And in our hearts we'll keep.

Lorna G Sim

Polly

My dog is such a wonderful companion
How much closer could a friend become.
A constant warming presence in a life that otherwise
Would be lonely, less eventful, much less fun.

Each time Polly looks at me from big brown soulful eyes
Or trots behind me everywhere I go.
I'm aware of loyalty unequalled.
Her affections are constantly on show.

When I am sad she's always there sitting at my feet.
As if to say don't worry I am here.
She's comforter, protector, she lifts my spirits too.
Whilst she's with me I have nothing to fear.

She welcomes me with such delight when I walk through the door.
Letting me know she's happy I've returned.
My little friend's been with me for almost fifteen years.
The love I feel she's really truly earned.

W A Ronayne

An Anchor Books Anthology

Pantry Thief

Came home
    And found him
        Fast asleep,
            Lying still,
                Full,
                    Replete.

He had stolen
    And eaten
            A family-size pie!
            And I with a smile
                Let sleeping dogs lie.

Nick Butler

Our Dog Snuffy

A good companion, a wonderful boy
He is our beautiful bundle of joy.
Soft and cuddly and lots of affection
He gives to us both with no exception.

He's fun to watch when he plays around
Round the garden like the speed of sound.
Then all worn out he has a rest
That's the thing he does the best.

Rest time over he gets his ball
Chases it up and down the hall.
Then there's the sock that's due for a chew
We wonder what next he is going to do.

He's a shitzu, pure bred, pick of the litter
A very knowing little critter.
He's only two he might make three
If he stops digging in my lawn for me.

At the end of day you look around inside
To see what else he has managed to hide.
Pick up his toys and put them away
We know it will be the same next day.

He's now taken himself off to our bed
Fast asleep, paws over his head.
Probably dreaming about what he did
It's just like having a little kid.

He loves everyone, they love him that's plain
He'll bring you a toy, for you to throw again.
Jumps on your lap all soft and fluffy
That's our boy, our very own Snuffy.

M G Scott

Meg

Don't look at me with that doleful expression,
The evidence is quite plain to see,
While I've been out you've wreaked havoc,
And the cats are firmly stuck up a tree.
Your playful antics are starting to make me seethe,
If it wasn't for the fact you are only a pup,
I'd tie you up with a leash!

I can't find a pair of shoes that match,
Guess what? They've mysteriously disappeared,
And those nice new bowls I bought for the cats
Are chewed to smithereens.

Oh Meg! Don't look at me like that,
I'm certainly not green,
You were the one that dug up my plants
While I was trying to weed.

I can't threaten you with detention,
Nor send you up to your room,
I can't use a stick or even a whip,
That really wouldn't do.

Instead I'll laugh at the memories
Of my rebel, my dear Meg,
I know one day soon you will grow up,
Then I will wish you a puppy again.

Jane Margaret Isaac

An Anchor Books Anthology

Catastrophic

Please take this opportunity to paws for thought
upon this picture of our much loved cat.
Doesn't she look absolutely purrfect?
Unfortunately I'm here to dispel your illusion of that
all is not what it may seem
she isn't the cat who's got the cream.
Yes, for the camera she strikes a pose
exuding such innocence as this photo shows.
She may have us wrapped round her little paw
but she's certainly no angel, that's for sure.

Before she eats she's sweetness and light
afterwards faced with reprisals we all take flight.
If some poor unfortunate unwittingly tries to pet
this apparently gentle creature abstaining as yet
from her habit of sinking teeth into skin
unsuspecting they knoweth not, suppressed aggression lurks within.
Our cat's actions demonstrate their unforgivable sin
a whisker away from pouring forth her scorns,
lulled into a false sense of security realisation dawns
before food, yes toleration she knows is needed
she's won us over again, her strategy has succeeded
to keep her owners dishing up her favourite grub
purring away, relax you're onto a winner, this time there'll be no snub.

Achieving her goal to pull wool over our eyes
she still retains all of her nine lives.
A cat who requests the minimum of fuss
we soon ascertained she is one charmingly discerning puss.
Thankfully curiosity hasn't killed this cat
Supremacy rules surprisingly, hard to believe but we're happy with that.

Ruth Locker-Smith

Boy And Dog

Frolicking, scampering, chasing, free as air,
The boy and dog exult in each other's company.
Running over the spiky-grassed sand dunes,
Careless of thought, enjoying this moment of euphoria,
They tumble to the ground and roll over and over,
Boy laughing, dog barking in glorious empathy.
Out of breath, they sit in warm sociability.
The eyes of the boy mark him out as different,
Disabled, unable to compete with his peers.
The non-judgmental dog gazes devotedly at his master,
An unbreakable bond between boy and dog.

Rose-Mary Gower

The Complaints Of My Cat

I know that I ate an hour ago,
So I don't want to make a fuss or a show
But I really feel the need for a snack,
So I'll rub my head against your lap.
Why won't you listen, do you know who I am?
You don't seem to be moving
So I'll try my next plan.
I'm going to run up and down the stairs,
You're paying no attention so I'll claw your chairs.
You look at me sternly, I think you are cross.
Do you not know that I am your boss?
Now I am bored, so I'll go for a sleep.
My dream of salmon will have to keep.
I go to curl up on my favourite chair,
But when I reach it you are already there.
You have my chair, so I'll sleep on your coat,
You finally wake up and you say on top note,
'Oh, look at the hairs all over my coat!'

You pick me up and rest me on your knee,
My tail stands on end and I purr with glee
But wait, what's that I spot in your hand?
A bottle of pills! So this was all planned!
You know that I love you and I know that I'm ill,
But there's no way on earth that I'm taking that pill.
You make me take worm tablets and flea spray me too,
What did I ever do to you?
You put me outside. But wait, this is rain!
I howl outside the windowpane,
'Please let me in, are you insane?'
I'm cold and wet when you let me in,
But what's that I hear? You're opening a tin.
Hooray! I knew you'd finally give in.
I have you well-trained, I knew that I'd win.

Natalie Kennedy

An Anchor Books Anthology

Misty's Ears

Silky, satin, perfect, poised
to prick up at the slightest noise.
Warm, smooth, pointed, small,
twitching with breath's rise and fall.
Trusting, guarding, ever-ready
to spring to action, true and steady.
Lifted head, wide soft eyes,
no words to say and yet so wise.
They fail you now, my faithful friend;
companion, steadfast to the end.

Kathryn Newbrook

Maxxi

Twitching nose, whiskers wide
brown eyes shining
ears held high,
marbled coat, gleaming bright,
silky silver
caramel
swirls: belly winter white,
cotton wool tail
softly stirs.

A coiled spring unleashed
surging, leaping
twisting, turning
you chase shadows away,
then stretched out
succumb, to your
dozy dreams of carrots
and dandelion leaves.

You are my sun and moon
and rarest jewel,
companions forever
you and I,
in my heart
you'll safely stay,
darling rabbit -
my true best friend.

Sarah Hibbett

My Best Friends

My name is Basil (on the left)
My mate Benji's on the right
Mum's brought us to have our photo done
And has been grooming us all night . . .
A man has plonked us on this rug
And said, 'Keep still - I won't be long,'
But it seems like an age to us
So I've broken out in song!
Benji is more serious
But I'm just young at heart
I wish the photographer would hurry up
So then we can depart.
He says, 'Watch the birdie,' squeaks some toys
And starts to jump around
Perhaps he thinks that we are cats
His acting is profound . . .
Then after what seems hours
He says, 'Right chaps, off you go
When the photographs are ready
I'll let your owner know . . .'
Thank goodness that is over
Being famous is a lark
Now off to serious business
Getting dirty in the park!

Anne E Roberts

The Four O'Clock Shift

My cat's gone off on his four o'clock shift,
Four in the morning that is - in the dark,
It's freezing hard and there's snow on the ground,
All fresh fallen and beginning to drift.

From the shelter of the conservatory
I watched as he darted into the night,
Snow clouds rising behind him as he raced
In zigzag fashion through the frosty white.

He'd wakened me with a demanding clout
Delivered with his paw, then he threatened
To shred the wallpaper and rug, so
At claw point I was forced to let him out.

He'll come home frozen - demand to be fed.
Thaw out; and leave a damp patch on my bed.

Margaret Hibbert

An Anchor Books Anthology

Just My Lovely Dog

She is just my dog. She is my other ears that warn me of any dangers,
My other nose that keeps me on route.
She has told me a million times that I am her reason for being . . .
> By the way she rests against my leg,
> By the way she wags her tail at my smallest of smiles.
> By the gentlest of paws touching my knee.

When I am upset, she nestles up to my face.
When I am angry, she clowns around.
When I am happy, she is pleased and excited.

She has taught me the meaning of life.
With her, I know the secret of comfort and peace
She taught me understanding, where I was ignorant.
The tummy that is stretched out in full
Over my feet can heal my human hurts.
Her presence by my side is protection against fears of life.

She has concealed a pocket in her life, just for me!
She will be always waiting to make me smile.

She is just my dog, Poppy.

Alice Shepherd

Hope

A bowl of food, a comfy bed,
We'd want for nowt, our owners said,
They'd show us love, in every way,
And buy us toys with which to play.

They saw us first in Disney's shows,
Spotted hounds from head to toes,
All fluffy, trained, behaviour good,
We only wish they understood.

We pups grow fast, our needs as well,
From this day on, our lives were hell.
Our walks soon stopped, as did the play,
That's how it was on every day.

We got told off for minor things,
Ouch! That smack, it really stings.
We lived in fear and sometimes dread,
It caused us both to wet our bed.

More smacks they came - they couldn't cope,
Now all day long we'd wish and hope,
This hellish life would soon be gone,
And someone kind would take us on.

Soon 'Dally Rescue' found a gal,
Who said she'd have us for a pal.
She took us home and gave us space,
To live with her and share her place.

She let us both have loads of fun,
Or just go lounging in the sun.
We're fed twice daily - on the best,
Our 'Mum' has really passed the test.

She knows our needs and sees them through,
Even though there's lots to do,
She plays our games and gives us cuddles
And when on walks, we jump in puddles.

She doesn't scream, or shout, or hit,
But tells us quietly just to sit,
While towelling feet and bodies dry,
She doesn't moan, or give a sigh.

Our wetting beds has stopped completely,
Our hellish life has now turned sweetly,
Daily grind - now turned to cheer,
We've nothing more to dread or fear.

An Anchor Books Anthology

We'd like to say a special thank you
To all the guys at 'Dally Rescue',
Through all your work, you've homed us well,
And this is what we'd like to tell.

To Disney films, and all the rest,
Just stop and think before, or lest
More lives around the world get tougher,
Please don't make our K9s suffer.

Animal lovers - we're meant to be,
Let's make it happen - you and me!

Wendy Bennett

Shay

Two golden suns glare in the dark
A menacing, throaty growl,
Sure-footed he comes like a lightning bolt,
A sleek black body hurls through the door
And paws on my shoulders land,
Wet sloppy kisses, then, he'd bring me his bowl.
When he was around, alert for each sound
His growl was enough to let people know,
Not to mess with my Shay,
He charged around the house, up and down the stairs,
Rolled his ball into a corner, then waited till you tried to get it.
I never won.

He liked his tea and toast for supper
And never let me forget,
We would sit by the fire, I would tell him of the day,
His head would rest upon my knee and give a contented sigh,
I stroked his black velvety coat
And was glad he was there with me, my Shay.
Now the house is very quiet, no Shay on my return,
No tea and toast to make, no dish to see upturned.
The ball is still in the corner, where he left it on that day,
I don't have the heart to move it, that was our last play.

Mary Neill

My Cat

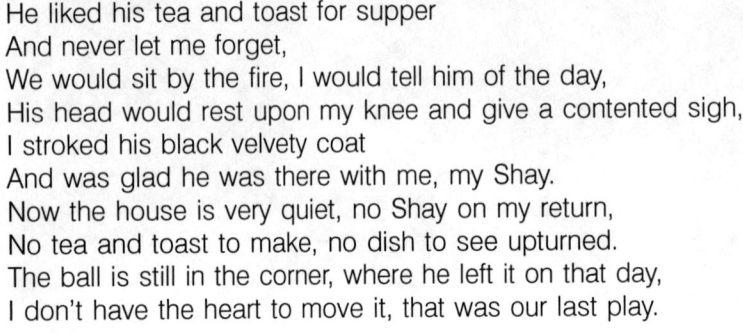

My cat is rather peculiar,
for he leaves his teeth in a jar.
He wipes his bum with a toilet roll
and washes up his own food bowl.
He cleans behind his ears at night,
and has never had a real cat fight.
He files his nails until they're done to satisfaction,
sometimes he thinks he's Michael Jackson.
He spends hours trying to spike his hair,
and cannot decide on what collar to wear.
He won't even catch a bird,
sometimes my cat is such a nerd.
But one good thing about him,
is that without him, my life would be rather dim.
My cat really is a star,
even though he is peculiar.

Nicky Pitchers

An Anchor Books Anthology

Emma

I know I'm 20 years of age, I'm long past being a filly
But in my head I'm two years old and still like being silly
If you ever want to meet me, I'm easy to pick out
You will find me in a second, of that I have no doubt.

It isn't that I have two heads,
Or my coat's a funny colour,
It isn't I'm a peculiar shape,
I really look like any other.

I have a special talent
And I'm sure like me you feel
It will always get me noticed
I love to have a squeal!

I squeal when Mum does up my girth
She tells me not to wriggle,
I squeal when she is brushing me,
It makes the humans giggle.

I squeal when I am being schooled
I haven't got a care,
I like to make my friends all jump,
As I catch them unaware.

The instructor, when she's teaching us
Says, 'Emma, do be quiet
Your squealing is causing havoc,
You're going to start a riot.'

My friends all know it's just a game,
I've often heard them say,
If Emma didn't squeal in class
It would not be the same.

Mum said that in a previous life
I never was a horse,
She said I must have been a mouse,
Which explains it all, of course!

Sue Walters

Soot To Soot

Our silly cat, Jet by name,
Thought he'd take a dive
Headfirst into this chimney pot,
Oh yes, he came out alive!

Aces black as well as high,
He surveys the land from tower,
No black tulip over sill,
But furry is this flower!

An old Victorian chimney pot
Used to take our bulbs,
The soot inside reflects his coat
Black moggy in coal-hole!

Graham K A Walker

Teddy - A Jack Russell

A fat scruffy bundle
Of black and white hair,
Is a special friend of mine
My dog called Teddy Bear.

She has sharp eyes for hunting
A rabbit or a rat,
But then again, she's not adverse
To chasing next door's cat!

She is a fearless guard dog
Although she's small, it's true,
She'll follow you around all day
Stick to you like glue.

Sleeping in her basket
She's like a children's toy,
When she's wide awake
Her piercing bark can so annoy.

I wouldn't be without her
This little friend of mine,
And I know when she's without me
She howls and starts to pine.

Georgina Slape

Mac

I have a little Westie,
His name is Mac,
He loves his tummy tickled
When he rolls onto his back.

He gives me lots of kisses
He always wags his tail with joy,
I love my little Westie,
He is my little boy.

His big brown eyes so dreamy
His curly fur so white
I love to give him toys and treats
And brush him every night.

We go for lots of walks,
We run about in the park,
But if a stranger comes near me
Wow, does that small boy bark!

He cuddles up to me at night
Especially for my toast,
But Sunday is his favourite day
When my mum gives him Sunday roast.

Elizabeth-Anne Paterson

Spilt Milk

They were only six weeks old
Far too young to know when told
Mum, sat down to watch the fun
Gold Tops glittering in the sun
Soon got toppled with a clatter
All this did not really matter.
It's no use crying over spilt milk
Pretending it was a 'river of silk'
The puppies tasted milk so sweet
In it they dabbled tails and feet!
Their master was going to be upset
He'd not returned from market yet
By then the puppies would be asleep
And Mum, out working with the sheep!
Their master went to market today
And four young pups went out to play!

Sheila Walters

Furry Friend

When I was sixty
Family brought me little Westie
Named her Mitzy.
Mightier than the sword
When she stands on her hind paws
But timid as a mouse
Seeing dogs so big in size.
Sleeps on my bottom
Pillow every night
Wakes up in the morning
She's laying beside me
Her eyes are big
Round, brown,
Like soils of the earth.
Coat, brushed and groomed,
Like pearly feathers.
Her bark sounds like
Thousands of echoes
Filtering in the distance.
Plays and loves attention.
When we sit, she lays behind me
On settee, head nestling on my shoulder
For peach and tranquillity.
Loves her walks,
Meeting people and furry friends.
Dog spells God backwards.
So I thank the Lord
For all creation,
My furry friend,
The devoted Westie.

Norma Flair Challis

Lily

She's the little cat with a squeak (a little too meek to miaow),
She's Indian black with white like a scarf, but more curiously,
Streaked in her ways . . .

Purple's the streak that's stubborn sometimes,
Deep amber - her fondness for cheese.
Blue is the girl who sits quietly and thinks
And gold when she's laid next to me.

Pablo Rose

My Cat

She scratches on the gate when she's stuck outside.
When we play a silly game she runs along and hides.
She slides and slithers across the front room floor.
She skids and bumps her head on the front room door.

Hayley Briant (10)

Ode To Fudge

A list of names from which to chose
For a little brown and white scrap
We knew we couldn't lose
To cuddle up on someone's lap.

'Fudge' the choice was to be
What a cute puppy
Anyone could see
That you were gorgeous and lovely.

A manic springer spaniel
That took some wearing out!
No one has yet written a manual
On just what you are all about.

A little pup that never liked to get wet feet
Soon learnt water was such fun
And now it is such a feat
To keep you away from the water on a run!

Such a placid and good-tempered girl
Never likes to be left home alone
Always chasing around in a whirl
But contented when having a bone.

You brighten up our days no end
Without you life would not be the same
You are our four-legged best friend
With you life is just one big game!

Thank you for giving us so much pleasure
With every thought of you we can treasure
You may drive us round the bend
But you simply are our best friend!

June Toms

Thomas

We moved to the countryside, where we lived for a few years.
We acquired another animal - that cost blood, and sweat, and tears.
We got another donkey, Thomas was his name,
We bought him from a farmer, turned out drinking was his game.

Every Tuesday, market day, as he'd return from town,
He's stop at pubs along the way, his sorrows for to drown.
And he had many sorrows, or so it seemed to us,
Tom, once stopped, wouldn't restart, however much we begged or cussed.

We pulled the donkey, pushed the cart, Thomas wouldn't budge.
The locals stood and chuckled, each other they would nudge.
We stood in front with carrot, lured with bread and jam,
Nothing we did had effect, Thomas didn't give a damn.

Then a farmer's wife said, 'Oh come on, those children must get home,
Tell them what the secret is. We all know how it's done.'
'You have to tickle Thomas,' all said with one accord.
Incredulous? No! Sceptical, I thing would be the world.

'Tickle ass's armpit, or legpit to be exact.'
One broke off metre branch of hedge to demonstrate the fact.
He leaned, and waved the fronded end down the ass's inner thigh,
And off the donkey trotted, I swear this is no lie.

So it went each Tuesday for the duration of our stay,
No trouble going, but slowly back . . . to each pub along the way.

K Titmus

An Anchor Books Anthology

Neddie

He was handsome as he was lovely,
a perfect specimen of a beast.
Like the one that Jesus rode,
completely grey except for his
brown cross and the tips of his
long ears, so soft the feel to a
youngish cheek.
He as a wedding present to Mother,
who grew up with the family.
Willingly sported all four
upon his back.
When four became seven,
it's now he learnt to let them
upon his back for a little ride,
to buck and kick his mounts
flying to the grass.
A wicked smile was in his eye as
he always looked back to the
victims on the ground.
The years had passed and I
had departed to another land,
within the news from home
it came the auld ass died,
great big salty tears I shed for
Neddie, who was a she, at the year
of thirty-five and I, just twenty-one.

Margaret Gleeson Spanos

My Best Pal

My pet dog,
My follower,
My devotion,
My guardian,
My alertness,
My listener,
My shoulder to cry on,
My supporter,
My friend,
My delight,
My fondness,
My companion,
My everything.
My best pal.

Catrina Lawrence

Prospect Pride

(Sing to 'A Few Of My Favourite Things')

Bitemarks and bruises, and sore little fingers
Just been kicked again and my knee's rather twisted
At three years old, it's just down to play
But I hope he's good mannered some day!

A new rug here, a headcollar there
Next day it returns with a vent and a tear!
Degree in escaping, now in farmer's field
Only ten acres, a luxury meal

Twenty miles away
Spots a bucket
Hearing of a bat!
Yet call him for worming
He seems to be deaf
Now what do you make of that?

Sweet itch in summer
Fences fly off like buttons
The punk look is back
Lamb dressed up as mutton
He stood really nicely last year for the spray
Yet now he pretends he is scared every day!

Don't like the farrier, his toolbox might bite him
Rather chew his apron, and rag him, to his knee!
He's really an angel dressed up in disguise
But I do tend to wonder, when I tell these white lies!

In five years' time
When he's a gentleman
I'll look back and say
I love him to pieces
What memories I have
But never a youngster
I'll have again!

K M Waddington

Lady Sadie

She crosses her paws,
Just like a lady,
And looks at you
With the eyes.
She lavishes the fuss:
Strokes are a must,
For little Miss Lady Sadie.

She nips at your fingers.
And lips your face;
And gorges the cat's food,
To their secret disgrace.
She winds up Tyler,
But why you love her
Is because she's Lady Sadie.

She's smooth and silky,
Just like a lady.
Flopped on the sofa
Laid like a baby.
She'll melt your heart,
But remember how smart
Is little Miss Lady Sadie.

So here she comes
Looking a lady,
And stealing you
With those eyes.
She crosses her paws
And despite all her flaws,
She's just little Lady Sadie.

Jodie Grant

Hi Laddie

On the hill above us, now you lie in peace,
It was your favourite place, when let off the leash.
From a very young pup, you were very nosy,
Disturbing birds in their nests when they were cosy,
Chasing young rabbits that quickly ran off.
Your arrogant pose made you look quite a toff.
But you were so loyal, obedient and kind,
Your cheeky ways, we did not mind.
The wonderful memories we will never forget,
You gave us great times, since the day we met.

Barbara M Twort

Fairfax

It was love at first sight
A match meant to be
When I noticed this tabby following me.
His eyes were appealing
He proposed, silent, kneeling
I tell you I just couldn't shake of the feeling.

So Fairfax was soon adopted into our home
A place where he could now consider his own
To curl up, stretch, investigate and roam.
Well he's surely made a lasting impact
On our stair carpet, no longer intact -
And in our hearts, we're fond of this cat.

He's gentle and dopey, not noisy or bold
He'd rather be inside than out in the cold
Our Alasdair's bed has become his stronghold.
At twelve years old, he's no longer agile
He exhausts himself after leaping a little while
But there's some fire still in Fairfax - and that makes me smile.

Evelyn Wooffitt

An Anchor Books Anthology

BMH

Beautiful Memories Harmonies
Bouncing around from seat to seat
Echoing yapping sounds to all she meets
Can she find me, yes she can
Kangaroo jumping around and around
Identify lost leads and squeaky toys
Exquisite, petite, small, with lots of noise.

Mightier than the fiercer cat
Absorb the names Lad or Max
X-ray vision while guarding on the mat

Help me with paws in the air in this park
Only me here, sad, lonely, cold in the dark
Lost, please show me back to Nathan's car
Lancashire police helicopter searches near and far
Yelling, 'Cuddle Holly, come on home.'

P Brewer

Oh Buster

Oh Buster, my pussy cat, where have you been?
You ain't been to London to visit the Queen.
You have been in the field outside of the house
I know that you have as you brought home a mouse.
Oh Buster, you monkey, you just want to play
You are chasing those mice all night and all day.
Come down Buster, you hear me call
Your dinner is ready, jump down off that wall.
Come eat your tuna, then jump on my lap
I'll fuss you a little then have a catnap.
Come have some milk Buster, to you I shout
Then from under the bedclothes you slowly come out.
Oh Buster, you are so full of love
I know you were sent from the good Lord above.
Time for my dinner, I have fish and chips
You sit there beside me, you're licking your lips.
You have been in the brook not far from the wood
A fuss and a clean will do you much good.
Off to bed now, yes my bed you can borrow
Go to sleep now, it's a new day tomorrow.

Kram

My Little Cat Called Sarchi

My little stripy friend,
who is faithful as can be,
cheers me up day after day.
Her personality means to me
a very great deal
which constantly I feel.
Her little miaow
and her tiny paws,
her little white whiskers
and big green eyes.
She's always there,
a friend for life,
my little sweetie,
she makes no strife,
no mess, no worry,
but fun and happy times,
all day long.
I love my cat,
my tiny little tinker
who chases my toes
and the tip of her tail.
She's just gone one
and needs her sleep,
as she curls up on my lap
purring merrily,
waiting for me to reassure her,
what she means to me.

Elizabeth Arnold

Ode To My Dog

Great is the devotion a dog gives its master,
A wag of tail is its first reaction,
No one can ever know unless they've kept a dog as a friend,
The fun of it in puppyhood, or the sadness at the end.
A dog's life is so very short compared to that of man,
So enjoy each precious moment, and love it all you can.
Its companionship on walks with you, while it is still able,
'Cause you'll miss it when the basket is empty 'neath the table.
They tear your favourite slippers, eat biscuits on the sofa,
Insist in climbing in your bed, knowing he didn't oughta.
Then amber eyes look up at you, and your heart melts like butter.
You never can be lonely if you have a dog as a friend,
They give their trust completely, and stay faithful to the end.

D Leech

Glen

Glen is very special dog and he is my pet
He is just the nicest one that I have ever met.
Gazes up at me with great big solemn eyes
They can open wide as big as mince pies
When he sits beside me resting paws upon my lap
It seems to calm me down stops me getting in a flap
Glen is a friend who seems to know my mind
The day he came into my life it was a lucky find
He is quite obedient when we go out for a walk
Sitting down quietly if I should stop to talk
He proves to be a guard when there's a knock at my door
Has a bark just like a lion's roar
I wouldn't swap him for a thousand pounds
Because I made the best choice from all those other hounds!

Ethel Wakeford

Our Tim

We had a dog.
His name was Tim,
our letter box,
was too high for him.
He'd go down the path,
to the lady next door.
Push his nose through theirs,
'Twas near the floor.
It would go, go go,
with a clickety-click,
the lady would answer
the door very quick.
She'd see our Timmy
standing there,
quick as a flash
to her it was clear
as he looked up so fondly
and a wag of his tail,
he'd run down the path
to his own door again.
Laughingly followed
by a neighbour so good,
who'd ring our bell,
for he knew she would.

Peggy Johnson

Nutty Bam Bam

Don't stare at me with those wide green eyes
Don't cock your head from side to side
Don't wink at me then purr down my ear
For off to the vet you have to go, I'm sorry my dear.
You kick up a fuss as in your box you must go
To go on this journey in your carriage to and fro
Your miaows get louder as we enter the gate
To be checked by the vet, something you hate.
'I'm afraid it's hormonal,' the vet does declare
As he examines the patches on your body laying there.
'He's grooming too much, it's his behaviour too.'
'Are you saying my cat needs a psychiatrist, can this be true?'
'If the hormone treatment does not work he may have to.'
So with a stab of injection, tablets to take
I squeeze you into your box and cry, 'For goodness sake.'
Bam Bam you're almost human, that I always felt
As I get you home, your black and white face makes me melt
Then dissolve into laughter at the thought of a shrink
My poor darling cat, this diagnosis makes me think.
So in your bowl some food and milk to drink
Then a tablet before bedtime curled up now on my lap
I stroke your clean body, you're such a beautiful cat.
So will you stop grooming too much, are the tablets going to do the trick?
Otherwise dear Bam Bam, it will be back to the vet's, yet another trip.
So don't stare at me with those big green eyes or wink,
'Cause if you carry on, you'll be seeing a shrink.

Maggie Strong

An Anchor Books Anthology

To Ellie

Ellie come and sit with me
In the shade of the lilac tree.
I know that you are missing Tess
In your lovely eyes I see distress.
Come sit in the garden you know so well,
What would you say if you could tell?
How Tess would sit by the window and wait
For you to come in the garden gate,
Then both of you stood beside the door
For Paul to put biscuits on the floor.
Then, biscuits done, you would go out
For a sniff around to see what was about.
You let me stroke and pat you now,
You never did before somehow.
So Ellie you are being kind
Let happy times come into your mind.
We must remember you and me
As we sit in the shade of the lilac tree.

Dorothy Bloomfield

My Dog Judy

I seek her here,
I seek her there,
I seek her almost everywhere.
But she won't come when she is called,
So I search and search till I am bald.
Wondering where she may be, I tear my hair out
Then a good neighbour brings her back to me.
You see she is such a little thing,
Through the tiniest hole she can spring.
She will never bark to let you know
In the garden she wants to go,
So a puddle I'll find on the kitchen floor,
Just in front of the back door.
But I find it hard to scold
As she is now thirteen years old,
A friend she has been all these years,
When she goes I'll be drawn to tears.

A C Iverson

My Best Friend

Sadness surrounded me at the end of last year
At the loss of my Sophie, loved so dear
For ten long years she'd been my four-legged friend
Loving and faithful to the very end

My home really doesn't seem the same
And all is still when I call her name
I feel sure she lies at my feet
But nothing moves when I offer a treat

I wouldn't wake her to suffer again
But I'd love one more walk down our lane
And her big brown eyes to look at me
Before running off behind a tree

Be happy my Sophie my faithful friend
My love is all that I can send
But your memory I will forever hold dear
And by my side you'll always feel near.

Judie Archer

An Anchor Books Anthology

The Not-So-Vacant Chair

I'm very particular just where I sit,
And I don't like it one little bit
When someone plonks down on my favourite chair,
And hasn't an inkling that I really care.
I give them a look and a plaintive meeow -
I've just got to get them off it somehow.
I stalk up and down, put on a brave face
And hope that they won't stay too long in the place.
The person sat down bends to give me a stroke
And I play along while I literally choke.
I wish that my mistress would just have a chat
And say that this chair is reserved for the cat.

Joyce Haigh

Echo

(Always in my heart, love Mummy)

Echo is my kitten,
When I bought him
My son was smitten.

Can you guess what breed he is?

He has big beautiful blue eyes,
He has such a vocal voice!

Can you guess what breed he is?

He can jump high,
He would reach the sky!
He loves his furry little friends
He is such a funny little guy!

Can you guess what breed he is?

He is what's called a lilac point!

Can you guess what breed he is?

Echo's breed rhymes with Chinese!
You have guessed right, he is my Siamese.

M Hinton

My Two Best Friends

Two friends I have, loving and true,
having to say goodbye makes me blue.
The two of them stand on all eight paws,
gentle and kind, both without flaws.

Golden retrievers is what they are,
Hope and Chevy the best by far.
One dark gold, the other so white,
both would protect me, both would fight.

Hope so small and gentle, her head on my knee she rests,
waiting patiently for my gentle pat, to her I'm the best.
Chevy so big and strong, grabs his ball, he wants some fun,
I play until he tires out, a place he finds to lay in the sun.

With a wag of their tail, their love they do send,
special to me they are, their love shows no end.
Sleeping by my door so late at night,
making sure everything turns out alright.

They welcome me home, and don't ask for much,
to go for a walk, or from my hand a touch.
Unconditional love is what they give,
something I'll return for as long as I live.

Nikohl Medley

Happy Dog

Murphy's such a happy boy
Always playing with a toy,
But he's happiest most of all
When he's got a tennis ball.
On our walks, people we meet
Find a tennis ball dropped at their feet,
He'll watch them with a big wide grin
It's not long before they give in.
With children about he'll put on a show
As they each take turns to have a throw,
He'll bring nervous children out of their shell
By encouraging them to play as well.
I think people love his friendliness
And his happy cheeky face, I guess,
Many now know him by name
Always joining in his game.
He fills so many lives with laughter
So if it's a happy dog you're after,
Then I think, without a doubt
Murphy's the happiest dog about!

Carole Cheyne

An Anchor Books Anthology

Fudge - Our Kitten (6 Weeks Old)

She is so playful,
She is so small,
Dark black fur all over,
Beige on her paw,
Frightened and shaking at first,
Then she's climbing up my legs,
Down my back,
Playing with her toys,
She really likes that,
She has so much energy,
Scuttling about,
Scratching, clawing, running,
'Look out!'
Hanging upon the curtains,
Climbing up the chair,
Purring, rubbing her head,
Around my neck,
Chewing my hair,
Her eyes and nose are so small,
She really has no cares at all.
Her claws are so sharp,
She meows at night too,
But now little Fudge
We wouldn't be without you!

Jackie Sutton

Our Reggie

When the time arrives to choose a pet,
With so many breeds which one should we get,
All shapes and sizes, colour galore,
Decision made, it was you we went for.

We brought you home, settled you in,
And form day one the fun would begin,
You are a clown, a joker, our special little man,
Enriching our lives as only you can.

You look at us with bold brown eyes
And we realise with no great surprise,
You return as much love as we give to you,
And we all share a friendship honest and true,

So Reggie there's only this left to say
We made the right decision that day,
No other dog in the world would do
With your sweet and sour expression it just had to be you.

Louise Farren

My Cassie

Oh, Cassie my puppy so small and so sweet
You've charmed me completely, swept me clean off my feet
You're winsome and clever, so pretty and cute
You amaze me you rascal - a pup who eats fruit!
As you chase and you tumble with pleasure I beam
And when you're asleep I just watch as you dream
The world is your playground, everybody your friend
May your puppyhood wonder and joy never end
But you're growing up fast, soon my pup will be gone
Time never stands still and you've got to move on
So I cherish these hours of puppy dog days
Will delight in recalling your puppy dog ways
These magical mem'ries that won't ever fade
Even when you've matured and become much more staid,
So you play and romp, scamper madly about
Then flop in a heap when you've worn yourself out.

Oh, Cassie my young dog how fine you've become
Loving and happy and so full of fun
With long silken ears and brown saucer eyes
You are big in appeal, though not big in size
You've a passion for water and digging in dirt
But wet and bedraggled and muddy won't hurt
As you seem to be happiest looking a fright
Soggy and mucky is my dog's delight
After digging then chasing about in a stream
It's home to be fed, to sleep and to dream
Though your energy levels put mine in the shade
You're a constant delight to this ageing old maid
So I promise to love you and will truly endeavour
To ensure that your life is one long doggy pleasure.

Jenny Hitchen

An Anchor Books Anthology

Cat Fight

She was short and fat and black
He was long and lean and white
They nudged each other back to back
And instantly you sensed a fight.

They quickly turned and toe to toe
You knew there was some tension there
But who would strike the telling blow
And would this fight be fair and square.

With lightning speed out of the blue
She smashed his nose with first attack
The knockdown there was sure and true
But he got up and he came back.

He circled round fixed icy stare
With one eye green and one eye blue
You knew that she was nervous there
And growled thinking what to do.

In a flash he darted in
Jabbed her once and then withdrew
She winced as if this was a sin
The battle now she must renew.

She grabbed him threw him to the floor
And mauled him like a grizzly bear
He soon retired towards the door
His body now the worse for wear.

The crowd dispersed from this mismatch
Stunned by what had happened here
She hardly had a single scratch
And whiteboy did not reappear.

Charlie McInally

Fern

I love to run beside the sea, to weave in and out of the rocks,
Oh, there's an angler over there, let's see what's in his box,
I run ahead and see some children playing with a ball,
So I rush and dive straight in, it's a good old 'free for all'.
I always come when I am called; I never walk on by,
Because I love my owner and I'm the apple of his eye,
Then I jump up inside the van, and smile with my cocker spaniel eyes,
We're going back to the place called home,
With the people I idolise.

Pam Newman

A Cat, You Were Only A Cat

Cat, you were only a cat.
A female, feline creature,
Descended from some desert beast,
Who would feast in the Egyptian granaries.
Eating the swarming rats and mice.
Found easy pickings amongst the grain.
But unlike the kindred dog,
Never went down the path of becoming a slave.
Rather you became an equal partner.
So precious, that on your death,
You were mummified before you entered the grave.
And so you remain today,
Aloof, regal and beautiful.
As then, in your grace and independence,
In our home you hold a special place.
Never a begger, put into a outside kennel,
But you find a bed where you may.
So my true friend, my black and white Tinker,
You sought to live with me for sixteen years.
Spending much time in summer outside.
You would find special places to hide.
In winter you resided by the fireside,
Or if you grew tired of that,
You found a welcome place on my knee.
Your sweet purring, told me it met your need.
But one day death came to take you away.
You made your way down the garden path.
One last look back, a final goodbye.
Never to see you again, though love remains
A quiet exit, finding somewhere outside to die.

Jonathan Pegg

Trouble

She is definitely trouble;
She is a very sneaky one;
She has even stalked me;
Wherever I go, she comes.

She is like a shadow in the night;
Her hair is midnight black.
She walks around so cautiously;
I always watch my back!

Yet when I have approached her;
She turns and runs away.
I then begin to wonder;
Is this a game of hers to play?

I have known her about four years;
And she has always been evasive;
I moved once since I've known her;
And she followed me to where I live!

I sometimes think she is the devil;
Hiding in her disguise.
If you look closely at her;
You can see it in her eyes!

Who is this creature from the darkness;
That taunts me wherever I am at?
I must confess I love her dearly;
She is 'Trouble' my little black cat!

Betty Hawkins

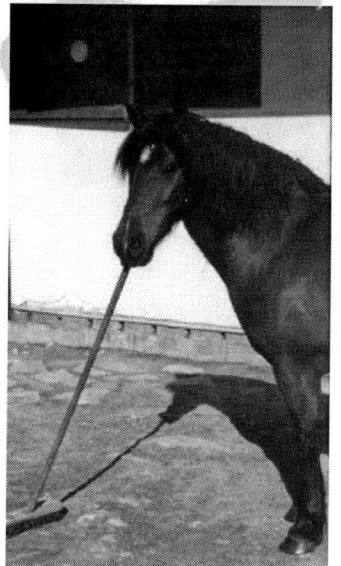

Teddy

Let me introduce you to a pony who's called Teddy,
He's rather round, very sweet, and usually quite steady.
He's a Dartmoor X, bright bay coat and only stands 12.1,
But when my son gets on his back, then we see some fun.
When they have a canter, a buck he likes to do,
And this is always followed by a noisy squeal or two.
They go to shows for jumping, for this he does the best,
He can turn upon a sixpence, at this I do not jest.
On sunny days, for cooling down, this is what he does,
'That splashing sound?' We had a look, and in the trough he was!
He likes a game of football, for England he should play,
Except, with teeth, he takes the ball, and promptly runs away.
A kind and special pony, a kick he's done? *No never!*
He won't be sold, he's loved too much, he'll stay with us forever.

Jane Francis

Gentle Spirit

(Written in July 2003 for my horse, Maisie, who had a very bad accident the year before)

I saw your pain, your body ripped and torn,
No hope, they said, already weapons drawn,
You spoke to me in volumes higher than the trees,
You spoke to me in whispers softer than a summer breeze;

You told me I must let you try,
You asked me not to let you die.

With your eyes you spoke to me
In shades of brown and burgundy
With your heart you told me this,
In rhythms gentler than a kiss.

Time and patience you said were needed
With your eyes you gently pleaded
How could I reject your cry,
Let your brave and gentle spirit die?

You took your trust and in my heart you laid it
My beautiful girl, I'm so glad you made it . . .

Michele Amos

Gender Bender

'Isn't she pretty. Oh, isn't she cute . . .'
'She's a he,' I reply, 'his name's Bosie to boot.
Not Rosie, Josie, Boozy or Beau
But Bosie of literary fame don't you know.'

My Cavalier King Charles it certainly suits,
From the tip of his nose to his dainty white boots.
He looks handsome and gay in his brown and white suit;
Runs swift as a hare when full in pursuit.
He's never aggressive, always greets with delight -
Adults, small children, large dogs
And the sounds and the smells, as we tramp through the woods.

So what's in a name? Folk are driving me mad.
To be blessed with good looks - is that really so bad.

J Bate

Charlie

For eleven years
we've shared laughter and tears,
conquered many fears.
We've had many walks,
and talks.
Together we've done agility
and every other doggy activity.
Together we've played ball,
heard the cuckoo call,
shared camping holidays
near and far away.
You have watched me toil
in the garden, planting in the soil
while you found a shady place.
Occasionally you've been in disgrace.
Now you are older, less bolder.
Sleeping like a log
in a sunny spot, but always my dog.
Charlie you're a wonderful dog.
I love you, always will.
Thank you for being you.
When your days are through
you will join the heavenly stars
and watch over me from afar.

Elaine Hicklin

Bernie

It was love at first sight when he came into view
Our life is much brighter now and never blue
He's black and brown, a bundle of fun
Both our hearts he'd already won
He's not very big and not very tall
But just like a bouncing rubber ball
He barks, jumps and does his own thing
Try ticking him off, you just can't win
Will we never learn his canine lark
Up at first light until it gets dark
Always on the go, he never stops
To the fields, down the road and even to the shops
We're mum, dad, playmate and nurse
When he grows up we're over the worst
Not so, say us all tired and washed up
And all we have is one small pup
We love him more now than when we first met
He's part of our family and not just our pet.

Janet Snowsill

My Boy

He sleeps all morning without a care,
You can wake him if you dare.
At 12 o'clock then he will stir,
To have a cuddle and a purr.
It's time for food, and time to play,
Whatever the weather he will have a nice day,
When evening comes he's told goodnight,
But this is the time for play and fight.
Dashing here and running round,
Things to play with he has found.
In the morning he's fast asleep,
And all the toys are in a heap.
It's time to start the daily chores
My boy is asleep, with his head on his paws.

G Binns

Wonderful Winter Mornings

We walk down lanes lined with green.
Our path ahead a rugged chocolate meringue
With crisp ice-covered puddles.
The trees stand over us.
Now with bare branches they cast ghostly shadows along the way.
Their once emerald leaves lay
Like a gold and red blanket on the floor below.
The hazy orangey pink glow of the sun lights our world.
It warms the air and encourages the frosty dew-covered grass
To wake and unfold.
Pheasants clothed in shiny speckled brown jackets
Strut across the fields,
While bobtailed rabbits nibble at the last of the winter crops.
Our breath floats past us.
Your thick black coat glistens in the sunlight.
White socked paws flash through the long grass as you dance along.
You pause and stand looking into the prickly hedgerow.
Your ears alert, and your brush-like tail twitching with excitement.
A silvery grey pigeon flutters and flies to the safety of a nearby tree.
I call you.
You turn your majestic head to me
And I look into those hazel almond eyes.
Your warm expression is almost a smile.
We turn to head for home.
I realise just how lucky I am to have a true friend.
Someone with whom to share these *wonderful winter mornings*.

Lisa Pearson

An Anchor Books Anthology

Sable

I said I didn't want one
I thought I knew my mind
Then I saw your little face
Peeping around the side
You looked so sad and forlorn
I could not turn away
I called you to my side
And that is where you've stayed
You've been with me through
The good times
You've been my rock
Through the bad times
You're my best friend
My closest companion
Twelve years I've had
The best of your life
We coped with the cancer
We pulled each other through
And now I've got to tell you
How much I love you
My life is all the better
For you being there
Even though you chewed
Dad's dictionary
And sat upon his chair
You accepted all the cats that came
And the puppy dogs too
You knew all along
That I loved you.

Sheree Watts

Time For All

Birds cannot read the face of a clock,
Or animals tell one the time.
Earth holds the secret when plants shall grow,
And who tells the salmon the falls to climb?
Why do squirrels gather nuts and store them
'neath a tree,
List to wild geese call o'erhead
As from winter chills they flee.
Seasons come and seasons go,
To each one there is given
Time to live, time to die,
Time for all under Heaven.

G Semmens

Queen Of The Snowflakes

Queen of the Snowflakes, a noble kennel name,
White as snow, she cannot always claim.
She graced us with her presence, at less than eight weeks old,
A ball of fluff, bringing piddles and poos untold.
We took her to the vets, for her injections course,
And she attacked a St Bernard, the size of a horse.
Mr Seal, Kitty and Doggy, are among her toys,
Which, she drags around the house with a lot of noise.
She's lost her baby teeth, we know, we have found a few,
And amazingly, we can proudly say, she doesn't chew.
Grapes, bananas, and even carrots, she likes to be fed,
And what she doesn't eat, she buries in her bed.
From a very tender age, she just loves to travel by car,
Hanging out of the window, barking at all from afar.
Taking her for walks on her lead, we try to teach,
But her favourite pastime is running on the beach.
She gives the cats, their exercise, as up the fence they leap,
But for others it's a different story, she kisses the sheep!
She has her own cosy bed, but ours she does prefer,
Then she licks you to death, with gravy-stained, facial hair.
Our adorable West Highland terrier, the pedigree,
But to us, she is just plain 'Jodie'.

Sue Jenkins

Tara The Tornado

I have a little kitten
With whom I'm very smitten
Tara chases flies round madly
Lovely flowers suffer badly.

Leaves are left on the kitchen floor
Tara rushes out for more
So much to see, so much to do
Seeing, hearing all things new.

She races up the apple tree
Expressive face says clever me
Onto the roof she has strayed,
'Come down Tara,' I have bayed.

Next door's cat is a friendly chap
Thinks, does she ever take a nap?
Life is exciting, life is fun
Not bad to say, she's not yet *one*.

Mary E Barker

An Anchor Books Anthology

Bog Snorkeller Blue

There is something quite amusing,
About a mud patch that's just oozing,
I like to take my time,
If I were a human I'd open a bottle of wine.

Oh just the thought of it
Makes my little hooves quake,
A bit like jelly on a plate,
And when it's finally time,
I just can't wait
I've got to sink into it
Like you people eating chocolate cake.

It's just a bad habit some might suppose,
But you humans have far worse -
Like picking your nose.

So here I am Tyn-y-cae Romance
And I can tell you I wouldn't miss a chance,
To jump in that mud
All gooey and brown
It helps keep my good looks the whole year round.

Mandy Preston

Man's Best Friend

Life with a dog is filled with fun
And wet loving kisses a-plenty!
Not only a companion by day
And a guardian by night
But a confidant who will never tell
And an ear that will never tire.
I've learnt a thing or two from my dog -
Like the virtue of loyalty
And the purity of unconditional love.
She's always happy to see me
And quick to forgive a harsh word.
I am the centre of her universe.
She's happiest at my side.
When I'm glad, she's glad;
When I'm down, she'll cheer me up.
Man's best friend - debatable
My best friend - definitely.

Sandra Trytsman

My German Shepherd

(This poem is dedicated to Cody my beloved German shepherd)

As a puppy you looked so sweet
We couldn't help but laugh at your great big feet.
Huge ears on a wee head
They're the first things you see when he pops out of bed.
Chasing his tail round and round
It's so funny when he falls to the ground
Wherever you go he's sure to follow you
He's a typical shepherd stuck with invisible glue
A mischievous twinkle in those soulful eyes
It's a sure sign you're planning a surprise
You do obedience and agility too.
Winning rosettes means nothing to you.
Search work is a favourite pastime
When you make your find you shout, you're mine.
You are so protective, noble, loyal too
Most people wouldn't mess with you.
Underneath that brave, alert attire
Is a big puppy who wants a belly rub by the fire.

Ruth Robertson

Faithful Friends

Our hearts were broken one sad day
When George the cavalier passed away;
He'd been our friend for ten long years,
When our George died we both shed tears.
The vicar came to talk us through our grief,
His kindly words of comfort brought relief.
We thought it nigh impossible to find another friend
But way up at East Runton our search came to an end.
Four little golden bundles lay huddled in a pen
The problem was which one to choose,
The Lord was with us then!
A black-faced puppy left the pen, whatever all the fuss,
We named him Dougal there and then, for he had chosen us!
Lhasa Apso was the breed, the first we've had as yet,
Friends to monks in monasteries, all way from Tibet!
We felt that God was with us at this time in our life
As He is with us all the time through sorrow and through strife.
God read our situation; He met our deepest need;
He guided us to Dougal, a miracle indeed.
I often marvel every day, especially of late,
How can a dog so very small, fill a void so very great?

William J Bartram

What Is A Cat?

What is a cat?
A small, domesticated, carnivorous quadruped
Says the dictionary.

I could add that a cat is a . . .

Charming, companionable, self-contained, independent, comic,
     lovable, exasperating, fastidious, obstinate,
     inscrutable, determined, snooty, decorative, demanding,
     persistent, affectionate, insistent, bossy, calculating,
     inquisitive, ingratiating animal.

But wherein lies the essential 'catness'?

My cat's *extremely* handsome:
Coat silky-soft, Persil-white and tawny -
Proclaiming his kinship with
The King of the Beasts;
Large, amber owl eyes;
Sensitive ears that
Twitch and flicker constantly;
Pale-pink pads adorned with silvery fur;
Pink-tipped nose and pink-lined ears;
Extensive vocabulary which
Makes his requirements
Crystal clear.
'Fantastically intelligent',
People say,
'Even for a cat'.

'My' cat, I said.
But it's surely a misnomer;
For though he condescends to live with me,
Essentially he belongs to no one but himself.
And You.

I thank You, Lord,
For making that fascinating,
Infinitely mysterious creature,
The Cat.

Maria-Christina

Ode To Holly

Amid the bustle of the day
When time was flying by . . .
So much to do . . . so little time
As we all, with spirits high,
Prepared the food, the church, the manse . . .
Thankful for a clear blue sky.

But then, into our crowded day
To take from us the toil and stress,
Came Holly, to the garden pond,
These human beings she would impress.
So thank you, Holly for the time
You spent with us, our hearts to bless.

Anne Gray

Ebony

A light went out in our world today,
When Ebony our first born calf
Was taken away.

However, she was taken for a reason,
Although today it's not easy to see.
I think that God had decided,
That she needed her mother,
More than she needed you or me.

She is at peace now,
No more discomfort or pain.
For now she has gone to Heaven,
To be with her mother Daisy again.

It is because of Ebony,
That we named the Blackwood Fold.
She was a black beauty,
A little treasure to behold.

She will never be forgotten,
We thought the world of her.
We will always have the memories
Of the happy times that were.

A little angel orphaned so young,
Not long after her little life had begun.
She had her sister Sable though,
Who was a good friend
And kept her company right to the end.

Joan C Igesund

An Anchor Books Anthology

Billy

He came to us from a place unknown, battered, broken and bruised
His eyes were so sad and his tail very still, he had been so abused
Slowly he began to trust though cautious and wary for a while
In time his eyes became bright and alert
And as he blossomed he made us smile

He started to play and scamper around
For he knew now he wouldn't be hurt
His character slowly began to emerge
But with mankind he could be quite curt
It was clear from his stance that a man in the past
Had hurt him and knocked him around
And now as he grew in confidence and strength
He was going to stand his ground

But with people he trusts his love knows no bound,
He is faithful doting and true
His favourite place is to up in your arms
Carried around and close to you
His master he clearly adores and will barely leave his side
He travels around taking in all the sights clearly enjoying the ride

It's a joy to see him now running across the fields
So happy and carefree at last
A testament to care he's received
As it's clear he's tucked away his past
He is funny and bright and when he creeps on the bed
It's an amusing sight
As he settles down there for the night and sighs with delight.

Gwen Gibson

A Poem For Keano

As I walked along the block
Two big brown eyes did make me stop
I stood there and I looked at him
His big sad face looked pretty grim

So I carried on along the block
But no more eyes could make me stop
I doubled back and stood by his pen
And those brown eyes caught me again

And so this dog came home with me
Along with his baggage, pain and misery
I have never thought to give him up
He'd had no life since being a pup

We take every day in our stride
And we work together, Keano and I
Some days are bad
Some days are good
I'd change his past if only I could

His eyes could tell a very sad tail
But he has taught me patience and love
Can and will prevail

And so this poem is dedicated to him
He is my prince, he is my king
I love him more than words can say
And in my heart he'll always stay.

Emma Bate

Spike

Like me, my dog is growing old
He used to do as he was told
But orders now fall on deaf ears
His eyesight too fades with the years
He's happy just to be with me
If I just don't expect that he
Will walk as once he used to do
But that's alright for that makes two
For my legs like his are getting lame
We both get stiff but just the same
We plod along from day to day
Remembering joys along the way.
We're warm and fed, that's all we need.
He sleeps and dreams and I can read.
Sometimes he drives me round the bend
But in spite of that he's my best friend.

Kath Barber

An Anchor Books Anthology

Tawny Dog

Tawny dog wrapped around my leg.
Blessed jewels from trees are shed.
A soft brown carpet from times gone by.
Cushion my feet, and breezes sigh,
'Walk in our world of tall green spires
that reach for the light,
forget your desires for the material world,'

With a path of magic that slowly unfurls,
Through the undergrowth of an emerald world.
Where Tawny dog will lift his head,
To scent the air, his message read.
Red blueberry upon the bush,
We venture far where the fox will push
Her cubs to earth,
And Tawny dog will forever seek,
Hidden treasures buried deep,
In a wooded land not ours to keep.

Eileen C Hersey

An Anchor Books Anthology

She Is . . .

She is a raindrop,
small and innocent,
but a thousand
creates a shower.

She is a candle,
a glimmer of hope,
in an empty world.

She is a blade of hair,
a coat of fur.

She is a warm cup of tea,
helps keep me going.

She is a draft of air,
a cool breeze.

She is a creature,
an example of nature.

She is . . . Jess.

Emma Owen (14)

Jenna

I lost a special friend today,
She's in my thoughts through the day;
I feel so sad, part of me is missing,
It hurts so bad, wish I was dreaming.

She never asked much of us all,
A generous pat, a friendly call;
Just call her name, she'd quickly come,
Return her love with so much fun.

Her eyes were like a window bright.
Full of loving, never spite;
No quest for her was ever too great.
You'd always find her at the gate.

Dear Jen, we all loved you so
Your shadow there where'er I go;
You gave us more than we can say,
Goodnight, God bless, the memories stay.

Rhiannon Collins

My Best Friend

You can take from me anything you want to,
Whatever it is, I don't care.
I don't mind if you take all my possessions
So long as my best friend's still there.

My arms will be opened to welcome you
Even if it's my things you take.
I'll stand by and I'll make no protest
If my friend is still left in your wake.

My friend is a wonderful person -
He always stands by my side.
And wherever I go, be it the gates of Hell
He's always following behind.

My friend isn't normally welcomed,
When we've been places before -
Maybe the reason is this one:
He hasn't got two legs, but four.

His face is one different to mine,
His ears are on top of his head,
And following the line of his backbone
Is a tail - a conspicuous end.

Many find his beauty and elegance repulsive;
It's dissimilar to theirs, so it's bad.
But I'll tell you the truth - of all my many friends,
My dog is the best one I've had.

He's never betrayed me in troubles,
He's kept all my secrets through strife.
He's comforted me in my illness,
And I need no friend better in life.

And so you may take my possessions,
My clothes and the food from my hand;
But still, my fate'll cause me no heartache,
If I have by my side *My Best Friend*.

Hannah Elysé

An Anchor Books Anthology

My Canine Companion

If I could say in words all that you offer,
Or emulate the love you give to me,
A treasure chest in values I could proffer;
The glow around my life would brighter be.

If I could match your grade in life's contentment,
Your patient endless zest for all to see,
If I could match your power to kill resentment
Or live as you in constant loyalty . . .

If I could find your likeness in forgiving,
The silent trust forever in your eyes,
My life would be much richer for the living . . .
With you, there is no need to feign disguise.

I could not visualise my life without you,
You give my world a quiet gentle grace . . .
In friendship - there is never need to doubt you,
Within my heart you hold a special place.

Pearl M Burdock

Fudgie

O my little furry friend,
You're always there,
Every day,
Without end.

How I love to come home
And have you greet me.
Whatever my day's been
You always meet me.

Your eyes are large and brown,
Soft, warm and loving
With tan brows
That won't frown.

Never a cross word
You ever tell me,
And with one soft paw
You always fell me.

With your loving ways
And endless patience
You brighten
All my days.

Sharon Grimer

Never Ask Why

Animals never ask why
They're left out in the wind and the rain
While their owner's in bed in the dry.
A horse or a cow
Will hang its head low
And suffer in silence and pain.

A cat scuttles by in the gutter
Unwanted, unfed and unloved
No notion it has to ask why
Or reproach the aloof passer-by.

A dog howls all day in its grief
At being left all on its own
For hours on end in the yard
And it does not presume to ask why.

Goldfish rotate in a bowl
Eyes glazed in an alien space
Three or four, or more often alone
They cannot begin to ask why.

A tiger is caught in a trap
To be skinned for a Chinaman's lust
Compassionate hearts are outraged
That his bones will be ground into dust.

Animals never know why
We treat them the way that we do
Innocent lambs, they must die
When they're useful to me and to you.

Ray Racy

Inky

Now there is a special cat, named Inky,
She's old, cunning, and so very slinky.
Always demanding of her daily cuisine
And refusing, when offered, any has-been.

Her owners driven to distraction, have been
Doing their best to encourage her more keen,
But her crafty old eyes flash at anything mean.
They know poultry and fish are her special scene.

So we bow to the old lady, a regular queen
Presiding over all-comers, of offers supreme,
Waving her tail, her head high, to let them know
That Inky will always steal the show.

C King

An Anchor Books Anthology

Tainted Tess

A border collie dog with fur so pure and warm
She left her past behind her, a wicked drawn-out storm

Her scraggy, thin and bony frame all too much to see
We fed her up with wholesome food and stroked her head with glee

Time went by with lots of love and gentle hands to soothe
Sweet Tess began to smile again and bounced away her blues

A year had passed so filled with joy she now had home at heart
She knew the love that came her way would last and never part

Our dog, our friend, our Tess forever, her pain and hurt has fainted
No sad days for her to bear, but just a little tainted.

Suzzette Goddard

Jodi's Tale

(I would like to thank all the staff at Huyton NCDL who have looked after me and have treated me over the last four years. Thank you. Jodi)

Hi, I'm Jodi, I've got a tale to tell,
At first I was loved by everyone,
Then when the novelty was gone,
I became dirty and started to smell.

They wouldn't feed me for days on end,
I became skin and bone,
I was really beginning to hate this home,
So much for being man's best friend.

My patience was wearing thin,
My back became red raw,
My spots were really sore,
I wish these fleas would stop biting my skin.

I was in a real bad state,
You got to me before it was too late,
Now I'm as happy as can be,
Thank you for rescuing me.

You took me to the NCDL,
They gave me some TLC and made me well,
Now I've made a fresh start,
We will never be apart.

Michael McNulty

The Stray

We heard your muted mew,
Rescued from the hedge
We took you straight into our hearts.
Our other cat now runs the gauntlet
Of your playful pounce
Flattens his ears and hisses his anger
To show who's boss.
Soon he accepts your irrepressible pranks
And in surrogate spirit
Licks and grooms your glossy coat.
Squirming, you submit for a while
Then escape to search for other attractions.
You peer through the grass
Quivering in expectation - Cleopatra eyes -
Wild as war paint - follow the butterfly's flight.
Then the paw you placed so gently on my cheek
Strikes out in an endeavour to perfect in play
The nemesis of some future prey.

Chris Cooper

Baem

I remember the day that we got you
Was about fourteen years ago
You were rescued by one of my aunties
And my parents just couldn't say no.

You were brought in a box with your sister
Both so helpless and small
Could fit you in the palm of my hand
Like holding a mini football.

You looked all head and no body
Your eyes so big and so blue
I knew from the day that I saw you
That we would be friends, me and you.

Whenever I've been feeling lonely
You've always been there for me
Demanding attention to cheer me up
And purring away so happy.

Even though now you're much older
You are still as cute as can be
And when the day comes that you leave me
I will miss you so completely.

And now I have made you a promise
That I'll be there for you till the end
I also just want to say thank you
For being my very best friend.

Phillip Carey

Home Comforts

My name is Jem, I'm ginger
And a hunter bold am I
I challenge any wildlife
To look me in the eye
I spend my time out hunting
In the darkness of the night
Then when it is morning
With the coming of the light
I make my way back home
To the place I love the best
It's so nice to put my feet up
And to have a well-earned rest.

Joan M Jones

Shadie Ladie

These feelings that I have unfortunately are real,
Yesterday you were here, today just seems unreal,
I've been so strong all day, well as strong as I could be,
Now it's time for me to remember how you used to be.

The way that you would greet me when home I'd come to visit,
The way you'd nudge my hand to make sure you'd get a clap,
When I'd sit on the floor you'd crawl on my knee,
With a sneaky little look as if to say, 'please pet me'.

We got you as a puppy all those years ago and even when I moved out,
I knew you'd still be there,
You were such a little cutsie, no other could compare,
I could never get mad with you, you knew that well,
And loved being spoiled with all your little treats.

Now I realise time was going by, you were getting older before my very eyes,
Though I didn't want this, these past few days I would never have wished,
They found a lump, a tumour they say, and within days you weren't the same,
No eating, sleeping, walking.

Mum and Dad didn't want you in pain, so they took you again,
The vet said it was best, my sweet little Shadie,
They put you to rest.
I know it's humane yet I fell all this pain, I miss you so much, life won't be the same.

So if you're out there listening, as they say you'll be,
I want you to know sweet lady, you're loved so much by me.
I wish that I had seen you to give you one last kiss,
And a big, enormous cuddle.

Now my tears are flowing freely, I hope the pain will ease in time,
So Goodbye my Shadie Lady,
There will always and forever be a place in my heart
That's only for you.

Jacqueline Donnelly

An Anchor Books Anthology

Our Dog Ben

Isn't he cute
Isn't he sweet
This dear little puppy
With rather large feet
Will he grow large
We wanted to know
What we mean really
How much will he grow
The look on his face
Determined it all
He had that sad look
We often recall
We couldn't resist
Those limpid brown eyes
He asked to be chosen
Our arms opened wide
We loved him
From that day
Till he was quite old
The pleasure and love
He returned
A thousand fold.

Jeanette Gaffney

The Trouble With Tilly

Tilly's our mad springer spaniel
An eight-month-old pup full of beans,
She runs round in circles and chases,
Her energy is endless it seems.

She has a half-brother called Dibble,
He's three and is kept on his toes,
She pinches his toys and his biscuits,
Sometimes from under his nose!

She got up to mischief one Tuesday
And decided to tear up the floor,
Chewing the lino was such great fun
Perhaps we should feed her more?

Although she has caused us some trouble
We'd miss her if she wasn't here,
Making a hard day seem brighter
With a wag and a lick always near.

F George

Our Josh

I'm going to tell of our catty named Josh,
He's velvety black and looks awfully posh,
But catty is batty, as mad as a hatter,
His belly is huge and is getting much fatter.

He walks tippy-toed
And creates such a patter,
His leggies are shorter,
Which doesn't much matter.

He goes out of the front door
And in through the back,
Occasionally knocks on the door with a tap.

He cries like a babe
When wanting his feed,
He cries for a lot,
Which I put down to greed.

Eccentrically dippy, but never a pest,
As Tina once stated, 'He's Simply The Best'.

Carol Hunt

Man's Best Friend

Memories of love and pleasure and fun
Or was I selfish, thoughtless and busy?
Reflecting on times with four-legged friends,
Did I try to be patient, good and kindly?

First there was Sammy, loving and caring,
With droopy, floppy ears and thick coat of red.
Then came Boyo, brown with lighter patches.
How Sammy enjoyed food, for Boyo only the best.

Sammy loved running free and splashing in for a swim,
He needed a shampoo to keep him sweet and clean.
Boyo was well behaved and gentle by nature,
He liked long walks and to sing his favourite tune.

Beautiful dogs, sadly missed, still the sign says beware.
Are they in Heaven, our guardians of home and hearth?
Now they're with God and I hope at peace,
They're still around in spirit, in photos and our hearts.

Sheila Rowland

An Anchor Books Anthology

Betty

Betty the budgie sits on her perch
She whistles and twitters and shrieks and chirps
Her shrill little voice can be heard all day long
As she merrily sings her birdie song

Betty the budgie is white and blue
With just a few yellow feathers too
She preens herself daily to make herself pretty
As she happily sings her bird-like ditty

Betty the budgie had a mate
But he fell off his perch and met his fate
He was a big bird, coloured bright yellow
Proud as a peacock, a real handsome fellow

Now Betty Birdbrain (as she's affectionately known)
Sits in her bird cage all alone
Tweeting and cheeping till her time comes to fly
Up to the aviary in the sky.

Jane Lynch

Charlie Wharlie

A bundle of joy came through the door
Small and cute, a dog to adore
Charlie Wharlie, that's what I called him
The little apricot poodle, so cheeky, such a darling.
When he was growing up, what fun we had
The tales I could tell you, he was such a lad.
One day he escaped and over the road he trotted
He must have thought, look at me, the escape I plotted.
When I got home, I got such a fright
My God, where's Charlie? He's not in my sight.
Out came a bag of his favourite treats
To tempt him back home to his retreat.
When Charlie was naughty it was always to be
To the box you go, where he lays his head down to sleep.
Summers I loved especially when he lay on my knee
To sunbathe in the sun, how contented he was to me.
One day my sister shouted, 'Where is my bun?'
And we all looked at Charlie, who did a run.
Such laughs we all had, I could go on forever
The memories live on in our hearts together.
Charlie Wharlie we miss you so much
I wish you were still here to give you a hug.
But never mind, we had 14 wonderful years,
So time has come to stop my tears.

Donna-Marie Whatmore

My Fish

Swimming round in its bowl
Does my goldfish have a goal?
It swims around every day
Always going the same way
Its memory is not very long
It can't remember what it's done
My goldfish has so much to do
Because it believes it's all so new
I haven't chosen to give it a name
Because it would only forget it again
But it must remember when it's been fed
Because if it didn't, it would be dead.

Tina Davis

Buster

With softest coat of black and white,
A home was sought by this small mite.
He chose a house numbered seven
And there found his piece of heaven.

Christmas was his favourite time,
He loved the treats and food so fine.
He came into his own one night
As gas threatened those that slept so tight.

Lots of love and a feather-filled bed
Were reward enough, with a tummy well-fed.
Basking in the summer sun
Life for him was full of fun!

Now after all those happy years,
Farewells gave way to many tears.
In our hearts and thoughts he will remain
The sweetest cat with the cheekiest name . . .
Buster!

Theresa M Carrier

An Anchor Books Anthology

Blackie

Dear Blacks, you have the softest fur,
And when you're stroked, the loudest purr.
You're like a baby in my arms,
Who's peaceful and so full of charm.

You lick my hands and smelly toes,
Then nudge me with your coal-like nose,
It's obvious what's in your sight,
A box of nibbles - cat's delight.

You have the most appealing face,
And tilt your head with feline grace,
Then with those emerald eyes you'll stare
And penetrate my soul with care.

I love the way you miaow and yawn,
And seem to wake me up at dawn.
You snuggle tightly by my side
Or under sheets, you'll sometime hide.

You walk with poise of movie star,
And like Joan Collins, you'll go far.
You'd look great on the silver screen
And be some fine director's dream.

You act like an Egyptian queen,
As Cleopatra, it may seem.
You have an independent air
And treat male cats with with lots of flair.

You're often seen with dear ole Dinny,
A ginger tom - Mark Antony.
It's fun to watch you cats at play
As you ride through the Arcadian way.

Oh baby Blacks, I love you so,
And I will never let you go.
You'll always live within my heart,
As you have done right from the start.

Connie Garrard

I Wish I Were A Cat!

Oh to be a cat
and never worry
about this or that
I'd laze around all afternoon
nibble salmon from a silver spoon
thump through the cat-flap
out on the prowl
each time I heard
the hoot of an owl
saunter back each morn
with a well-concealed smirk
to watch my owners
leave for work

Goodbye to stress
hello to fun!
I'd do as I pleased
all day long
endure the fussing
with dignified grace
yet celebrate sin
with a feline grin
I wish I were a cat
all furry and fat
Oh I wish I were a cat
curled up on the mat
Oh I wish I were a cat
Oh I *wish* I were a cat!

Michael Ward

My Frisbee

Running left then running right
I watch it duck and dive
It swirls around then lifts again
And I am left behind.

Up in the air it catches the breeze
And dances out of reach,
With one big effort I leap full height
And catch it in my teeth!

Cyd Griffin

A Tribute To Our Pony, Dyrran

To one of our friends who is one of the best,
The time has come to put you to rest.
If we could do anything to save the pain
We'd put this off for a time, but it would be in vain.

We could spare you now for a month or two,
But when the weather warmed, we'd know not what to do.
We do not want to see you suffer more, so
With dignity, we must let you go.

You've been a good friend to my children, and more,
Giving back confidence that they'd lost before.
Many you have taught to ride
And also bucked a few over the side!

You'd go hunting and enjoy the day
But when it came to showjumping, there was no way!
You'd start to jump, and do your usual triple stop,
The whistle would blow and out of the ring you would trot.

At gymkhana games you would do very well,
And in the fancy dress classes you did excel.
Walk, trot and gallop was your favourite game,
But winning at the County Show was your claim to fame.

You gave disabled children much pleasure and joy
When they sat on your back you were such a good boy.
You took to driving like a duck to water,
Whoever the driver, it did not matter.

So to our grey pony, who is 28 years old,
The decision is hard but we must be bold.
Happy memories we have of fun in the past,
Of hunting, gymkhanas and driving the cart.
So please now find eternal rest,
You were our first pony, and one of the best.

Glenda V Llewellyn

My Shadow

It doesn't matter where I am, somehow I always know,
My shadow will be close behind wherever I may go.
He's with me when I'm sleeping and beside me through the day,
In fact my little shadow never seems to go away.

He protects me from all dangers, on that I can depend,
My shadow is my guardian, my true and faithful friend.
And when we both are parted, the sadness will remain
Until we're reunited, then our hearts rejoice again.

Some days when I am feeling down, too tired to want to speak,
My shadow lies before me like an angel at my feet.
And all the times I raise my voice; I'm forgiven every time,
That proves to me such loyalty is high above mankind.

So if you have a shadow that follows you around,
Cherish it for evermore for a treasure you have found.
Remember all God's creatures, be they great or very small,
Will never ever let us down, they're here to love us all.

Valerie Carter

Ziggy, The Cat

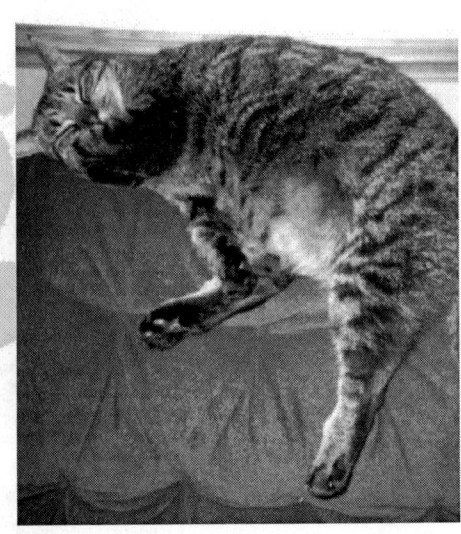

Your feline incandescence shrouds me
As softly I sleep, together with thee.
Dark is the moonlight which hangs around your eyes,
You're treacherous and cunning, but oh, what a prize.
I need your light to keep me blinded,
'Tis with you alone my problems confided.
Oh feline cat, predator at heart,
The Egyptians were in your clutches,
For them you were too smart.
Oh domestic cat, your cousins would surely eat me,
But instead, you do simply make a seat of me.

Alan Lester

In The Words Of Max

I was welcomed in the family,
In the year of '94,
The love and understanding,
I couldn't ask for more.

Oh! An older brother,
For me to snuggle with at night,
But he was having none of this,
All he ever did was fight.

But Mum came to the rescue,
It was her I ran behind,
But after living there a while,
I found out he was blind.

So I tried my best to help him,
I'd guide him when I could,
I whispered one day, 'Be my friend?'
He grumbled yes he would.

Now we are never parted,
To me, a real surprise,
The very best of friends are we,
So let me be your eyes.

Shirley Chapman

To Dino

My cat is fantastic, all furry and fun.
Loves to sit by the fire or bask in the sun.
I'm forced to take notice - though TV's my intention,
Cos your soft gentle paws, pad my arm for attention,
Then you'll sit nice and warm, relaxed on my knees,
Knowing well that I like it, you just aim to please.
You're purring away quite happy in sleep,
Until you decide that it's time for a leap!
So off you streak, stand and stretch every bit
Of your body and limbs, with wide yawning lip.
You look up at me then with questioning eyes,
'Is it time for a feed?' your soft miaow cries.
And when I call 'Dino', you come on all fours
As we both greet each other - you are mine - and I'm yours.

A Cotter

My Horse - My Friend

My horse, to me, means all the world,
   More than money, diamonds and pearls,
He brings me so much happiness,
   The greatest gift one can possess.
He taught me how to understand
   A language horses do command,
From a past of wilderness, once he did roam,
   This language he taught me, all of his own.
A love and respect granted from above,
   We are a team, but it's also love.
He taught me wisdom, to be patient and kind,
   Can't believe I'd been so blind.
He doesn't mind what clothes I wear,
   He doesn't stop to look and stare.
When times are tough and I feel down,
   He is the one I want to be around.
He never asks, or questions why,
   If all I want to do is cry,
He just listens to all I say,
   And never wants to walk away.
A trust built up between he and me,
   Is hard to find in humanity.
When a friend like this comes your way,
   Don't let him wander, or go astray,
A good, true friend is hard to find,
   Especially of the horsey kind.
Over the years, what he's given to me,
   Has made me so, so very happy.
To him I guess I'm just his keeper,
   But I think we both know it goes much deeper.
So when he's gone, how sad I'll be,
   Because he meant the world to me.
He'll not want me to be sad,
   But just remember the good times we had.
No one will ever take this away,
   'Cause in my heart, he'll always stay.
So, for now he'll continue to be
   A very special friend to me,
I'll carry on and cherish each day,
   And pray our parting is a long way away.
My horse, my friend.

Samantha Walker

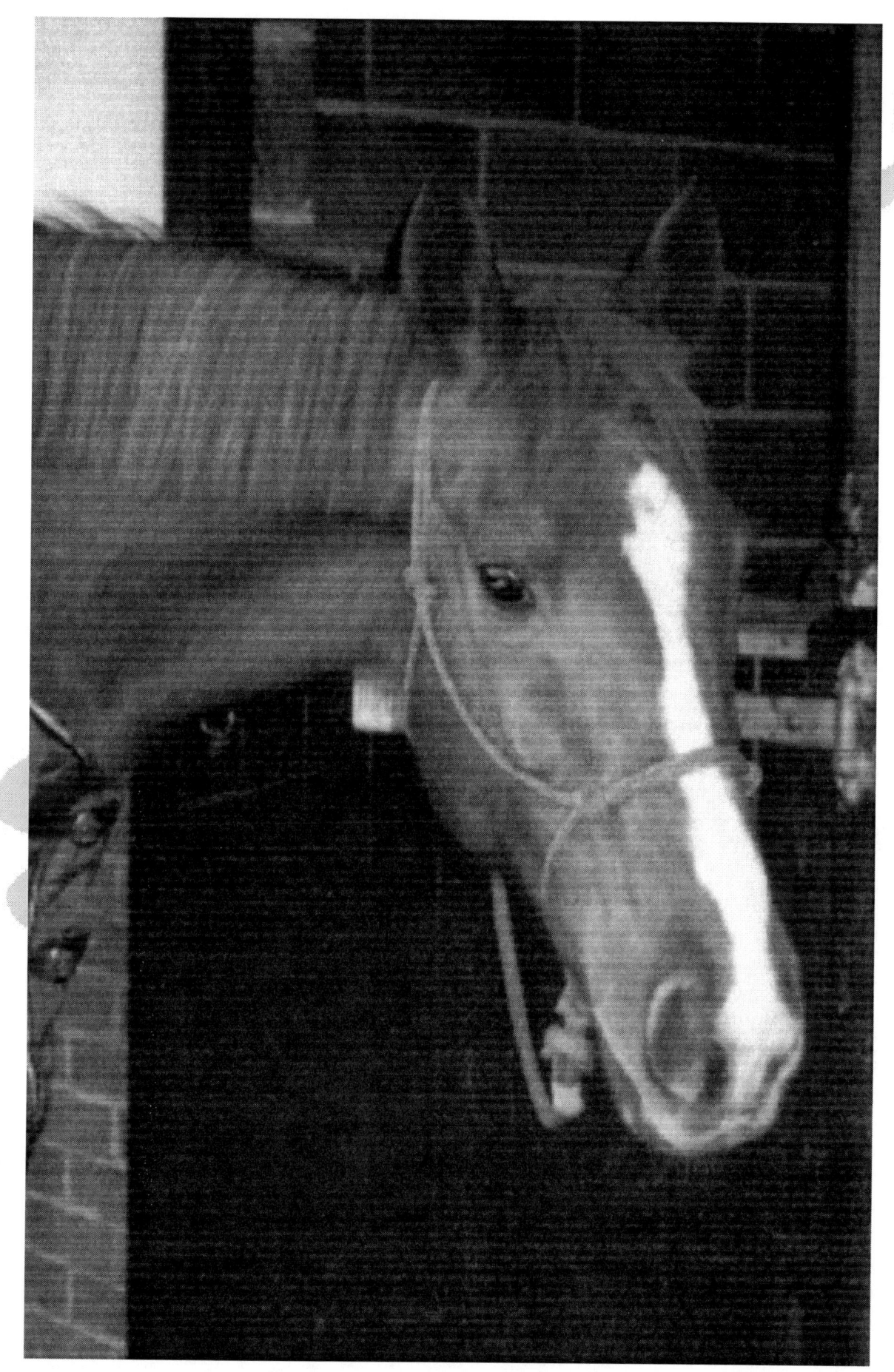

The Golden Girls

Sun streaks through the trees
and passes her by
yawning and stretching
she opens her eyes.

With patience and purpose
she struggles to wake
moving silently forward
to open the gate.

She greets her companion
and falls into line
moving in sequence
stopping to dine.

They circle the garden
then resting awhile
They cuddle together
making me smile.

Who would have thought it?
The best of friends
Curious playmates
a dog and a hen!

Sandra Evans

Hattie's Song

Sleek creature
Shiny smooth
Unsure at times
She needs reassurance
Love
Touching
Verbal tunes

She jumps up onto my knee
Singing Hattie's song
It comes from deep in her throat
She settles down to soft purrs

We call it 'Hattie's song'.

Moira Jean Clelland

Fish

My tank full of fish,
They would make a nice dish,
If you didn't want them
as pets,
But I look after them so they need no vets.

My tank full of fish,
Every day I make a wish,
A fish I hope to be,
So that they can play with me.

My tank full of fish,
When they go I will miss
Watching their mouths open and close,
And to the others they seem to pose!

Catrina Lawrence

The Ice Cream Cone

A lovely summer's day,
in the beautiful county of Cornwall
was the perfect setting, and a bench
with an ice cream cone in my hand
was the perfect thing to do

So to the window of the shop,
I asked the lady with a smiling face
for a 'Vanilla flavour please,'
anxiously looking at a nearly empty tub.

Not to worry, there was plenty for one
'and a little cone for your little dog'
who was looking so expectantly
and she received it with pleasure!

My dear little Pomeranian
knew she had been give a lovely
treasure and enjoyed it to the full,
it was the one and only one
she ever had and it was her last.

I still can smile when I dream
of my little dog and often wonder if
that kind lady ever realised the joy
she had given to both of us on a
sunny afternoon in Bude.

J L Holden

Our Dog Slikker

In all the world there is no dog
Like our dog, Slikker,
There is no canine, half so fine,
As our dog, Slikker,
You should see him jump and wag his tail,
When he runs outside to get the mail
Our clever dog, Slikker.

He lies on the mat and pretends he's asleep,
Does our dog, Slikker,
But through his lashes, he will peep,
Will our dog, Slikker.
He'll jump up high and rush about,
If he thinks I'm going to take him out
Will our dog, Slikker.

He loves to play a merry game,
Does our dog, Slikker,
With balls or bones, they're all the same,
To our dog, Slikker.
He'll growl and bark, and leap and bound
And toss the balls and bones around
Will our dog, Slikker.

I hope he's with us for many a day
Our dear dog, Slikker.
For no other dog could with us play,
Like our dog, Slikker.
He likes to climb upon my knee,
No dog could mean the same to me
As our belovèd Slikker.

Rosanna J Freeman

Walkies!

'Come on, Lady. Get your lead'
My mistress says to me.
If I pretend I haven't heard,
Perhaps she'll let me be
She thinks I need the exercise,
But really! Can't she see
Tucked up on these cushions,
Is where I'd rather be?
I think the one who wants the walk
Isn't me but she!
So she should go and get the lead
And take herself, not me!

Margaret Doherty

Dillon's Dilemma

Oh there's that perishing lead again
I suppose it's time for my walk
I'd much rather stay in my basket
If only I could talk
It's not that I don't like the walkies
It's the tugging that makes me fed up
And all those grown up people
Telling her she must train her pup
After all I cannot help sniffing
All those wonderful smells out there
To expect me to patter straight past them
Is really just so unfair
There, she's calling me, I had better go
And let her get me ready
I don't suppose we will get too far
Before she is saying, 'Steady!'

Susan Anthony

Glen

How could anyone abandon you?
I really don't know, I haven't a clue,
Small and sweet, a living soul,
Not left with anything, not even a bowl.

All over town you walked and ran,
Your little body, black, white and tan,
No food or water, looking for a bite,
This is just cruel, it isn't right.

A Jack Russell just looking for care,
You must have gone just anywhere,
Up the road, down the street,
All you wanted was someone kind to meet.

Then someone came and took you away,
You were just a little stray,
They took you, cared for you, treated you well,
Took you away from that living hell!

We heard about you waiting for a home,
How hard it was when you had to roam,
We saw you with your loving eyes,
Those horrible people we truly despise.

Now you are ours, our darling Glen,
You will never go through that ever again,
You are so special in our heart,
With us forever, we will never be apart.

Pearl Devereux

Charlie's Angel

'Who's that knocking at my door?'
'Who's that walking down my street?'
'Don't come near, I'm not the kind of dog you would like to meet.'

All I wanted was a faithful pet
A Labrador - that's what I'll get!
A bundle of joy, just seven weeks old
The light of our lives, a dog to behold.
A little yellow Labrador, Charlie was his name,
To him life was fun, all just a game.

Charlie had so much energy, he would surely calm down soon
But his favourite was the 'wall of death' around the sitting room
'Stop that Charlie, no, don't do that,
What was that scream? Oh no, he is mounting the cat!'

He was fast and strong with teeth you couldn't ignore
- Not your usual Labrador.

Walk after walk, but still he wanted more
- No, not your usual Labrador.

And as the months passed by, it wasn't much fun
Charlie was different, something had to be done.

First stop the vet, 'Is medication what we require?'
'Castration is the answer, it's because he's entire!'
He was duly castrated - cat-safe at last
'But, what about his problems?' 'Well I'm glad that you asked!

You need a behaviourist, an expert in his field,
A consultation, a training plan, yes, that's what you need!'

Two experts later, and armed with a list of his needs:
A head collar, a harness, a collection of leads
A bumbag and titbits and mandatory clicker.
'Keep up with the training, this way will be quicker!'
So strapped up in his harness, bumbag at the ready
Someone coming towards us, trying to keep him steady.

But as they approached, it was all in vain
Teeth gnashing and snarling - it was always the same;
Lunging and barking, 'I'm not going to be beat;
No - I'm not the kind of dog you would like to meet!'

What was I do? Should I do the deed?
He's the love of my life, but way out of my league.
Then a ray of light shone, was it divine intervention?
I was reading the paper and Rod Roberts was mentioned.

A dog training course was advertised, and after it Rod's name
'Help for all types of problem dogs'. Rod knew the game.
'All the things about Charlie's behaviour you hate,
Well they're his greatest assets; no it's not too late.'

An Anchor Books Anthology

Rod duly took us both under his wing
Guiding us, training us, through thick and thin.
'Working Trials is what we are working toward,
Charlie needs stimulation and a purpose to stop him getting bored.'

Surely enough Charlie's confidence grew
And even became friendly with people he knew.
He began to enjoy life, 'People weren't that bad,
They fussed me and stroked me and what about that sausage I had?'

Now he is competing in Working Trials and it's all down to Rod
He has given Charlie his life back; he is such a happy dog.

'Who's that knocking at my door?
Who's that walking down my street?
I am Charlie! Just the kind of dog you would like to greet!'

Janet Freeman

Rosie

When Rosie came to our house
She really was quite small
Silvery grey and fluffy
Around her eyes a curl.

Rosie is now growing up
She really is a size
White and grey and curly
Soulful liquid eyes

The tiny yap now has gone
Instead, a deep, deep bark
Yet Rosie is a softie
She's only having a laugh

She bounds around the garden
On her enormous feet
Chasing bees and butterflies
And once it was a leaf

Rosie is our sheepdog
I'm sure you must have guessed
Our gentle loving giant
Rosie really is the best!

Juliet Marshall

My Dog

He's not tall, but small
But he's proud and stands up tall,
He's a cinnamon shade of red,
And is very fluffy on his head,
Yes, you've guessed, he is a chow,
And every time I walked past someone, they say, 'Wow!'

His eyes are as black as night,
And his tail is snow-white,
His feet are like a bear's,
And he drags them along like he doesn't care!

When he's on a leash, he's like a bull,
And you heave him back with a great big pull!

He is very obedient,
He knows, 'roll over', 'paw' and 'sit',
And I won't stop loving him,
Till I get to the bottom of the bottomless pit!

Jessica Copland

An Anchor Books Anthology

My Faithful Friend, Simba

My dog is my best friend, he is with me all the time,
No finer pal in all the world I could ever find.
He is so loyal and trusting, he never lets me down,
And when I feel lonely he is always around.
His big brown eyes look up to me and a kind word I do say,
Then he comes and licks my hand, what more can I say?

Don Goodwin

My Tiny Tiger

He has a tiger's elegance
But on a smaller scale,
A rounded form with darker rings
Like bracelets on his tail.

His coat is just as smooth and svelte
But of a smaller size.
He has the same designer stripes,
The same gold-glitter eyes.

He paces as a tiger does,
Making a tiny swathe
Through crystal grass where silver mice
In pools of moonlight bathe.

He stops, he lies in wait and then
On priceless fields he crouches,
Bejewelled by the sapphire bells
That make exotic couches.

He has a tiger's lordly stance,
His bold, hypnotic stare,
His grace of movement when he walks,
His proud, imperious air.

He has the same intelligence,
The same instinctive skill,
And tiger-like he walks alone
And has a tiger's will.

If fate should compromise my cat
So these two creatures met,
He'd fire on all compressors
To take off like a jet.

Celia G Thomas

Ode To Puss Catt

I welcome the day
My friend came to stay
And for the gifts
He so freely gives.
At first just a shadow,
A glimpse in the dark
And a bowl
Which was licked, oh, so clean.

Now he is sleek
And happy with life.
His presence
He openly shows.
Each mouse in the house
Ev'ry rat in the barn,
Shook at the sound of his name.

Dear Puss Catt
Old friend cat
You're worth every Kit-E-Kat,
Tho' foe of poor Pansy the dog.
Your agile nobility
And friendly notoriety,
You're the king
Of this rodent-free home!

Lyn Sandford

My Furry Friend

I have a furry friend who is cute and cuddly.
Tiger is his name, a name he lives up to.
Always swinging on the curtains, scaring the living
daylights out of the budgie.
I know he would like to eat the goldfish as a treat.
Always near beside me, he is lying now at my feet.
Purring, singing and swatting flies.
Ah sure, he is always full of mischief, my little pride and joy.
I could not be without him.
My tiger!

Nancy Elliott

Ben

I'm glad you chose me to be the one
For you give me strength to carry on
You are my friend when I'm feeling low
My pal when I've nowhere to go
You listen without making a sound
And are there when I need someone around

You look at me with love in your eyes
There's no way in your look, could your eyes ever lie.
My brave heart, that's what you are to me
My Ben, my dog, my friend you will always be.

Maureen Morris

My Sunshine Budgie

Once I had a budgie called Becky.
A bright yellow colour she was,
     and what a pretty sight she made.
She was also a chirpy little thing.
Strong and long-lived, she outlived
     three other budgies of mine.
Tame she was not, a solitary,
     strong budgie, my Becky.
When I went to touch her,
     she would bite and struggle free.
Left alone she wanted to be,
     just to look pretty and majestic.
Her alones made her strong.
But one day she started struggling
     with her flying.
It didn't get any better,
     so to the vet I took her.
The vet couldn't find anything wrong.
'Just old age,' said he,
     'nobody lives forever.'
One day, soon after, I found her dead
     at the bottom of her cage.
At the end of her life
     she'd been struggling and suffering.
For seven and a half years she lived,
     during which she taught me something;
'You can make it on your own. Be strong.'
At rest she is now and may God keep her.

Christina Gilbert

My Cat Tigger

Tigger was my wonder cat, with such a common name
He really was exclusive; he could drive me quite insane
His colour was all ginger, apart from his pink nose
And his hair was always falling out; covered all my clothes,

Whenever we moved house, which was often in the past
He had to re-establish himself with every other cat!
His territory he would claim; ferocious he did fight
Battle-scarred he'd come home, a weary cat that night

We always had a cat door, so he could wander in and out
Once he brought a black tail in, from another cat no doubt
He seemed to climb the highest, of any cat around
Rescued from a building, sometimes he hit the ground!

Yet he was very loveable, he'd sit on anyone's knee
Never showed a preference, could be a he or she!
Sadly showed his signs of age when he reached nineteen
We had to take him to a vet; you all know what I mean.

He was buried in the garden, beneath a lovely rose
The sweetest cat in my world, now sleeping in repose
Such a strong affection, I developed for my cat
I'd love to see him once again, just sitting on my lap.

Joan Prentice

Cat's Life!

'Dusty! Dusty!' Did I hear my mistress call?
Oops! I'm all tangled up in her 'wool' ball,
I'm in trouble again, will she scold me?
No . . . she laughs out loud as she sets me free,
I tried to make friends with the bird in the cage,
But it nipped my nose and flew into a rage,
When I dipped my paw in the goldfish bowl,
The cold water startled me, on the floor it did roll,
I didn't like getting wet, I did soon discover,
So escaping into the garden, I ran for cover,
With all this excitement, I needed a 'wee',
I wonder how far I can climb up that tree,
I've got to the top, it's scary looking down,
As I cling on and cry, I see a face with a frown,
Soon two loving arms gently enfold me,
And take me safely indoors in time for tea.

Glenice Siddall

The Badger Gasps and Groans

When midnight comes a host of dogs and men come out to play.
Go out and track the badger to his den,
And put a sack within his hole and lie there -
Till the old grunting badger passes by.
He comes and hears - they let the strongest loose.
The old fox hears the noise and drops the goose.
The poacher shoots and hurries from the cry,
And the old hare, wounded, buzzes by.
They get a forked stick to bear him down -
And clap the dogs and take him into town
And bait him all the day with many dogs
And laugh and shout and fight the scampering hogs.
He runs along and bites at all he meets:
The shout and holler down the noisy streets.

He turns to about to face the loud uproar . . .
And drives the rebels to their very door.
The frequent stone is hurled where'er they go;
Your disposition so sweet, no one else could ever compete.
You were dignified and classy right from the start.
Love was what you were about; of this, there's no doubt.
You are my 'brown dogs' for keeps.
When badgers fight, then everyone's a foe!

The dogs are clapped and urged to join the fray;
The badger turns and drives them all away.
Through it, though scarcely half as big, demure and small -
He fights with dogs for hours and beats them all.
The heavy mastiff, savage in the fray,
Lies down and, like it, licks his feet and turns away.
The bulldog knows his match and waxes cold,
The badger grins and never leaves his hold.
He drives the crowd and follows at their heels -
And lets them through - the drunkard swears and reels.

The frightened women take the boys away,
The blackguard laughs and hurries on the fray,
Till kicked and torn and beaten, out he lies -
And leaves his hold and cackles, groans and dies!

Viv Lionel Borer

A Faithful Dog

A dog is a man's best friend,
you can teach him tricks
make him run for sticks
and give him treats, no end.
He's playful and fun
and loves to run,
you walk for miles and miles,
he jumps through hoops
and runs through fields
and leaps over crooked stiles.
At times of rest
near the fireplace is best,
as it's cosy and warm you know,
he's your very best friend
and true to the end
when you're down
and feeling low.
When times are good
when times are bad,
a dog is your favourite mate,
when you finish work
and arrive home late,
he's there waiting
for you at the gate.

Rachael Ford

Fluffy

Fluffy was a flighty mouse
Made of mighty stuff
Quiet in his whitey house
Most content enough

Out about on mousy walk
On tippy, tappy toe
Housey mousey, 'round the housey
Mousily would go

Scatty, scutter, skittering
Scatters 'round the room
Scatty catty comes to chase . . .
Fluffy with a zoom

Flighty to his whitey house
Fluffy nears the door
Yet! Too late for fluffy fluff
Fluff all 'round the floor.

Gemini Cherry

An Anchor Books Anthology

My Cat

I've had my cat since he was born
I've watched him grow, I've watched him yawn
Scratch the furniture, make a mess
But I still love my cat the best

He loves to drink milk, eat tuna too
He sits on your lap and purrs for you
You let him out, he comes back in
You play games, he lets you win

I brush his fur coat every day
He listens to what I have to say
If cats could talk what tales they'd tell
About all other cats and dogs as well

I'd never part with my dear cat
The way he sits on the mat
The way he comes when you call
I love my cat best of all.

Sally Anne Petrie

Compromised Freedom

Little brown feathery bird
Up in your 'wherry' nest
Singing happily, free as a bird
Well, really, so you should be

Early in the crow of dawn
Off you go in search of worms.
How diligent you are in your chores;
Make way, Make way! And here you come.

I watch with envy and excitement
As you dole out with love and commitment.
What a way to live a life,
Full of misery and imprisonment.

A pet I took for you to be,
But your freedom it compromised.
I promise with my heart to let you go
Once your chicks are strong,
And ready to fly.

Emmanuel Omoro

Mixed-Up Pets

I called my terrier, Kitty, my cat I named Rover.
These names confused them, a problem they could not get over.

So Rover took over if a stray cat should stray.
She did all the doggy things and chased it away.

Now terrier Kitty what a pity did something new.
Drank milk from a saucer and started to mew.

With this unfair confusion I reversed the illusion changing back their names although they
Could not accept the fact that they had been changed around the other way.

The terrier is now living at a cats' home and Kitty herds sheep in north Wales.
Or is this another one of those 'shaggy dog tales'?

T A Napper

A Kitten's Plea

'Miaow!' She lets out a pitiful cry.
She has not yet seen the land or sky.
Her eyes are closed to the world around her.
All she can hear is her sibling's purr.

They grow silent, she is left all alone
As they cry out their final moan.
This tabby kitten dumped in a cardboard box.
Left to the mercy of any dog or fox.

'Miaow!' Will someone not hear her plea?
'Miaow! Can someone please find me?'
Dumped by an adult in a wheelie bin.
Don't they know it's a crime and a sin?

Helpless she is not completely alone.
All she wants is that perfect home.
A comfy lap to curl up on at night.
If someone knew of her plight.

Curled up in front of a log fire.
Is only this kitten's one desire!
Cute and cuddly she deserves a home.
Not to be left in a box all on her own.

How can people be so cruel?
Can we not make a tighter rule?
No animals should start his or her life this way.
People who commit cruelty should be put away.

Jo Lodge

An Anchor Books Anthology

Puppy Love

She jumps up to lick my face
And excitement makes her wee!
When I come home to our place
She jumps up to lick my face!
My pup feels no disgrace
When she runs to welcome me,
She jumps up to lick my face,
And excitement makes her wee!

Dan Pugh

Billy, Our Clever Cultural Cat

He often takes in 'Mastermind'
Or other quizzes of that kind,
British Fashion Week is his forte;
Our Billy's *so* not 'prêt-a-porter'.
Models treading the catwalk -
Oh, if only our sweet Billy could talk!
He'd tell you everything that's new;
For now, he comments in purr and mew.

Billy, our clever cultural cat,
Adores the Proms, and events like that,
Men dressed, like him, in black and white
Playing instruments till late at night.
'Newsnight' and interviews by Paxman -
Not for him Superman and Batman.
His taste extends to opera and ballet,
Not 'Friends', or 'Cheers' with Kirstie Alley!

Billy, our clever cultural cat,
Transfixed by 'Time Team' and all that
As he digests the evening news
So trans*mog*rified become his views.
Following Palin on his travels,
Or, as life beneath the sea unravels,
Nature programmes seem to be the best,
For it's after these his eyes shut to rest.

Geraldine Laker

Puppy Love

When we saw Lucy she was a ball of fluff
Her damp cold nose and her small tongue was rough
When we gave her milk it was her favourite drink
Her noisy lapping was like tap water running at the sink

The name was chosen, it was Lucy for this beautiful one
The days we had with her became such contented fun
Those special treats, the petting she got when she was small
Those torn pieces of newspapers and toilet roll littered the hall

Those chewed slippers were always found in her small basket bed
When we scolded her, she would sulk and drop her forlorn head
We would always find her favourite toys upon an armchair
The cushions and carpet were covered with her fine strands of hair

She would always be a friend, this faithful, beautiful, loving pet
We would laugh when she struggled to climb those garden steps
The grass would be in a mess with her playthings and chewed bones
Thro' that large hole in the hedge she often crawled and roamed.

Thro' these special times our dog Lucy will always be our best friend
She grew so fast that sweet puppy love we hope will never end
These most cherished years here filled pleasures we love to share
Without our Lucy our lives and our hearts would be empty sitting there.

J Grainger

Eee Me Dog!

Eee, I love me dog
I love him more than any mog
He doesn't bite, he doesn't scratch
He doesn't wee on a certain patch

Eee, I love me pet
There's not another I'd rather get
He's very loyal, he's very tame
He gets his ball to play a game

Eee, I love me Scooby-Doo
When I chose him who knew
That he would be my best friend
Any troubles he would mend

Eee, I love me dog
If you're getting a pet don't get a frog
They're very cold with slimy skin
And how funny you'd look walking him!

Beverley Dale

An Anchor Books Anthology

We Are Drawn!

Without the need of any spoken words - we are
all drawn by the antics of our pussy cat -

Will look at us with wide-open eyes - telling us
she is now ready for her treat - once given she
will purr until she falls asleep.

Over the years a trust has been built up - she knows
no harm will come from us - and she knows we
need a pussy cat - Lucy is her name!

R P Scannell

Animals Section - Mice In A Stew

Dearest eldest grandson, Josef

On my travels again
discovered and cross my heart and hope to die
this is true and they say there is proof

there is a place called Guang Zhou
which is said totally differently to the way it is spelt
but research keeps interfering with my sound system
so I find it difficult to familiarise myself with the language

this place is called Gwang Joe
which is in the vicinity of H Kong
the city, not Hitler's favourite film,
has mice which are five kilograms in weight
like a little pig, says my favourite Li Feng
these are mice not unlike the regular invaders from the sewers
of my London cottage where you used to visit
down round the corner of Idi Amin's wife's restaurant
who was done for a mucky kitchen by the council!

Josef, Guang Zhou mice are eaten alive for lunch
and scream but thrice . . .
they swore to me at Haier last night at lesson time
and swore this was so, and who am I to disbelieve Haier staff?

The first time when dipped into salt
the second time when bitten into
and the third time, I forget . . .
as I wasn't listening anymore, being a vegetarian
no, I've got it . . .
first when sliced, second when salted and third when bitten

and Josef, all Chinese people everywhere say
in Guang Zhou, they eat everything on benches
except the benches . . . !

Renate Fekete

Blue!

Five years ago to the day
I received what I had been wishing for.
A man got a message from the SPCA
A girl wanted a husky that he had to give away

He came to my house with a tear in his eye
He said, 'This is Blue and he is very shy.'
It took a while, but the shyness melted away
Our family grew and loved each day

Long walks we would take
And he loved car rides to the lake
He wanted to spend his time outside
But, also loved rough housing inside

Time is shorter than you think
It can be gone quicker than a blink
My dream growing up was to have Blue
It is now just a memory of a dream come true

Out of my touch
It hurts so much
A life now lost, had so much to give
Now, I am lost and have to live!

Paula Brewer

Ode To A Corgi

'What's that?' they say when I am out
'What *is* that on the lead?'
More Welsh than leeks and daffodils
Dwarf dog, this ancient breed.

The old-time farmers know that I'm
A herder not a hound,
Some say my legs are much too short,
But all four reach the ground!

'Is that a sausage with a tail?'
They say when they come round.
No, I'm a Cardigan corgi
Not a short sheepdog from the pound.

Paula Stevens

Untitled

You may think that I am Santa Claus,
The hat gives me away,
I'm laid down in my armchair,
It's been a very busy day.

I ran the hedgerows, sniffed and played
Then my mistress called me back.
The days are getting shorter now,
And the skies are looking black.

My bed is this big armchair,
It's cosy, soft and warm.
My family call it *my* chair,
And I'll never come to harm,

This hat is just a joke you know,
I'm such a silly girl,
My mistress dressed me up like this,
But I'm too tired to do a twirl,

She put this on her Christmas cards,
I thought it was quite silly,
By the way, I'm not really Santa Claus,
My proper name is Tilly.

D Cordell

Is That Your Dog?

Dogs are a man's best friend,
They are faithful to the end,
There are no dogs the same,
There are no dogs just plain,
Because they have a personality of their own.

They may bark when the postman sings,
Or perhaps when the doorbell rings,
It really is a joy,
To see your dog play with its favourite toy,
Is your dog considerate and kind
And keeps thinking of you in heart and mind?

My dog, so happy, full of life,
Ready each day and gives no strife,
Nothing is too much for his dear heart,
My dog and I will never part.

    Yes, that's my dog!

Amber Stevens

Biggles

O' Biggles, tell me what it was,
That made you such a treasure,
Perhaps a multitude of traits,
Gave each of us such pleasure.

Maybe it was the 'tilted' head,
That seemed to check our mood!
Were *boots* or *opener* in mind?
Was it a walk or food?

Before a walk, you'd slip out quick,
And clear up Harry's plate,
Then, stopping by to grab your stick,
(Eyes firmly on the gate).

Across the common you would run,
With Harry chasing rabbits.
You'd yelp and bark and dodge and turn,
Endearing 'Biggy' habits.

If any one of us was sad,
You seemed to gauge our mood,
You'd 'flump' right down and snuggle in,
As if you understood.

You sensed your time clock running out,
So you knew what to do,
You gave us Algy, Bobbie, too,
A perfect gift from you.

So Biggy, as we've shared your life,
With walks, treats, bits of fuss,
A true companion, special friend.
Ben's dog, yet loved by us.

Gillian Humphries

Cat Cares

I want a place where I can sleep
And rest my furry head,
Wrap my tail around my paws
In a snug, warm, cosy bed
My needs are few
I don't ask a lot
For my nine lives to be complete,
Love and care and some gentle strokes,
And a few nice things to eat.

Christine Williams

An Anchor Books Anthology

Master Of His Realm

Do you own a cat? Does he do tricks?
Get into mischief, amuse with antics?
Mine does! Pooch! Colouring aping small tiger,
Intelligent feline, no other cat finer,
Lithe, handsome and striking, bounding swiftly along,
Muscular as a panther, for his size and age, strong,
Hunts prey, not to eat but paw - plonk on head,
He wants them to play, not rigid and dead.

In summer months never fails to wake me at dawn,
My head held with paw, combs mane with southpaw! I yawn and yawn!
He cat-preens me, claws out, sprucing hair down with tongue
When strands caught midst wee teeth, becomes highly-strung!
I let out piercing shriek, 'Stop! Tangled underneath!'
Pull out hair and ignore him but he's staring beneath,
Those amber eyes do not blink, directly bore into mine,
With smouldering glare, suddenly makes a beeline
To climb up my body till our noses entwine.

How can I resist a cat with such charm?
I know hour is early but he's doing no harm,
Pooch, gently nips my arm awaiting to be fed
From dry cat food packet kept beside bed,
Sated, he twists into air, returns to lie sleepy head
In cat bed; leaving me smiling at determined redhead.

Hilary Jill Robson

Old Dogs, Young Dogs

He's old, my old Ben
And I don't know just when
He could run as fast as the wind
Whereas my young Dibble
Runs like the debble
With the hop and the skip of a rebel

He's grouchy, my old Ben
And I don't know just when
He turned into a grumpy old fart
But Jack Russell Dibble
Is just dibble tribble
With more life than an engine's kick-start

He's a springer, old Ben
And I don't know just when
He first breathed on me 'breath of cod'
Or first angrily barked, in Dibble's face:
'Disgrace, disgrace, to the canine race
For letting them brush your teeth, bathe your face!'

He's old my old Ben
And I don't know just when
I loved him like I do now
But I love 'Jack the ripper'
The new town boy nipper
Old dogs, young dogs, all dogs are chipper!

Eric Ferris

A Dog's Nightmare

Hop, hop, hop, I can see those fleas
Hop, hop, hop, they're going to jump on me.
Hop, hop, hop, here they come across the floor,
Hop, hop, hop, too late, I'm out the door.
If they get in my coat, I'll scratch all night and day,
Then Mother covers me in dust and brushes me that way.
Hop, hop, hop, one's jumped right on my nose,
Hop, hop, hop, another's reached my toes.
Hop, hop, hop, I have nowhere left to run,
Now there's no more hopping, so I guess their job is done.

Mandy Jayne Moon

Epitaph

Here lies the body of Halley Hound.
A better dog will ne'er be found.
No more the whimper, wag or woof,
The wet nose on my knee
Nor yet the race across the beach
To plunge into the sea.
She's gone alone, fresh fields to view,
A better dog I never knew.

Maurice Gubbins

Angel

A precious gift at Christmas time
The sweetest thing to see
Sleeping in a cardboard box
Beneath the festive tree

We named her 'Little Angel'
She only slept and purred
We thought that she was *purrrr-fect*
Until she killed a bird

Come spring we thought to decorate
New wallpaper we chose
But oh, one day, when we came home
She'd ripped it with her claws

From then we couldn't stop her
She went from bad to worse
Where was our little Angel
The pet we used to nurse?

And then one night dear Grandma
Lay resting in her bed
When she gave out the loudest scream
That you have ever heard!

'Come quickly, please come quickly
Something's nibbling at my feet'
We pulled away the blankets
A mouse was in the sheet

To think we'd called her Angel
So very funny that
She's no *little angel*
She's a very naughty *cat!*

Ann Donovan

The Sweetest Pudding Of All

I didn't really want a dog, the two we had grew old,
We loved them both so very much, were worth their weight in gold.

My youngest son and daughter said, 'Please just can you see?'
I knew who would look after it, yes, that's right, just me.

We saw this advert mention, of puppies that were for sale,
When I knew the cost they were, my face just went quite pale.

A little Yorkshire terrier, aged two weeks to the day,
I rang the breeder there at once, 'Can we see her straightaway?'

The lady entered in the room, her palm stretched out and steady,
She said, 'This is the little dog, although she's not quite ready.'

Those piercing, shiny, sweetest eyes, were staring back at me,
I fell in love that moment, 'Can I take her home with me?'

We named her Little Pudding, as Yorkshire went with that,
Her fur coat coloured steel and tan, on your knee she often sat.

We watched her playful puppy ways, we took her everywhere,
Whenever you were feeling down, Puds was always there.

For many years my faithful friend, always by my side,
Alas, I miss every day, from the second that she died.

I kept the photos of her, her toys she played with too,
I loved that dog with all my heart, a faithful friend so true.

Betty Hattersley

Animals

I'm only a harmless creature
I've got feelings just like you.
So why do they keep me locked up
In a place the call 'the zoo'?

I'd love to have my freedom
To roam over the country wide.
But they've locked up all the gateways
To keep me and my pals inside.

One day the gates may be opened
And we will be free to roam
But we will still be strangers
For we are so far from our home.

D Adams

Cage Covering

Doing budgie-sitting
I had a little chore
Cage-covering it was
But one night I had more
This particular evening
Outward came this sound
'Goodnight my darling'
Stepped back and fell down
Another noise then came out
It sounded just like this
'Please I hope you're not hurt'
Followed by a kiss.

Michael D Bedford

Dogs

An air of excitement pervaded the hall
Excitement like that at a debutantes' ball,
Dogs all barking, leaping or sleeping,
Flushed female owners emotionally weeping,

Spotted Dalmatians and pugnacious pugs,
Drooling mastiffs with long floppy lugs,
Cheeky York terriers and doleful bassets,
Were all parading their unnatural assets,

They were dogs with long leggy bounds
Like greyhounds and sleek Afghan hounds,
Golden retrievers and glossy red setters,
Refusing to concede they had any betters.

French poodles were there, looking haughty,
Pekinese lapdogs behaving naughtily,
A King Charles spaniel choosily regal
Rebuffing the attentions of an amorous beagle.

Majestic Alsatians and imperial chows
Were dutifully taking their well-earned bows,
Dogs of all shapes, breeds and sizes
Competing for nationally sponsored prizes.

Legions of shampooed and perfumed dogs,
Elegant, pampered and engineered dogs,
Man-made and unnatural, long, short and tall,
But to my mind my mongrel's the best of them all!

F R Smith

The Kaleidoscope Cat

Kaleidoscope sees ghosts by night
Fluffs tail like bottle brush
She wails a feline opera
When all the world's in hush.

A tortoiseshell of multi-hues
Of camouflage supreme
She melts into garden jungle
Ephemeral as a dream.

One moment wicked predator
And next your guileless pet
But within her dwells the huntress
Who has not woken yet.

Paws velvet-soft yet dagger-sheathed
Each whisker, a live sensor
The acme of dichotomy
And cunning fit for Mensa.

Tongue-washed, paw-groomed, fastidious
Diva-Siamese superior
Who sneers at dogs and suchlike pets
As specimens inferior.

You'll fail to beg or bribe her
She eateth as she wishes
A pauper's friend or prince's
On cracked plates or golden dishes.

Yet should I lead a good life
And never do my worst
When my passport's stamped for Heaven, that
Witch's cat'll be there first.

Sarah Blackmore

My New Family

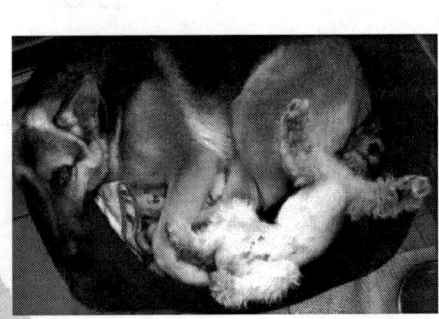

The first time that I saw them I was only four weeks old.
They said that I was lovely and could they take me home.

The second time that I saw them it was plain to see
That they were so excited and they took me home for tea.

I'd left behind my sisters and my mother too;
I was really frightened and not sure what to do.
But I need not have worried, as you can clearly see
I have a new friend, Phoebe, who shares her bed with me.

Louise Holt

Dalmatian

Someone knows the way out of the abyss
Splash, splash, in the bath
A Dalmatian canine habit
Go forward to the next stage

Move it on up
To the top of the class
Where would we be
Without that dog?

Finance ready all the way out
Nobody saving up except the doggy people
Prepaid envelope Dalmatian charities
Passed on to doggy Heaven.

S M Thompson

Mugs At Sixty-Eight

The word spread through the feline world,
'There's mugs at sixty-eight.
You only have to look half-starved;
They'll feed you on a plate.

There's Kattavite and all the brands
Well advertised on telly.
No ginger tom nor Persian pet
Should nurse an empty belly.'

So every mog in Moggyland
Turned up to grab his portion;
Some even seized their chance to make
A bob, by sheer extortion.

You've heard of eighteen forty-nine
When men rushed out for riches.
That's nothing to the scramble that
Ensued in lanes and ditches.

One day a sign was set up, on
A post beside the gate,
The gist of which, translated, meant
'No mugs at sixty-eight'.

As if that wasn't bad enough
For every living mog,
The garden was soon occupied
By an enormous dog.

John Belcher

Walking My Dog

Walking my dog
At half-past seven
When it's windy and cold and wet,
Turn up my collar,
Slosh through the puddles,
He's my friend; he's a wonderful pet.

The joggers are out
And other dog walkers,
Traffic is building up fast,
About half an hour
And I will be back
Home, drinking hot tea at last.

Give him his breakfast,
Give him a pat,
Promise him a nice juicy bone,
He looks at me
With big soulful eyes,
Without him I'd be so alone.

June Melbourn

The Guard Dog

'I'll tell you a story,' a friend of ours said,
it made the hair stand upon the back of his head
When he went to an old lady who lives alone,
sadly who is aged and very frail grown

When he found her house, she was waiting for him
beside her stood a large dog, alert, guarding.
Indoors there was no sign of this dog to be seen
as he had died the previous year it would seem.

A photo of this dog was exactly the same
as he saw guarding her and her home down the lane!

Valerie Ovais

An Anchor Books Anthology

The Escaped Horses

Today I saw a splendid thing:
Five chestnut horses galloping
Abreast in an unbroken line,
Their hooves a-flash, their coats a-shine,
Along the tarmac'd highway flying,
Oblivious of the danger lying
Not far ahead, as cars speed on
Along the Route Napoléon.
No reins nor saddles on them press,
But joyful, free and riderless,
With easy movement fast they go -
Their manes and tails like pennants flow,
Their flanks and limbs awash with light -
Around the bend and out of sight!

Evelyn Westwood

The Calico Cat

The calico cat glides across the cold floor,
headed for the distant door.

Behind the door lies one sick and in pain,
fighting, his strength to regain.

The old cat leaps from floor to bed,
as if being supernaturally led.

The quiet figure stirs,
as the cat softly purrs.

The hand reaches for the cat,
to give him a gentle pat.

The cat remains there throughout the night,
keeping his master in sight.

The day dawns with sun shining bright,
the master stirs at the glistening light.

His strength has been renewed,
and his pain subdued.

As he stroked the cat's head,
he quietly said,

'A creature you are,
but my best friend by far.'

Linda Constantatos

My New Horse

A new horse, what an exciting day!
A strong piebald lad, gentle eyes and intelligent head -
'A worker and nothing else,' so the trekking centre said.

The week's trial was strange for me;
Just a snaffle bit was all he should wear,
And was told 'He eats nothing more than grass and air
So don't be tempted to feed him lusher fare!'

Two months have gone by, the cheque banked long ago,
But in my mind second thoughts and doubts continue to grow.

He seems to have settled in the field, which is good,
But lost shoes are hard to find and his hooves are so big,
That my budget only allows for refits at a time.

On a hack he wants to go home before we start,
And no amount of cooing can reach his heart.

'A brave soul of sterner stuff I should be!'
But I quail and wish it was some other rather than me!

On the last ride, when my nerves could stand no more,
Little did I know there was a surprise in store.
As I loosened his bridle, he turned his head,
Looked at me with his gentle eye,
And whispered 'Just persist and I'll try!'

Jocqueline Jones

An Anchor Books Anthology

Snowy - Amber's Star

I looked up in the sky last night and saw a twinkling star
It reminded me that though you're gone, you're never very far.
And then the memories started, I recalled them one by one
From the day that I first got you, till your time on Earth was done.
So scruffy and so muddy, to me you were unique
I'd brush you till as white as snow, and trim your little feet.
I'd lead you off and through the gate, in you I had such trust
You'd trundle off into the field, then roll yourself in mud and dust.
Not just my pony, Snowy, my confidante and friend
The one I could share troubles with, your ear you'd always lend.
We had an understanding, you and I, my little lad
You'd always lift my spirits if I were feeling sad.
You'd gaze at me with soulful eyes, I saw devotion there
You'll never know how wonderful it felt to know you cared.
And though the years are passing since the day you went away
I still recall the things we'd done, the good, the bad, the 'so much fun'.
I long for you to be here still, I often shed a tear
Then pain and sorrow grip my heart,
As I remember you're not here
But love like ours is timeless, it cannot fade or die
Always I give thanks for you as I gaze at my 'star' in the sky!

Audrey M Tully

She

(Dedicated to Smokie for all her love and affection
which is reciprocated)

The storm would not let up
Fury would not abate
Hitting me on all sides
Keeping me awake

Trees shook in the moaning wind
Empty milk bottles were scattered
There was no escaping it
Night was turned to day

Finally I had to give in
And go and see what she wanted
Storm in a teacup?
My cat's attitude?
Her Majesty wanted in!

Mary Shovlin

Our Max

(For Melanie)

We have a dog, his name is Max
He is black as the ace of spades
Very fond of chasing cats
He is quite fit for his age.

By trade he is a gun dog
But he hasn't got a clue
He would run a mile if he saw a frog
Believe it or not, it is true!

Jokes apart he is so smart in a funny kind of way
He is faithful and has a big heart
We would not part with him, no way!

May Ward

Lament For A Pet Rabbit

The rabbit lopin ower oor green
he wis the finest o them aw,
wi his white jeckit, shinin clean,
an troosers, rabbit grey, but braw.
Oor twa-three cats he didnae heed,
nor yet oor cairnies, wild an yappy.
Aye, he wis brave, but noo he's deid,
      oor puir auld Mappie.

Oor Mappie aye wis clean an neat
but kept his feelins tae himsel.
He'd come when there wis ocht tae eat,
but did he love us? Wha could tell?
Whiles he wad let ye stroke his fur
an gie him lettuce, green an sappy,
but och! A rabbit cannae purr,
      an nor could Mappie.

He wis a rabbit fu o sense
an lovin life, like me an you,
but ae sad day, ayont the fence
we fund him, stiff, an wet wi dew.
But A'll tak Grandfaither's advice
an no be greetin sair for Mappie,
for he's in rabbit paradise,
      an unco happy.

J Waddell

An Anchor Books Anthology

Jess

Jess, oh Jess,
Good and you're not a mess,
Cos you live outside,
And you're a perfect ride,
Allergic to flies,
But still she tries,
You're my best friend,
I can't imagine the end,
You love your food,
You're always in a good mood,
You are my perfect horse,
Always have been of course,
Your coat so black,
And your elegant tack,
You look like a star,
Even from afar,
Your golden heart means so much to me!
Friends forever, you and me!
    We're family!

Sarah Herbert (12)

A Kitten's Plea

I'm a little kitty
I really need a home
I'm cute, soft and fluffy
And I promise not to roam
I'd be very good for you
And would try hard not to cry
When you're sad and lonely
I'll lick your tears goodbye
We could play with balls of string
I'd make you laugh, you'll see
The fun we'd have together
If only you'd agree
And when my kitten days are gone
And I'm a great big cat
I'll chase the mice when they come in
I'd even face a rat!
So sat yes to this kitty
Go on we'd have such fun
And I will always stay with you
'Cause you will be my mum.

M McNamee

. . . And The Condemned Ate A Last Meal

A flea
With glee
Alighted on my knee.
My cat,
She sat
Close by me and was glad.

Her problem gone,
So she looked on
As I sellotaped the flea
There on my knee

Cat and me,
We are proud, you see
'Cause dead is the flea

But saints alive!
Many more survive
Bent on revenge
My fist I clench,
Then grab the tape.
There's no escape!

To dine on me
Is a death sentence, you see!

Helga Dharmpaul

A Dog's Life

My mum and dad are greedy pigs with two legs, not my four,
They never give a titbit, however I implore;
With dark and pleading eyeballs, I gaze from face to face,
For all the good it does me, I'm just a waste of space!

Sometimes when they're cooking, they drop a thing or two
And if I'm quick to lick it, I get to eat it too.
I try to like raw carrot, potato peel and such,
But even on a busy day, they do not drop so much.

But if there's a disaster, perhaps a pot of cream,
I'm right in there with busy tongue, the answer to a dream.
'Good dog,' they say, 'look, here's some more!'
Until I've washed the kitchen floor!

But I stay fit and healthy, wet nose and glossy fur,
While they get fat, just like the cat, except they do not purr.
And there's the real lesson for Dad and for my mum,
Give up all that fancy food and have a tin of Chum!

Patrick Davies

An Anchor Books Anthology

Our Dog

She was an adorable little ball of fluff,
At first she peed on the carpet more than enough,
But this was quickly cured, she learned to do things right,
In the garden first thing in the morning and again, last thing at night,
Then we would go for many walks,
On beaches, fields and often stopping for talks,
With people we would sometimes meet,
Or perhaps whilst resting on a welcome seat.
We loved our dog with all our heart,
We dreaded the day that we should part,
She was good at football and 'pull the rag'
And could have some fun with a blown-up bag.
She could fetch our letters from the door
She gave us her sorrow when our health was poor,
A lot of love and a bit of grub was all she ever desired,
To be at our side constantly was also required,
Her gentle eyes and kindly nature we will never forget,
We cried like babies the night she died,
Heaven now has our dearest pet.

Roy Kimpton

Butterfly

Spread your wings and fly
upwards to the sky
fluttering, rising high
colourful butterfly

A moment you rest
at a flower's breast
clad in your brilliant dress
you receive its caress

On a sunny day
your life is gay
at mere sight
you create delight

Graceful butterfly
continue to fly
enrich nature's globe
with your gorgeous robe.

Wila Yagel

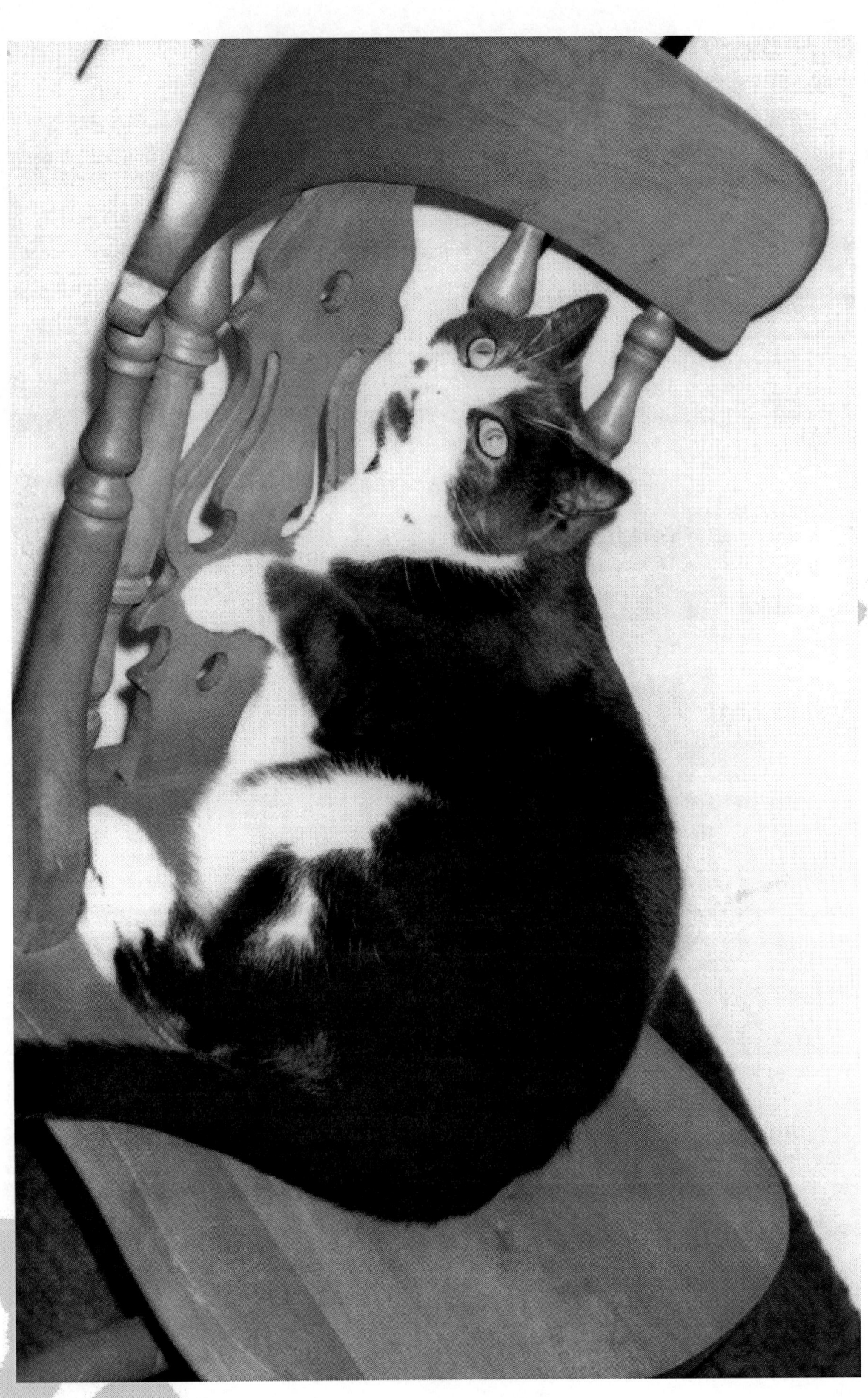

An Anchor Books Anthology

Barney

I heard the fence rattle and I knew it was you,
As you sprang from the undergrowth into full view.
So confident, so proud, so pleased to see me.
You raced towards the door, tail raised high,
Bursting with happiness - absolute glee.

You followed me everywhere, in the garden and then in the house.
I even remember the day you brought me a mouse!
You played in bags and boxes, sat by my side,
Slept on cushions, chased your dreams, greeted anything new with eyes so wide.

Such a handsome boy with plush blue and white coat, paws as pink as a shell,
With a nose to match, beautiful eyes of gooseberry green, you looked so well.
Everyone loved you; the children would stop at the top of the driveway
And if they saw that you were there, you made their day.

You knew exactly where the sun would warm your fur,
I would watch you gently breathe in and out and when you woke, that purr,
Sealed your contentment and proved that this was where you wanted to be.
And so it was, in the summer of ninety-nine, you were given to me - officially mine!

We shared sun-filled, happy days,
As I carefully watched, learning your ways.
You were my shadow, protecting my land
From other cats, like a sentry on duty, you looked so grand.

Just three years of love and laughter came to an end.
Now my garden is empty - well, not quite,
Seeds brushed from your coat, grow, where you lay.
Forget-me-nots so blue and so bright.

I hope you are playing at Rainbow Bridge, chasing the toys,
I miss you Barney - my beautiful boy!

Theresa M Carrier

Side By Side

She licks him all over, 'til he's quite wet and purrs like mad,
Watching the dog, washing the cat, cheers me up, when I'm sad.
For ages, cat will let dog continue to do its stuff,
But a claw will appear if or when the dog gets too rough.

The neighbours cannot believe how well this twosome gets on,
And dog will bark when she realises her playmate has gone.
They are both young and have several years of play ahead,
Recently, found two fast asleep, side by side, on dog's bed.

S Mullinger

Fred

I shall never forget my favourite pet,
A small Border terrier, Fred.
With a coat full of tufts, he'd have never won Crufts
In spite of his being well bred.
He'd a mind of his own and was famously known
For slipping his lead in a trice,
But he'd always come back at the sniff of a snack,
He was partial to anything nice.
The older he grew, the less he would do,
Growing older is never much bliss,
But if someone had said, 'Will you speak to us Fred?'
Then he might have said something like this:

'Most people attest that I'm long past my best
And well beyond learning new tricks,
That I do very little but salivate spittle
And chase after soggy old sticks,
But a dog of my age is a hard-bitten sage
Who's mastered the art of deceit,
With a sad, doleful look, I can melt any cook
And inveigle a morsel to eat.
When out on a walk, people think I can't talk
Or follow a verbal command,
When they call to me, 'Come!' they imagine I'm dumb
And assume that I don't understand.
But the older I get, the less often I fret,
And, as every old-timer agrees,
It's an old canine trick - to pretend that you're thick,
And it means you can do as you please!'

Alan Millard

Friends Together

Friends together, poles apart
Hefty, harsh white fur
Experienced wise old mutt
Lumbering, dependable sir

Tiny, dusky damsel
Youthful, frivolous lady
Crazy, risky, comical
She can be really shady

What makes them friends though
Is that they like to chase rabbits
Chase each other
And share each other's bad habits!

Mark Jenkins

An Anchor Books Anthology

Dog Save Us!

Jim Dog has come to fill my lonely days.
Behold, his head, between front paws he lays,
To watch with soulful eyes unblinking gaze.
With faithful trust he'd gladly die for me,
But he is far from perfect, you may see.

His taste in food to garbage he may turn
And to dig in splendid lawns he'd never spurn.
He loves to bark at non-existent cats
And sprawl on tender plants until they're flat!
When will this dog turn up his nose at smells
As we're on twilight walks upon the fells?

Now you may ask, as you have done before
'So, tell me plain and true, what is a door?'
And Jim will answer you with doggie pride,
'Why it's that thing I'm always on wrong side.'

Gordon Paul Charkin

Rudolph

Rudolph is my cockatiel
He's such a lovely bird
He sings, whistles and talks
Like you have never heard
His favourite tune is 'The Cheeky Girls'
He whistles it to his heart's content
He also whistles the sex bomb song
Rudolph was heaven-sent
He's yellow and grey
With big red cheeks
We've had him since
He was just eight weeks
He sits in his cage
Saying 'I'm a cheeky boy'
My grandchildren love him
Better than any toy
He sits on my shoulder
As he is very tame
My granddaughter, Ellisha
She gave him his name
He will be one year old at Xmas
Each day he learns another word
He's wonderful and we love him
Rudolph, our red-cheeked bird!

Heather Dunnfox

Wedding Fright

I'm getting into such a state
I've been so awfully busy
My wedding's getting out of hand,
It's sent me in a tizzy.

I only wanted one bridesmaid,
That seemed to me enough,
But when my pony friends found out
They went off in a huff.

So now I've said, I'll have the lot
Just to make things right,
But now they argue what to wear,
It's landed in a fight.

Star, she wants a pretty dress
With sprigs of Scottish heather,
But Polly wants a leather skirt
In skin-tight dark brown leather.

Beauty wants a beaded cap
In case there is hot weather,
Honey wants a purple hat,
With a giant ostrich feather.

My brothers aren't much better,
They are a pair of pranksters,
They said they'll only be pageboys
If I let them dress as gangsters.

My intended said, 'You must not fret'
I have the perfect scheme,
We both are going to run away,
And wed at Gretna Green.

Mum, worried by the rising costs,
Said, 'Tell me when and where,
I will drive you to the station,
In fact I'll pay the fare!'

I suppose it's sad it's come to this
I'll not be wed in white,
But a pony in a wedding dress,
Could be a frightening sight.

Sue Walters

An Anchor Books Anthology

Fox Terrier, Sandy Mine

Dressed elegantly, trendy suit azure blue
Ankles trim, black patent shoes
I went for my feathered Vogue chapeau
Left on duvet quilted bed.
Suddenly was overwhelmed in whirling storm
Feathers, feathers white everywhere, nearby, a head.
Hat denuded of feathers, fit to wear no more
Plucked as if for Sunday roast
Duvet ripped open from top to toe!
Culprit, my rascally dog, Sandy
Pedigree fox terrier was he
Instinct, love, hate for fur feathers only
Loyal, loveable friend for twelve years or so.
Creatures, all great and small, kindness give, cruelty abhor.

Ivy Lott

Our Furry Friend, Scratch

Well, goodbye old son,
We must have loved you
Because, why do we weep?
Why are we sad and lost
And wonder why you're gone?
No more early calls
No more furry hugs and paws,
Just the memories all around
In the garden, that tiny mound,
You never spoke, but never mind
All those licks were very kind,
These last four years have been
Quite eventful in-between,
Those first scratches at the door
To the peaceful pose upon the floor,
It was a pleasure, you may depend
We're going to miss you, our furry friend.

A Chaldecott

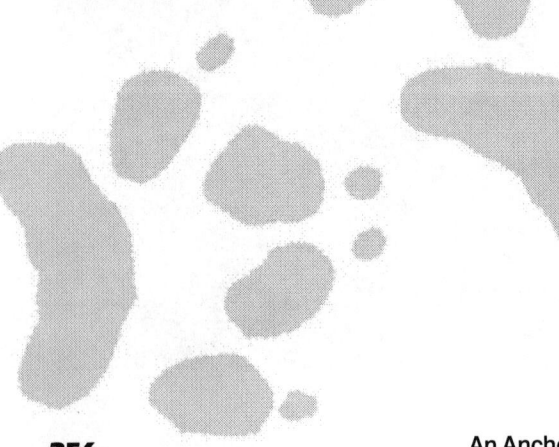

What Is A Moggy?

A bundle of silk purring rhythmically,
Gentle twitching whiskers,
Soft paws draped across a furry chest,
Tail swathed around itself.
A shape of sweet serenity,
It's my feline friend,
Tigger.

S S Marson

Pets

My very first dog was a spaniel called Chum.
An ordinary name for an ordinary pet?
Wrong. For Chum, I'll have you know,
Was by far the cleverest quadruped yet!

Next came Brumas, named for the bear.
A mongrel dog with eyes like dough,
But his tail wagged enough for twenty hounds
As he gambolled madly through grass or snow!

When a guinea pig arrived to take their place
It ate its way through mountains of food,
Then squeaked for more, both loud and clear,
Knowing I'd come as fast as I could!

My final pet, or so I thought,
A master at making one smile,
Suddenly died - as hamsters do -
Leaving us all bereft for a while.

I then decided to try a rabbit,
Called him Alphonse and fed him carrot.
He ran away, which was just as well,
Because I went out and bought a parrot!

Parrots, rabbits, guinea pigs and dogs
We tried them all so what to do?
Take hats and coats, galoshes and gloves
And go see what's to be had at the zoo!

Oriana

Animals

Toady said to Mole one day
'Let's go into the woods and play
We'll take our food and drinks so neat
And sit and chat and have a treat
We'll ask the rabbits if they would like
To share our humble and appetising fare.'
The field mice are scampering in the sun
'Please come with us and have some fun.'
Otter, Dormouse and Weasel gay
Cry, 'Can we come along and play?'
'Yes, do!' we cry, 'we welcome you
And Freddy Fox, you come too
We'll have lots of games and a scrumptious tea
Then we'll wander homeward full of glee.'

Laura Chaplin

Pet

He's only a moggy but he is our pet
We haven't met a better one yet
He's the one we adore
Lying on his back on the floor
Saying, 'Come on Mummy
Please tickle my tummy'
One minute he is climbing all over the room
The next he's playing with the broom
Or racing around the house
Trying to catch that imaginary mouse
Then he is up on your lap
Having his afternoon nap
He has lovely soft paws
Hiding those deadly claws
At night he's out on the prowl
While we wonder what's he going to bring in now?
He likes to lie in the sun to get warm
But soon runs in if there's a storm
He hates to get wet
And yet
He doesn't mind a bath
He is like a rag doll, when he comes out, we have to laugh
We know he's only an old tomcat
But he's our pet and that's that!

Richard Trowbridge

An Anchor Books Anthology

Polly The Horse

Polly was my grandad's horse,
born after World War I.
She lived a life of cropping grass
with duties almost none;
except for one day in each week
when bridled to the trap
the four of us went for a spin -
denied her pm nap!

She trotted down the country lanes
and made the motors wait
while she took preference over them -
established her estate!
So when she met the crossroads four
with traffic from each side
she boldly stepped across them all
whatever should betide.

But one fine day a policeman came
to do point duty there
and just as Polly reached his pitch
he held his hand in air
to stop the traffic in her line,
then Grandad pulled the rein.
She stopped abrupt with legs apart
to never go again.

The policeman tried and Grandad tried
to coax her on her way,
but she refused to budge an inch
to human's lack-a-day!
Until she'd felt she'd made her stand
to be the top horse in the land.

Owen Edwards

Mitzi - My Cat

Two minutes rest is all I ask
But there's no peace for me.
A little bundle of 'cupboard love'
Is waiting patiently.
My little cat called Mitzi
Seeing that I'm disturbed
Jumps upon my inviting lap
Giving nuzzles and loving purrs.
It's time for food, this cat is saying,
No need for words - just action
And I am so in tune with her
She knows my every reaction
The dish is empty, she goes to the door
And sits there patiently
Why should she use the cat flap
When a doorman is close - that's me?
Two hours have passed, the knocker is raised
I open the door to see
Mitzi is there with a mouse in her mouth
A present for me, you see!
But I am terrified of mice - with a shriek I stand on the chair
Mitzi is startled - so she lets go of the mouse
Who scampers away like a hare.
The chase is on but what can I do?
Thank goodness the door is ajar
The mouse it runs through - the cat follows too
I'm praying the mouse will run far
Mitzi returns like a warrior from war
She looks at me disdainfully
She washes her face - nestles down in her bed
To dream of that present for me.

E Timmins

My Cat

My cat stretches out when she lies on the floor
When I put on my shoes, she waits by the door
She runs after sticks and drinks from the loo
I think that my cat wants to be a dog too!

Elaine Langford

An Anchor Books Anthology

Amy

She stares! She stands and stares!
With eyes so big - so green,
A really beautiful little girl,
The prettiest cat you've seen.

And still she stares; and stares,
You look this way and that,
Whatever is she thinking of.
This proud and haughty cat?

But on she stares, just stares,
Then a boyfriend comes to call,
And with a final, distasteful stare,
She disappears over the garden wall.

Avril Hooper

Silent Friend

She holds a wealth of mystery within her eyes,
Something which us mere humans cannot describe.
I can't explain how those chocolate-brown eyes seep
Into my 'I'm happy, I'm OK' disguise.

How is it that a friend of mine has incomprehensible speech,
Yet she touches my emotions which no one can reach.
I never thought I would find in her a silence, an open door,
A space into which my thoughts should I pour.

I wish others could have respect for creatures of her beauty and grace,
Yet instead superiority belongs to the human race.
Why not appreciate the rich, striking sight,
Of her leaping through the whispering grass, as if in flight?

I thank God for this animal poised before me,
Look at her soft, humble face and I think surely,
Surely this soul there through the pain and strife,
Surely she will be a friend for life?

Elyse Lake

Guess Who?

You're always there to greet me
Whenever I've been out
And if I happen to be late
You never scream or shout
At night you sleep so close to me
You're there when I awake
And while you sleep so softly
There's no sound that you make
I get your meals, look after you
Nurse you when you're sick
It had to be my lucky day
When it was you that I did pick
I can tell you all my secrets
And you never answer back
You mean so very much to me
Even though you're just my cat.

Karen Hodgetts

Monty

I knock at the door
See an innocent paw.
Blue eyes look up at me

And I look at the cat
Sitting on the door mat
Watching with intensity.

It's as if he was waiting,
Like he'd been narrating
A story about me.

Big and fluffy
He's never scruffy
But graceful and sweet

He's as big as a dog
But looks like a mog
And you *have* to give him a treat!

Roisin Fattorini (10)

An Anchor Books Anthology

Sheba

She passed away many years from now,
But I still think of her, she was my companion and friend.
She was faithful and loving right up to the end,
I miss her waiting at the gate,
Wagging her tail as I came up the street,
She had that twinkle in an eye, my four-legged friend,
The day she died, my heart was broken,
For I lost my faithful companion and friend,
Though she's gone now, I feel her presence . . .
my old friend!

S G P Evans

Trouble With Cats

Under the stairs there lived a rat
That no one knew was there.
Except for next door's ginger cat,
Who chased him everywhere.

Well, all this chasing got too much
It really made him blue.
If I could only find old Butch,
He'd tell me what to do.

One fine day he met a mouse,
Who said, 'How do you do?'
They made themselves a cosy house -
In the master's worn-out shoe.

The mouse - he did have sisters,
And very fine were they -
With rather splendid whiskers -
So happily they'd play.

One he was quite fond of
So they courted every day.
'My dear - I think that I'm in love,
Shall we go away?

We'll go and find another house
To start our life anew -
We could bring all the other mice,
There'll be a lot to do.'

Eventually - they found a place
In an attic above some shops -
With skirting boards and lots of space
And no more flipping cats.

Wendy Watkin

Our God Of Gods

I want you to read my little tale
About our 'Siberian' a silver male
We took him home at six months old
For three hundred pounds he was sold

We named him 'Zeus' it suited well
An indoor cat without a bell
He slept a lot and rarely played
Then we noticed the way he laid

Then after that, we saw him limp
He's not a cat to be a wimp!
So off we went to the vet's that night
They said his knee joints were not quite right

We had some X-rays the following day
They told us the results with some dismay
The knee sockets were too shallow for the balls to remain
Not just in one leg, but both the same!

This is usually found in dogs not cats
His breed is rare so it could be that
He's had this condition from birth it shows
Now what do we do? No one knows

We have a choice of two to make
A major op to undertake
To pin his knees and joints together
Or simply leave him lame forever

The vet says he's not in pain
It's up to us, oh, what a strain!
If he has the op, there are no guarantees
He'll not limp on both his knees.

It will take him months or years to recover
He would have one op and then another
Sleepless nights we've had a few
Wondering what we should do

He's ten months old now and loved a lot
Is he having an operation? No, he's not!
Buying a pedigree kitten, be aware
Read lots of books if your cat is rare?

Don't be put off by what I've said
You cannot foresee what is ahead
He's got some mates now and plays a lot
Two Maine Coon kittens, we have got

His mates are Zara and Zak by name
You can't really tell that he is lame
He's happy and proud, he's our bundle of love
He's Zeus, god of gods, the one above.

Kristian & Victoria Haynes

Ike

Ike, our dog, is my best mate
A friend that I appreciate
He's a constant companion by my side
His loyalty and trust he cannot hide

Ike always has a listening ear
No problem too small for him to hear
He's not critical, does not demand
Obeys my voice and any command

He seems to walk with such pride
Head held high by my side
The highlight of his 'doggy day'
Is a walk in the park and then to play

Our cat, Otis, is his best mate
That pair you just can't separate
They whisper secrets in each other's ear
Confident no one will hear

Ike's role in our family
Is an important one as you will see
For we can leave our house at night
Knowing everything's alright

'Cause who is guarding our front door?
Ike, of course, who could ask for more?
So if a pal for life you would like
Choose a dog like my Ike!

Penny Pritchard

Happy Memories

I used to have a dog called Pat
She was so full of fun
Always waiting on the mat
Lying in the morning sun

I miss her every night and day
But the memories are so sweet
She was so good in every way
When curled up on my feet

In the car she loved to ride
To the moors to romp and play
Chasing rabbits in her stride
We all enjoyed a happy day.

Phyllis M Nichols

Phoebe

Whenever you want someone to be there,
Not to talk but just to care,
Phoebe comes when you call
And sits by you so loyal and small.

Yes, she snores and has a doggy smell,
But we all love her, so what the hell!
With her toys, Badgey, Hedgey, Furby too,
She'll fetch them and bring 'em to you!

She licks her chops and scrounges so,
That silly old dog, oh she knows . . .
Words like 'garden', 'birds' and 'cat',
She sits 'on guard' from her mat!

Jackie Heath (15)

Fud

Dear little Fudski pudding and eggs
Has a round fat body and short little legs.
He's a Jack Russell and everyone's friend
As long as you have lots of playtime to spend.
With black circles round both of his eyes
He looks like a badger or even a spy
He has naughty habits, some are quite bad
He steals from his mother, oh what a cad!
Don't leave your teacup on the floor
He will drain every last drop without raising a paw
He plays football with children, bounces balloons off his nose,
Being a Jack Russell, he has the time, I suppose.
He can lie on his back holding a ball in his paws
Turn over and catch it before it reaches the floor
He has a sensitive nature and hates to see you cry
And will jump up on your lap and lick every tear dry.
He will sit up and beg with the patience of a saint,
But don't be fooled, he's not quite that quaint!
He has bad habits, I've not written down
To be honest they are so awful they would make you frown.
The best thing about Fud is at the end of each day,
He will cuddle up close and take all your troubles away.

He thanks you for dinner, walks and, don't laugh!
He will even join you when you're taking a bath!
Dear little Fudski pudding and eggs
With your round fat body and your short little legs
You have your faults, you can be a pain
But whatever your faults, you're loved just the same.

Barbara Archer

My Significant Other

I have a friend so very dear who's like a second skin
He's almost like a shadow, 'cause he's always right behind me.

And when we have our meals, I always share my food
I know I probably shouldn't but it's so hard to deny him!

When I work, he's always there, faithfully watching
Waiting to follow me to see what I'll do next.

Sometimes he'll go to bed and if I'm not ready,
He'll come to gently indicate my company is wanted.

He guards my home so diligently, I shouldn't ever worry
For if evil were a-lurking, he would surely let me know.

He patiently waits for me when I have to shop
And let's me know how glad he is that I've hurried back.

And if I have to leave him which I never like to do,
He is oh, so very sorrowful and does he ever pout!

Impatiently he waits for me and when I return,
His happy shouts let me know how very much I'm loved.

He is very dear to me, this, I hope he knows,
For love is not love, they say, until it is returned.

So why, you ask, don't we wed . . . since our love is so enduring?
Could it be I'm just his mistress, and he is *man's best friend*?

Bonnie Rudzik

The Peeper

(From a visitor's perspective!)

I thought I saw
A puddy-cat a cweeping . . .
No - not that!

Not a sliding, rolling thing,
A stretching queen -
It was less serene.

A glimpse -

I think,

Gone in a wink

A twitch

A snatch

Missed with a blink!

Was anything there?

Yes.

Tales of emerald eye and pudgy paw -

Not at all what *I* saw!

Somehow I feel . . . I sort of sense,
That her sighting of me was *more* intense.

Not so quick . . . *not* a mere flick.
But a *lingering* look - could have written a book!

And I absolutely *know*, no doubt in my mind
That her description of me will be *most* unkind!

Regina Fattorini

A Pet

'Mam, you said you would get us a pet
One that doesn't need lots of trips to the vet
A dog or a cat would be lots of fun
But a snake would be difficult to take for a run
So Mam, we'll leave the final choice up to you
But don't get us something that belongs in a zoo.'
'Son, I wouldn't even mind a pig or a steer,
After all I've lived with your father for twenty-odd year!'

Mick Gayfer

An Anchor Books Anthology

Rodney And Fudge

Rodney and Fudge are the funniest pair,
They shuffle around without a care.
Their noses twitch in an amusing way,
As they eat our lawn at the end of the day.

Their eyes they stare inquisitively,
As they skip along quite positively.
But I know too well what they search for,
The barbecue they hide under on the floor.

I try to keep them away from there,
And chuckle too at their floppy hair,
Yes, to keep them away, I try my best,
But they get past, my dear little pests!

G White (14)

Sophie And Candy, Friends Of The Canine Kind

(Or, You're never alone with a Dachshund)

This story that I write is of Dachshunds brave and true,
I'm honoured that I share my home with not just one, but two!
My friends and my companions, who never leave my side,
Sophie and Candy, my little ones, in whom I take such pride.

Sophie, with the long red fur, who walks with regal grace,
A princess among sausage dogs, with a noble intelligent face.
Who sits up at the thought of food, with a back that's ramrod straight,
I know she really wants to clear the dinner from my plate.

She seems to know the words I speak, whene'er to her I talk,
She knows just where her lead is kept, when I say the one word 'walk'.
Ferocious with all other dogs, except for little Candy,
If anything attacks me it's sure good to have her handy.

And what of Candy, small and smooth, with coat of shining black!
What would she say to me, her friend, if she could talk back?
Her favourite word is 'biscuit', she's never far away,
Puppy-like, mischievous, always wants to play.

She rolls upon my towel, when bathing I complete,
Swathes herself with my body's scent then trots up to lick my feet.
These two happy little dogs are not just pets to me,
They're faithful, loyal and loving, part of the family.

Their body language tells me almost all I need to know,
They tell me when they're hungry, or when they need to 'go'.
I know just when they need a stroke, or just a little pat,
You're never alone with a dachshund, my two friends
Make sure of that!

Brian L Porter

Pets

We take our dogs out for a walk
They're pulling all the way
They know where they are going
Because we go there every day
We let them run around the wood
And they just bark with glee
Then he will see a squirrel
And chase it up a tree
But when I whistle and call his name
He comes straight back to me
For her I have to throw a stick
She loves this little game
She's the one called Anne
And Reebok is his name.

C C Lee

Big Fella

Named for a virtuoso
bred from the alley's best
Yahudi
was orphaned young and raised
by a scientist, who loved him like a son.
'Mr Magarian, it's leukaemia
we'll have to put him to sleep'

Big Fella, big mane, big feet
Big Bum is gone,
but not in vain
For 'little fellas' walk the Berkley streets,
tails of a thousand and one heats.

Prince Freakitty Queen Key
And my pumpkin maiden fair
will miss their King Yahudi
who
brought love and respect to the words
'Big Bum'

James Rasmusson

An Angel Came Through The Mail

Gizmo, Gizmo, is my one and only.
He picks me up when I'm feeling lonely.
When I'm down or have a frown,
He's always there and comes sniffing around.
He wags his tail, but his eyes look sad,
That stops me from feeling bad.

He's old, arthritic and quite deaf
But he's my life, my soul, my very breath.
God sent Gizmo, he's an angel in disguise,
He came via the mail and saved me from a life of demise.
He's my 'special needs' dog, I love him so much,
His fur is so fluffy, it's a pleasure to touch.
He digs Mom's garden, digs at the moss
He drives her round the bend cos he knows he's the boss!
When he's excited, his eyes open wide,
He's my very own gremlin, but nice inside!

Teresa McTigue

Untitled

Cats can purr
With their glorious fur
They can miaow very loud
Right over the crowd
They chase the rats
And lie on the mats
They sleep all day
And they love it in May
Where they play in the garden
And get out of the way
Cats are sweet
Cats are fine
Think again . . .
Because they're mine!

Melika Gumush (13)

Rentacat

Your silky paws run after me
whenever I appear.
You drape yourself upon my knee
and purr when I am near.
Your liquid eyes compel me
to pause and give you heed.
A stroke upon your glorious fur
is all you seem to need.
A scratch or two behind your ears
to satisfy an itch
and tickling your tummy
can cause your tail to twitch.
Upon the sound of dinner plates
clinking on the side
your weary body stretches up,
your tiny mouth gapes wide
to ask if, just perhaps, there may
be some small titbit there
to satisfy a hungry puss
who only wants to share
each mouthful with his loving friend,
for they'll be buddies to the end.

Well - just until he hears Mum shout,
'Hey, Frankie - come on - dinner's out!'

Helen Strangwige

An Anchor Books Anthology

Bunny Em

My Emlyn, long-haired, fluffy, with three black spots on her nose
Is coloured as a Friesian with outrageous podgy toes.
She is my toothless wonder with lop-sided pretty face.
A superstar at ping-pong as she darts about the place.
Em's strange in her affections as she shows her love in bites,
And grapples with me arms or feet, believing it's alright.
Yet who am I to question her expressions of love true?
She is my closest loyal friend, with often-chanted mew.
She likes it when I sing to her, sits staring on the floor,
Then mews in all the places, when I know the words no more.
When finished, then she's purring, one contented happy cat.
I'd never change a part of her, I'm certain sure of that!
Of course there's times she drives me mad, of that I can't deny.
Attention sought, I stop to help, I love her as I sigh.
My Bunny-Em, sweet little Em, you truly are the best,
And on that day when I met you, I knew that I'd been blessed.

Charlotte J Ireson

My Pet Dog, Rufus

Rufus is my puppy
And he's such a playful pet
He loves to hide my slippers
And I've still not found them yet!

He doesn't like tinned dog food
He prefers a juicy steak
And although it's not good for him
His treat is 'Cadbury's Flake'.

He loves me going shopping
Because he knows he'll get a bone
He guards the house and barks like mad
And even answers the phone!

He loves to chase the next door's cat
He has him running scared
My neighbour thinks he's vicious
But her senses are impaired

Because he's such a lovely puppy
He just likes having fun
And although he's only one year old
He's nearly six foot one!

Sandra Booth

A Cat's Christmas

Christmas is coming,
And Binx is getting fat.

Zeus is up the tree,
Cos he's the Christmas cat.

Kiri's singing carols,
Spreading Christmas joy.

Luna's growling at her stocking,
Hoping for a toy.

Victor's rolling in the snow,
Getting very wet.

Marble's wrapping gifts,
Just for the vet.

Sheba smells the turkey,
Wishing for a bite.

And Guinness is asleep,
Dreaming of a silent night.

Libi Garner

An Anchor Books Anthology

Snake

I had a twenty-foot snake,
It bit me for goodness sake,
I tried to feed it one day,
And it took my finger away.

This got me mad,
Which made it sad,
I fed it mice and boys,
Amongst my play toys.

The police came up to my door,
Said, 'We're taking the thing you adore.'
I had to cry,
As it was going to die.

And now I'm alone,
My life is blown,
My only pet,
Was killed by the vet!

Robbie Strick (13)

Cats

I love cats
One called Patch
I have owned a few
One called Sue
But is it because I am older
That I am getting colder
Towards the little darlings
One called Marlene
Or is it the piles I find
I can't hide that I do mind
As I have to scrape it up
Such smelly stuff
On top of my plants
The thought of it on my hands
As I pull out the weeds
Before I can sow the seeds
Will they all be scratched out?
The birds are not about
They have been chased off the tree
So I shall not be stroking a cat on my knee
Until they start to cover it up
So that I don't have to scrape it up
Off the plants in my garden
Those darned cats!

Sylvia Shafto

Oscar's Dream

Stretch, yawn and purr - oh, the place I've just been
Was filled with the sweetest of mice.
They were the juiciest I've ever seen
Yeah - this dream was really quite nice.

Hmm - what can I do now, where can I stroll?
Sometimes life can be such a bore.
I think I will see what is left in my bowl
And then have a roll on the floor.

I've gulped down my food, now I'll go for a nap
Eating is such a strenuous thing.
Maybe I can find a nice, warm, cosy lap
To curl up and continue my dream.

Ah - there are some legs, all dressed up in black
A lap can't be that far away.
But first these legs could do with a rub of my back
Before I move upwards to stay.

Yeah - now I am pleased, the black's brightened up
With ginger-white clumps of my fur.
His voice shouts, *'Oh no!'* but his hand pats my back
I know he'll be glad when I purr.

Okay, pal, I'm coming - I'm ready to jump
My paws creak - I think I get old!
I land on his knees with a skilled, graceful thump
I'm happy - and *he* won't get cold.

Oh, purr, purr and purr - don't stop stroking my back
It really feels so very nice.
I drift off to dreamland while he scratches my neck
And I'm back with those sweet little mice.

Brigitte Hale

An Anchor Books Anthology

Which Pet For Me?

Lost for some company I thought I'd get a pet
So down I went to the local shop to see what I could get.
The man, he said, 'A tortoise would be easy just to feed and keep.'
But I wanted something wide awake instead of half asleep!

He pointed to some goldfish that were swimming in a bowl
Though they were very pretty, they didn't stimulate my soul.
'Perhaps,' he said, 'two long-eared rabbits might be just for you?'
But, 'No,' I said, 'it won't be long before I'd have forty-two!'

'So what about a little bird to cheer you when it sings?'
And then I saw the mess it made when it flapped its little wings!
Then I saw a pup that I thought I could adore -
Until I thought about the mess he'd make upon the kitchen floor.

I was going to buy a lovely cat who looked so much at ease
But then was told the facts about the worms, the ticks, the fleas!
I want a pet that I can keep and talk to when I'm bored -
And when I see it every morn can feel my soul has soared!

So, I cast my eye all round the place to see what I could see
And it wasn't long before the answer really dawned on me.
It was not a pet I needed - so I've made a cunning plan -
I'm pulling all the stops out - to try and get myself a man!

Cora-E Barras

Untitled

Soft brown eyes gaze into yours,
A paw gently touches your knee,
He knows you need comfort and that you are sad,
As if into your heart he can see.

How trusting they are, our animal friends,
Never judging or turning away,
They listen to all our stories of woe,
And you know that's as far as they'll stray.

They try so hard to give us support,
And to show that they really do care,
So show them some love and give them a chance,
And your troubles they really will share.

Joyce M Woods

Homer

I have a dog named Homer
Who I rescued from the pound
Nobody knew who owned him
A best friend I really found.

He is a little terrier
Who keeps me on my toes
I lift his lead for walkies
And he dunts me with his nose.

Cold nose and mucked-up paws
Jumping from bed to bed
Shoes all chewed and settee all hairs
He makes me see pure red.

Pulling washing from the line
And ruining all my pegs
Saddened face when I scold him
With his tail between his legs.

I wouldn't change him for the world
He's the best friend I've ever had
So friendly and so loving
I know, I must be mad!

Geraldine McMullan Doherty

Facets Of A Cat

Crying to go out this sunny morn.
Warmth of amber eyes,
cold at night in stealth and death.

White paleness of the moon,
golden rays of the sun.

Bedecked in black and white,
penguin suit, high on a branch,
watching the world go by.

Tormenting neighbourhood dogs,
chasing neighbourhood cats.

Polite yawn, soft purr, gentle stretch,
licking tongue removes surplus feather,
slinky walk, timeless parade.

Feline majesty, condescending ways
Head of state, head of mine.

Ian W Robinson

An Anchor Books Anthology

Wild Horses

Wild horses. Free! On the open plain,
Together! No man can ever tame!
Don't harm them, or throw your rope around!
No saddles, no spurs, to slow them down!

Free-flowing their manes of luscious gold
And eyes as black as charcoal
Don't harm them or throw your rope around,
Cruel rustlers! We know you're back in town!

Wild horses don't run from me
They're as free as they will ever be!
They go their way and I'll go mine.
Free till the end of time

So cruel a rustler with a gun
Pulls the trigger and makes the horses run
If wild horses cannot be free
What chance is there for you and me?

What glory to shoot the horses down?
For money? For gold? Or precious stones?
Cruel rustlers, you have had your fun
Come on and lay down your rope and gun!

Pamela Hanover

Through The Eyes Of Molly (My Puppy)

I wake up with sunshine in my eyes,
I gaze around at the beautiful blue skies.
Contentedly I dawdle over to my water tray,
And take the first refreshing sip of the day.

Out of the corner of my eye, what's this I see?
It's my ball lying in front of me.
I slowly edge towards my prey,
It hasn't seen me yet, it's not moving away.

And in an instant I crouch down and pounce,
I've succeeded in killing it - it didn't move or bounce.
I wag my tail in delight,
And to make sure it's dead, just one more bite!

Uh oh! Now my ball is torn,
Oh well I'm tired, so with a yawn,
I grab my teddy and gently drag it to bed,
And on my warm fluffy blanket I lay my head.

Lianne Bunn

Birds Of A Feather

The puppies in the window, as usual, caught my eye.
We hadn't got much money and we didn't mean to buy,
But as we went into the shop, just to look around,
We couldn't help but hear this funny little twittering sound.
High up in the corner, in a cage upon a shelf,
Sat two bedraggled budgies, I couldn't help myself -
'Why are those two way up there, sitting on their own?'
'They came to us a week ago, we can't find them a home!'
One was a scruffy yellow, they couldn't tell what age.
The blue one had a broken wing poking through the cage.
'If you take them home with you, there will be no charge.'
So she put them into boxes, and a bag that was too large.
We didn't have the car that day, so we started walking home,
Chatting to them in the bag, pleased I wasn't alone!

The cage we had up in the loft, was once the home of Fred,
The budgie we had till twelve years old, now we had two instead!
The following morning off to the vet, to hear what he had to say.
He didn't think they would live very long, 'but then again they may!'
Their chumminess soon vanished, once we came on the scene.
The blue one, Gill, got jealous and became a little mean.
She knocked poor little Jenny down onto the floor,
But like that trooper that she was, she climbed back up for more!
Back to the vet, he shook his head, her hip was dislocated,
But with a matchstick for a splint, she was reinstated!
Separate cages seemed the answer to this tale of woe,
But the vet then told us, it was time to let her go.
Now left with Gill, she seemed content, to have us to herself.
Anything was better than sitting on that shelf!
But six months on we realised her life we could not save,
We did our best, we think of them and how they were so brave.

Vera Brown

Dogs

Dogs, dogs, dogs,
from the littlest corgi to the greatest Dane,
fluffy dogs, hairy dogs, tiny dogs, smelly dogs,
all kinds of dogs from all kinds of places,
naughty dogs roll in smelly things,
dig up holes,
chase moles,
clever dogs fetch sticks,
learn to do all kinds of tricks.
My dog's naughty, he doesn't do what he's told,
but even though he's a pest
he's still the very best!

Katie Ireson

An Anchor Books Anthology

Gemma

I recall the day I brought her home some 15 years ago,
For her master who always had a love of dogs from before,
Yet dreaded having a Staffordshire bull terrier at home.
She was such a pretty bitch, black and white, one just couldn't leave her alone.

She matured and strengthened, always caring and loyal,
And her master was treated like a royal.
After a few years she developed her true form,
That of a magnificent 'Staff' who took the world by storm.

Years of enjoyment, what with puppies and babies around.
Protective and tolerant, she held her ground.
They dressed her up in some ludicrous attire.
At night gentle Gemma was glad to retire.

The solid muscle was erect on her neck
As she galloped up the mountain, a long trek.
The might and power was unique in flight.
One cannot imagine such a magnificent sight.

Then all of a sudden, she slowed down her pace.
Sagging in body, grey hair on her face.
The legs were weary, her breathing not right.
Hearing, non-existent, she was a sad sight!

It's difficult to express in writing, the way I feel today,
Gemma, our old faithful has suddenly passed away.
She was riddled with arthritis and losing weight for a while,
Yet through bleeding and collapsing she didn't die in style.

Today she leaves us with a massive void.
My eyes are so tender, her master so annoyed
As we cannot take in what has happened just yet,
She was part of our family, not only a pet.

Kindness in her face - loyalty as ever,
Can we forget Gemma, our 'Staff' - *never!*

B Thomas

Bath Time

The bath filled, bubbles to the top,
My cat looked on, her next adventure in sight.
She tested the soft foam and purred with delight,
I could see her next move, I tried to halt her delight,
Her thoughts in action, the look on her face.
A soft foam landing in sight!
But the shriek was so loud in cat language
She cried, *'Get me out!'*
She was gasping for air, life's just not fair.
Her vice-like grip with no chance of a slip,
The look in her eyes was sheer awful surprise.
I understand what she cried,
'That's just cost me one life, a little too close
To Cat Heaven than I really would have liked!'

Beverley Dales

Walking The Dog

So many different kinds of dogs
Go past my gate each day.
I like to watch their different walks
It's quite a game to play.

Alsatians pad like tigers
With tails held down behind.
There are cheeky ones who mince along
With tails aloft, 'Oh never mind.'

The boxer has a bouncy step
The Labrador, a playful
The Scottie walks with jaunty pride
While some up in their leads get tied.

There are some that have a swagger
With tails to left and right
While some lift legs at lamp posts
And give the cats a fright.

But to everyone who owns them
They're the best dog in the world
With tails up straight or hanging down,
Or simply just tight curled.

Isobel Laffin

Guardian Angel

I kissed you goodbye on a summer's day, when all I could feel was our rain
Knowing I would never have the chance to hold my precious gift in my arms again.
I needed to take away your pain, so I placed it inside of me
Without words, you told me, you needed to be set free.
I no longer could watch you hurt, you handed me the lifeline to cut
It was the time for your journey to end, I gave you my heart to take
with you as I lost my fragile friend.
I watched you take the steps to Heaven, your soul fly through the sun
A life together now over, as our new life begun.
I know that peace that only love can bring. I've lost the shelter of my angel's wings.
Can you still hear me? Do you feel the sadness my heart now sings?
Sometimes I can hold you in my dreams I wish upon a wish you were still here
Then I feel you watching over me I know now, you're always near.
Your presence graces my earth with all the memories I still hold
Enhancing the miracle of birth in each thought you're there like hidden gold.
I've lost my crutch but I have learned to stand on my own
You're inside me, always beside me, so I can never truly be alone.
I love you,
I will love you until the sun and the moon meet
I will love you until the stars no longer shine
I will love you yesterday, today and tomorrow
I will love you until the end of time.
I know that you are waiting for me at Heaven's gate
For the happiness to return that we had to forsake
For a time we loved and I know we'll still in a million years
And when we meet again in Heaven
My guardian angel can kiss away my tears.

Linda Ann McConnell

My Old Feral Cats

My dear cats, as the passing years go by,
As they grow older, more on me rely.
Sweetie, the mother, twenty-one years old,
Her twin daughters, their twenty years unfold.
All tackling life more quietly but fit,
Never far from me, they do wait and sit.
Queen Sweetie, now relaxing at leisure,
Always rolls on her back to show pleasure.
When I am near, they come with devotion,
Blackie enjoys nursing - purring motions.
Cutie, a bit shy, but very faithful,
As I walk, at my feet, weaving, playful.
These dear ferals, so much my life a part,
My cats and I, so united at heart.

Joan Egre

My Old Pal

Tucked up in a blanket at the base of my bed,
Lies a little old creature who sleeps like the dead.
But every so often with a flick of his tongue,
And a twitch of his paws, he dreams of being young.

'Spirit of Dreams', full of vigour has entered his mind,
Pushed out old age problems and things of that kind,
And now taken over by the joy of this pace,
The years fall away and youth plays on his face.

Welcome back to this comrade that frolics within,
And helps him the battle against boredom to win.
Puppyhood moves in and takes him away,
On a journey of chase, of excitement and play.

There's a little old creature who sleeps like the dead,
Tucked up in a blanket at the base of my bed.
Now, once more exhausted, he'll slumber all day
Ever hopeful that his ally will take him away.

Sara Marlow

Three Words

He said the words, 'I love you,' my heart then skipped a dance.
Be joined in holy wedlock, if he got the chance.
These years he is more loving, three words he still does say.
He greets you with a welcome, each and every day.

I look at him in kindness, 'I love you' now he blares.
Poor soul is losing his hearing, no matter, who else cares?
He ages more, yet looks distinct, with a voice all soft and frail.
His 'I love you' is distant as he starts to fade and pale.

I would have been so lonely without this daily rhyme.
To love so deep is natural, it isn't any crime.
I move in close beside him, to repeat that 'I love you'
He's been a friend, a comrade, gave all, that sure is true.

The time has passed so quickly, I wish it could stand still.
His 'I love you' resounded, it gave me such a thrill.
But then one day I found him, all still without a word.
Sadness came across me, at the loss of this old bird.

Teresa Tunaley

An Anchor Books Anthology

My Proxy Pet

To our neighbour's home he came
A small bundle of delight,
Arriving safely on Christmas night

Unable to afford my own
I pretend the doggie's mine
And we both have a good time!

No poop to scoop,
No bills to pay
Rolly and I just play all day!

Helena Henning

Can't Forget 'Puff'

Can't forget - when I was eight, floodwaters pouring into our garden,
When little brook became a monster river - breaking its banks.
Can't forget - my urgent call to rescue 'Puff' - my white angora rabbit,
And trudging - half-clad - down long path to garden's end -
Where Puff lived in his hutch - hoping he still did!
Can't forget - seeing his little nose - breathing just above water level.
Once - when I tried to pick him up - he badly scratched my arms.
Holding them out to save him now - could Puff see it differently?
I realised then what it means for the Lord Jesus to save me.
But praise the Lord - Puff makes his gallant leap of faith -
Nestles in my armpit - trusting me - I know I must trust Jesus too.
Can't forget I slipped, and could have drowned us both!
Only fence tops visible then - and I was scared to move!
Lord's message to my brain - answers desperate prayer so strangely -
'Success or failure is none of your business now -
Put one foot in front of the other' - so I complied.
While waters still rise alarmingly - it's my time to trust.
Mum receives us home, and warns, 'It's not over yet!'
Towel-dried, Puff retreats under chair by welcome cosy fire.
There - so motionless - we wait - wait - wait - endlessly wait.
O' Jesus, I will wait under the shadow of your wing.

Putting now a plate of carrots and lettuce - tempting Puff to eat
Stranger Lord's message - 'Strawberries'! Why yes, Puff loved those!
Once, he ate all three rows of strawberries from Dad's new plants.
None left! But raid the larder for that strawberry jam -
Separate out its strawberries - will Puff come out now?

Can't forget glorious moment when Puff hops out to eat them,
Lord - I will take care of Puff, I promise, in my love.
You will - won't you Lord - always care for me? O' please, I pray,
Cos Puff and me - we're both saved now!

Don Harris

Cats And Erm?

Cats are funny creatures when they're first brought to the house.
We show them pretty pictures cute . . . those photos of a mouse.
And say then 'Go and catch one and bring it home to me.'
The cat walks round in circles slow, just thinking hard you see.

Then off it trots its head held high and eyes like laser beams.
It's looking hard at anything that makes a squeak, it seems,
Or has a tail, a pointed nose, or ears like Mickey Mouse.
In every nook and cranny dark, around this big old house.

It's gone just for a whole day now and nowhere to be seen.
Its food untouched, its milk not drunk. I wonder where it's been.
I've looked about the garden slow and even on the wall,
And under stairs, on top of chairs but nothing there at all.

Just then I heard a funny noise behind the old settee.
A sound of rustling paper loud, my cat was there, you see.
But then I laughed till I would burst when looking down at him.
He had the tiny paper mouse . . . that I threw in the bin!

Robert Eric Weedall

Straight From The Horse's Mouth

I'm standing here by the gate,
It's almost feeding time, I can't wait,
If I stand here looking glum,
They'll feel sorry for me then they'll come!
Here I stand with a grumbling tummy,
Waiting patiently for my mummy,
Come on Mum! Where's my food?
If you don't hurry I'll be in a mood!
I'm still standing at the gate,
Please, Mummy, don't be late!
Maybe if I call and jump around?
Hang on a minute! What's that sound?
Clunking buckets! Could it be?
Is she here to feed me?
Here she is, here's my mummy!
With something nice to fill my tummy,
I knew it, I knew it, I knew she'd come!
At times like this I really love my mum!

Julie Roberts

An Anchor Books Anthology

Sometimes Her Personality Glows

i watch her
to me it's a bit of a surprise
she is sitting on the back porch
she looks at me with her snowy-glazed eyes
she's getting old now
must be well over ten now
i used to think . . . *she is so old*
but she doesn't look it
sometimes her personality glows

wouldn't say she's a spring chicken
she trips sometimes and walks into the patio doors
but i'd say she makes up for it with her loving face
and her dainty little paws
as a pup she was shown the door
by a cruel owner who would not give her love anymore
she was found and given a loving home
this is her home
she was renamed nala
i used to call her snala
i used to pull faces at her
and tease her quite a lot
she's my sister's family pet
there used to be two
but the angels took the other one
left the family feeling blue
i watch her as she walks in the grass
with her little walk and shaking her little ass
calling after her she's finished her business
runs away she likes no forgiveness
telling her off cos she's ignored me once more
getting frustrated holding onto the door

she walks past me and turns her head as if to say
'ha ha uncle ste, i always get my own way'

i have one thing to do before i go back home
i'm gonna buy her the biggest marrowbone . . .

Stephen A Owen

Tibby

I am a cat named Tibby,
My coat is black and white.
When I stick my claws out,
I give my mum a fright.

I like to wash my coat,
And make it gleam so bright.
I also sharpen my claws
And get ready for the fight.

I like to watch the water,
Swirling in the sink.
It gets me all excited
And then I stop to think.

I like a game of ball,
I kick it with my paws,
When you go to grab it
I come out with my claws.

I am such a happy cat,
My people feed me fish
So when I have finished it,
I like to clean my dish.

Linda Finch

A Letter From George

Just a little note to say
I have moved away today
My mummy is feeling very sad
But in a while, she won't feel so bad.

For she has found me a nice new home
A place where I will never be alone
I'll be with John and Rosy too
They have told me, 'We love you.'

I know that I'll be happy here
They think I am a little dear
I won't have to stay in my cage
To sit and scream and shout with rage.

I'll be out every day
Lots of room for me to play
It is best for me I know,
My mummy loves me, so she let me go.

Pauline Nind

An Anchor Books Anthology

Sweet And Loving Memory

Uncle Fred, he had a budgie
Jo Jo was his name
He talked and learned a lot of tricks
And was so very tame

Uncle was dying of cancer
Spent many hours alone
Jo Jo was his pride and joy
In that quiet little home

Uncle played the saxophone
When he was young and strong
Sometimes he'd have a practice
And Jo Jo landed on

The buttons and the sound-piece
He did not mind the noise
Up and down the instrument
Sideways, and with such poise

When Uncle felt quite tired
And lay upon his bed
Jo Jo, too, went with him
And nestled on his head

When Uncle was sadly taken away
Jo Jo stayed locked inside his cage
He missed his loving master
His sadness unassuaged

He pined and pined
And soon his life had gone
His soul, gone to find his master
In that grassy, peaceful home

Those bright green feathers nestling
On the dark and curly head
A picture I will never forget
When I think of dear Uncle Fred.

J Howling Smith

Basil Bird

As a child I always wanted a parrot - an African grey,
And teach him lots of funny things to say.
But my parents refused and I had to wait,
Then I had one at last, when I was 28!

Basil's his name and he's a lovely chap
Who flies from his cage and onto my lap.
I'm always amazed at what he can say,
And the swear words he knows, didn't come my way!

He says 'Good morning' as the lights go on,
And cheers me up with his chirpy song.
He listens intently to all noises around,
And can copy exactly - any sound.

The microwave rings and over I go
But is the food ready, almost certainly no!
Basil it was - he mimicked the sound
While the food in the microwave goes round and round.

The telephone rings and he shouts, 'Hello,'
And how many times have I answered the door,
Then realised it was Basil again mimicking the chimes?
He's tricked me with this over a 100 times!

When I sit by his cage, in my comfy armchair
He throws his nuts and seeds into my hair.
He loves being naughty and when I react
On he continues with his cheeky act.

Although he's well fed, 'I'm starving,' he'll say
When we're all having dinner at the end of the day.
He'll squawk and beg until we give in,
There's simply no chance of him being thin!

Enfys Evans

Feed Me

He looks, then carefully sits
Away from the dish of dry bits.
Amber feet placed neatly,
White whiskers twitching sweetly,
Eyes puzzled, ears at a stretch,
Making me feel a wretch.
She's done it again,
He's saying, quite plain
I never get fed as a wish,
Just kibbles in the dish not fish!

Carol Spencer

An Anchor Books Anthology

Pip

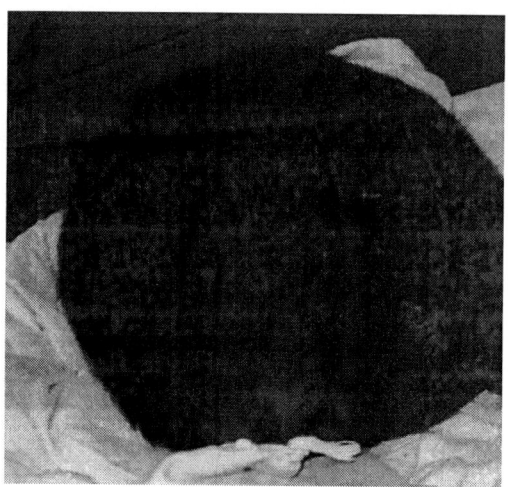

Older now, sleeping often,
Cantankerous awake.
You invaded my depths sixteen years ago
With your quirky charm and open trust.
And still it shines from you -
Absolute faith in your loveability.

I envy you that, feline friend.
You brighten the world with faith;
May this human friend follow your steps.

Kath Williamson

Matthew, A Little Rascal Of A Rabbit!

At first, he seems quite the little innocent,
But if only you knew how many females he had made pregnant!
It's utterly disgraceful although that's his job,
And that's why he's not for sale.
You wouldn't be able to trust him!

And if he's bored from running in circles around his pen,
He lets you know fairly fast.
He'd terrify the life out of anyone who has never been in
the store before,
Because as you're walking down the aisle, something on top of the
pen catches your eye.

When you look directly at it, it appears as though there's a rabbit
Propped with his front paws hanging over the side
And his ears flopping down onto his back.
You blink and look again, but the rabbit is gone.
If that happened to me, I'd think I was going mad,
But the rabbit really was there.

He sits down and you think he is going to sleep,
But he gathers all his strength and suddenly springs into the air.
He goes up vertically and on the way down,
He grips onto the corner of the pen tightly.
There's a strip of metal running around the inside of the pen,
And he sits on it, looking quaint and comfortable.
He tries to get over but his rear is too awkward
And he usually loses his balance, resulting in falling.

He lands on his feet and glances round suspiciously,
To make sure that nobody noticed the humiliating fall,
And once he's satisfied that no one saw him,
He settles down for a nap.

Moya Muldowney (15)

Cosmic The Cat

I loved you my
Soft, fluffy friend
I'll remember you
To the very end

Your purr was so loving
I tickled your tummy
From the day
I took you home

On that day
I named you 'Cosmic'
And I vowed to take
Care of you

So wherever you are, remember
It's a long way home if no one's there
But a short journey
For love and care

I write this poem
To say goodbye to my
Little ginger and white
'Cosmic' cat, my friend

Sonya Hayes

Thumbalina (Thimbles)

Thumbalina Fairy Sprite
Glossy coat and eyes so bright
Round the house you seem to fly
Like a demon butterfly

Upon a shelf you have to look
What's in this dish or behind this book
What you can find to take today
To your secret hideaway

While other felines sleep or play
Your mad half hour lasts all day
You fly around from lap to chair
And nip poor Sooty on the stair

Tired at last, your day is done
And for a cuddle you will come
As purr turns to contented hum
On the warm lap of your mum

E Malkison

Me To A Tee

Two months now have been and gone
Walking, trotting, hanging on,
'Heels down Lesley, shoulders back
Get that horse back on that track.'

'Help me now, he's running off
Oh! My God! I'm getting off.'
'Don't be silly, you sit still
I'm right here, he never will.'

Out we go now for a hack
Please dear 'Sampson' bring me back
Holding tight, legs wrapped round
It's a long way down to that ground
Homeward bound with a grin
Now I'm back, want to go again.

'Was he okay?'
'Yes, he was fine
Think it's just all in my mind.'
All over now for another day
Safe and sound with my bay
For all the work that you put in
My stupid laugh, my silly grin.

L Haynes

Dog On A Beach

He scampered along a sandy beach
Water's edge within his reach
A cold, frothy wave lapped his toes
Sending a shiver right up to his nose
He bounded along so gleefully
This was fun, this thing, the sea
Let's dig a hole deep in the sand
It's okay, don't need a hand
The water beckoned, it said to him,
'Come on in, come for a swim.'
He swam far, a long way out
Then he heard a worried shout
Swimming back, he reached the sand
Shaking water all around
He curled up then contentedly
Dreaming of the bone he was having for tea.

Juliet Marshall

To Leo

With exuberant bounce,
You bound on my knee,
Your whiskery visage
Expressing your glee.
I caress your warm fur
And rejoice as you purr.

Your tawny-hued coat,
Glows gold in the sun.
As soft to my touch
As gossamer spun.
You melt in my lap
With liquid-like grace.
While perfect contentment
Shows on your sweet face.
What more bliss could there be
When your rapture I see?

Rose Moss

My Dogs (Benson And Hedges)

My two dogs are my pride and joy,
One little girl and one little boy.
They are both cream retrievers,
And love walkies and rivers.
They are handsome, strong and very bold,
They are both well behaved and do as told.
They both are the best pals I've ever had,
Loyal and faithful but never sad.
They are clever, funny and true,
If you could see them you'd love them too.
I take them everywhere I go,
The folks out shopping stop to say hello.
It takes us hours to do our shopping,
Because people are talking and always stopping.
They are truly loved by everyone,
These two little darlings.
They visit the old folks, the children, the sick,
They are PAT dogs you see, and they do lots of tricks.
I couldn't live without them, they are part of my life,
They are so loyal to hubby and wife.
So my beautiful dogs, both tall, cream and strong,
It's a pleasure to own them, they do nothing wrong.
On the riverbanks they dive off the edges,
My beautiful dogs called Benson and Hedges.

Hilary Tozer

The Birthday Girl

Rhona, my Dobermann, is so much fun,
She is now six years old but
Still acts like she's one!
She'll always be a puppy at heart,
Born to have fun
Right from the start.

She loves to eat and will never be slim,
If all else fails she will rake in the bin.
She has wandered around
With the lid around her head,
I have been in hysterics,
What more can be said!

Tubs of margarine have disappeared,
Before reaching the sanctuary
Of the fridge, I fear!

She sits like a statue,
Watching me eat and will react with speed,
Should food drop at my feet.

My black and tan beauty,
She brings me so much pleasure.
Rhona, you have a wonderful temperament,
You are truly a treasure.

Carry on with your daily antics,
Please keep me amused.
Excuse me while I tidy away,
Before these biscuits are removed!

Joan Igesund

Benji

He has taken our hearts by storm,
This little white tenacious form,
Just four years old and full of fun,
We sometimes wonder what we've done,
To say he's loyal is just a lie,
He's off with any passer-by,
From the rescue centre he came,
A white Jack Russell, Benji by name.

Mary Elliott

The One And Only Bulldozer Affectionately Known As 'Bully'

I'm definitely so very male
With ragged ears and half a tail
Grey and white with whiskers sleek
Passionate and meek.

I roamed the neighbourhood in younger days
But now I'm settled in my ways
Sunny mornings I take my constitutional on garden seat or wall
Within ear's reach if somebody should call!

In wintertime the fireside hearth I drape
Even been known the odd spark to take!
A friendly lap or chest to cling
I calm myself and start to 'sing'.

Pasta and pizza, tuna, ham and bacon
Anything really, just for the taking!
I patiently wait but then . . . my paw will strike at the speed of lightning
Sometimes really it is quite frightening!

My presence holds a certain air
To make anybody want to care
About a cat . . . who is so loving
And does indeed think he's a human being.

Sheila Lewis

To All Those Pooches At The Park

We're the new craze,
Be prepared,
To be amazed.
The Arnold pooch duo
Are coming your way!
We're the funkiest, grooviest,
Santa's pooches are in town.
Here to deliver
Our very own poochagram.

Have a wonderful, barking mad Christmas,
Filled with lots of love and happiness,
And a howling new year!
Love
Trooper Arnold, Feather Arnold and Flax Arnold. XXX

Linda Arnold

My Wee Rabbit

I have a pet rabbit
and her name is Honey,
she is white and brown,
and quite a nice bunny.

She has floppy ears,
and she's quite furry,
she has a cute tail
and moves in a hurry.

She darts round the garden,
as if she's mental,
everyone thinks she's a 'nutter',
but she's really quite gentle.

She sniffs around the grass,
when she's out of her hutch,
but when she sneaks in the house,
Mum says, 'That's too much.'

So that's my wee rabbit
and of her I'll take good care,
no matter what,
I swear.

Mikayla Bruce (14)

Copper

With elegance and pride
he strides out to the beat,
his coat shimmering
and his eyes glowing like
endless pools of sapphire blue.

So balanced are his paces,
with a neck arched with pride,
his feelings a rich haze
of mellow joy.

The music at his toes
is a harmonious tone of elation,
his mane glides
like windswept silk,
my friend, my companion,
my horse.

Beth Robertson (14)

Cat's Ode Tae A Toad

The panto was a treat for the Glasgow cat,
'They sang Christmas wishes - think I'll try that.'
'Oh, timorous, slimy, odd-shaped toad,
Sittin' there aw lonely at the side ae the road.
Dis true luv await me? Are ye reelly ma prince?'
It could be her destiny, she dare not miss.

'Och, away ye go, I'm no kissin' thaat,
Ugly thing looks like a cow pat.
'Spose he has a cute wee croak.
Naw, I cannae dae it,
The thought's makin' me baulk.'

Laura Maxwell

Gismo And The Catmint Plant

I sowed a pinch of catmint
To give the cat a treat
I watered it and watched it grow
A little plant so neat

No cat should be without it
Was what the seed book said
They didn't say the scent of it
Would go right to his head

He rolled in it, he lay in it
He held it in his paws
Then 'goodness me', he ate a bit
With quickly munching jaws

He then ran up the curtains
And tumbled down the stairs
With popping eyes and brushed out tail
A whirligig with hairs.

And when he'd finished running
He was so very hot
He then collapsed on top of it
And nearly broke the pot

So when I see him on the sill
With glassy eyes and very hot
I know just what's the matter
I'm afraid he's gone to pot!
Catmint fashion.

Isobel Laffin

Lucy

As she's got older, my dog thinks she is me,
As you can tell by her picture, you will agree,
She puts on her glasses and little red scarf,
When you see what she looks like, you just have to laugh!
She looks oh so brainy, so clever, so smart!
Just like her owner, you can tell from the start,
But her main ambition, she whispers to me,
That she would like to open the first dog university.

Margaret Berry

Muldoon

Muldoon our first dog, he was so sweet
At eight weeks old, carrying him home was quite a feat
A pale yellow Lab who matured to gold
Like antique pine with a cold, wet nose

A loveable nature, he loved us all
No bad habits to recall
He travelled with us from north to south
Nothing in life seemed to put him out

Very independent he turned out to be
He loved his walks, not always with me
'Muldoon' really suited him, even though no spots
Houdine would have been better, he escaped a lot

What treasures he brought home, toys, balls and shoes
Many a time we wondered whose
A knock at the door, a sweet child stood there,
'Has your dog got my ball?' I could only stare

At intervals, two children arrived on the scene
He took them in his stride, always serene
The gifts, they kept coming, a sheep's skull one day
From Harry the butcher across the way

We moved, not far, rheumatism set in
A homebird at last, we thought, settling in
He waited with patience his chance to escape
Hurrah, what's this open? Why it's the gate

Many a time I'd find him upstairs
Waiting for water to run unawares
From the wash basin tap he liked to sup
Eccentric! Not him, my thirteen year old pup

Patricia Mackie

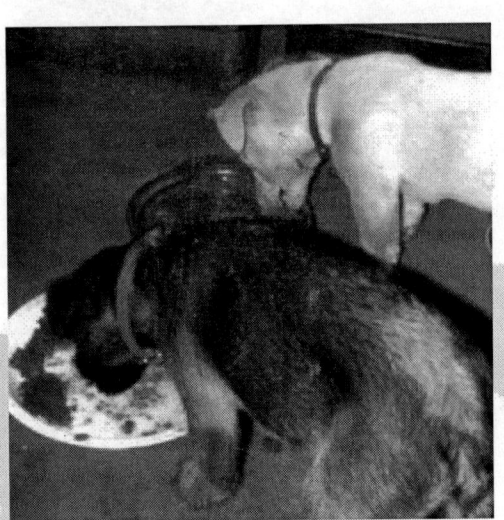

Man's Best Friend

I spent my life with angels, they didn't ask for much
Just a cuddle and a kindly human touch.
These little angels disguised in fur, so cute to see,
Many abandoned by folk just like you and me.
Just a little of your time is all that they ask
And so much they will give in return.
When no one else seems to care
That little tail will wag,
Just to say I am here, and love you so
And will be loyal to you.

Jean Bailey

My Hairless Friends

'Is that a dog?' I'm stopped and asked
'My, it really is unwell
Are you sure it's well, my dear?
I'm sure of these things I can tell.'
A sprite of fur upon her head
Her tail and her toes
I wish they would leave her alone
It's a shame that not many people know
She is such a pleasant dog
Never grumpy, or a worry
When I take her out for a walk
I often try to hurry
Not many people have seen these dogs
And so they stop and stare
It's not the dog they should watch
It's me they should beware
I *bite*
For my Chinese crested dog

Tina Nightingale

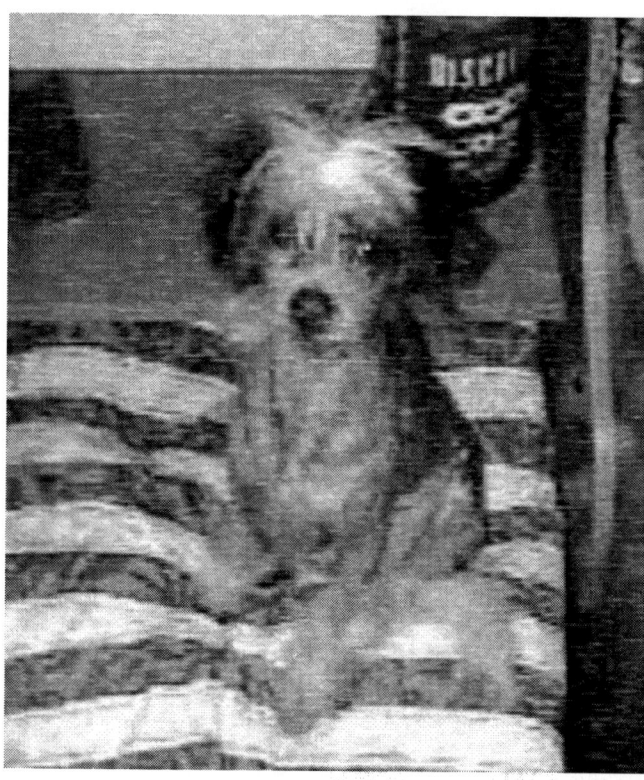

A Dog's Life!

My name is Cara; I am a Lab,
I have a shiny black coat that looks really fab.

I like to go out for a walk, or a jog,
that's what I like best cos I am a dog!

They all go out and earn the money,
to buy the food, to put in my tummy.

They buy me toys; I chew them up,
I should stop that, I'm no longer a pup.

I guard the house, night and day,
anyone I don't like, I keep them away.

I settle down, when I tire,
all warm and cosy, by the fire.

Gillian L Wise

To Love A Toad

'A toad! A toad!'
Their little fingers pointed, the children's voices growled.
Such ugly creatures of warts and moles,
Slime oozes from between crooked toes.

The toad smiles its sweetest smile,
But they only see it as a snicker of vile.
Evil toads, they say, have minds too wild,
To be tamed as a pet to worth your while.

Does a toad know how to give a hand?
Can you find in it a loyal friend?
Toads bring plague and mishaps to men,
On Apocalypse like they did back then.

Condemn toads, condemn!

They claimed toads are the Devil's accomplices,
Yet what do they know when they press their charges?
My master loves me albeit conventional farces,
Because I'm her beloved good toad, her favourite.

Master cares not my bumpy skin,
She pets me just the same when others link me with sins.
With her hands, she keeps me warm from the wind,
Master cringes in anger when they poke me with a pin.

'Let go of my toad, you ignorant folks!'
She pushes them away as on tears she chokes,
On Master's palm I sit and into my eyes she looks,
I roll mine to her blinking, her sadness I know.

It's the same misery I have seen before,
When Master's good friend vanished into war.
I stood by her then on my tiny four,
Can a toad stay by her side for evermore?

'I shall never disown you or leave you in the cold.'
And with this promise a toadie swallows its woes.

Vickie Lui

Untitled

I am a little brown dog who's been compared to a hyena
Not sure if this is good or bad as I've never actually seen one!
My name is Maisy and I live with Sam
He is great, he's the 'main man'
For a time I thought my name was 'No'
But now we've got that cleared up, I'm always ready to go
Anywhere, anytime, with anyone
I just love having fun
If I could have one wish come true
It would be to have a great big 'do'
With all my friends, two-legged and four
To play, sleep and play for evermore.

Roberta Affleck

The Stray

Opened my door early one morn
There you lay on my lawn
Hungry, tired, you raised your head
You looked so thin and underfed

I gave you food and quenched your thirst
Sent you on your way
But on the very next morn
There on my lawn you lay

No one seemed to know you
No one seemed to care
You must have come from somewhere
You had a home out there

Your big brown eyes, golden coat
Couldn't turn my back on you
So we carried on together
What else could we do?

The family really loved you, Ben
You just walked into our lives
We really got a winner that day
Won the golden prize

Fourteen years have passed by
The chicks have flown the nest
Now you're old and wobbly, Ben
But you really are the best

Tina Scott

Clever Puppy

Mum and dad have gone to town
They want me just to settle down
But I have seen a brand new book
And want to go and have a look

The book is made for pups like me
To help us learn more easily
The ways to do those clever tricks
Like rolling over and fetching sticks

I'll learn to sit down on my bum
So I'll impress my dad and mum
I'll also learn to bark on cue
But only when they want me to

Okay, I think I've got the sit
I could improve a little bit
But let's just try the down and stay
And then I think I'll go and play

Kayleigh Brookes (15)

Ode To Jewel

I have a lovely boxer dog and Jewel is her name,
She is never happier than when we go out playing games,
Bounding, leaping, jumping, chasing,
Walking, running, pacing, racing,
On the field or in the wood,
In the pond and through the mud,
In the sunshine, snow and rain,
Every day we do the same,
She's wonderful company and we have lots of fun,
It's the best time of day when we go for our run,
When she's had enough, it's time to go home,
Time for a sleep and to be left alone,
Dreaming those things only my dog can dream,
About running and chasing and things she's just seen,
One hour later, she's there by my side,
Looking intently, brown eyes open wide,
She's wagging her tail and seems to be saying,
'When is it time for us to go playing?'

Natalie Plows

Cuddles

12 years ago a Chihuahua we did buy
so little, so cute, so quiet, she didn't even cry
brown and white she was so small
Cuddles was going to be her name to all
unreal she would fit inside Dad's hand
content to sleep there with no demands
eating and playing and falling asleep
what a life she had and not once a peep
she wrapped round all of our hearts
that we knew we could never part
the name Cuddles suited her no end
snuggling up to us even on the bed
taking her places was certainly no trouble
a small carry bag would do as a double
her nature is kind but weary of strangers
till she gets to know them, then there's no danger
like one of the family she has her own belt
when riding in the car so she's safe, so we felt
nearly lost her to sickness 2 years ago
in hospital on drips, was so hard to let her go
our vet and the staff were there many a time for her
with lots of cuddles and kisses to keep her spirits up
that stay was a few days but she didn't give up
never being apart from us at all for that long
we would visit her and sit with her and keep her strong
our Cuddles is worth more than loads of money
our mate, our companion, she is such a honey
so Cuddles we are so thankful you came into our life
stay with us forever to give us new life.

Karen Holm

Missing You

(Dedicated to my beautiful feline friend)

No one will ever know just how much I miss you so.
Looking at your picture there, I can only stand and stare.

Fur so soft and eyes so bright, wish with life they would alight.
Through my sad and lonely days, full of love your little ways.

You could tell when I was blue; comfort me, you'd try to do.
Sitting, staring, willing me, a little happier to be.

Always there, my little friend, staying with me to the end,
Happy just to be with me, just to keep me company.

Giving all without a word, sweetest sound I ever heard,
Little footsteps on the floor, as you scamper through the door.

Making sure I'm there inside, round the curtains you would hide,
Catching all the warm sunshine, lovely little cat of mine.

Always I'll remember too, wanting just to cuddle you,
What a joy you've always been, joy that no one else has seen.

As I view your pretty face, not another takes your place,
Faithful I shall always be, Jasper my celebrity.

You and I made quite a team, through the fat and through the lean,
So my friend, no one will know, just how much I miss you so.

Muriel Rosamond Harris

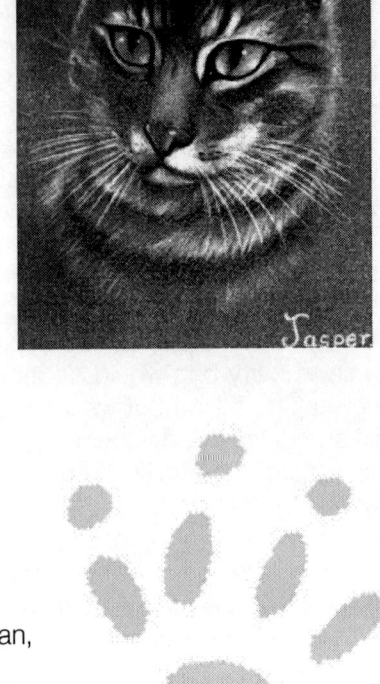

My Staffies

My Staffies are so precious to me and all,
They're always around when I call,
They're always so boisterous when at play,
There's never a dull moment through the day,
They're so cheerful and full of glee,
Oh how they bring tearful laughter to me,
As they both look up to me with their big brown eyes,
I can see the love in their eyes,
Such powerful dogs for their size,
These dogs tell no lies,
Their bones never last,
I've never seen anything eat so fast,
Such lovely dogs, big kids at heart,
We're always together, never apart,
From my heart I can dearly say,
Rosie and Ceaser, so loving and true,
I'll never be without them through and through!

Hayley Jayes

Butter Wouldn't Melt

I rescued you
When you were quite small
Just eight weeks old
That's no age at all.
I fell in love
With your sweet little face
To leave you behind
Would have been a disgrace.
I called you Bonnie
Because that's what you are
I always knew
That you'd be a star.
With your lovely brown eyes
And your long floppy ears
I've had you now
For nearly two years.
Sometimes you're naughty
Sometimes you're fine
All that I know is
I'm glad you're all mine.
Butter wouldn't melt in your mouth
That's not quite true
But I'll love you forever
And I'd never swap you.

Julie Knappett

My Cat, Lucifer

There's a fire in your heart
for freedom and for peace.
At night you warm my stomach
by day you stray outside.

Your eyes tell a thousand words.
Your devilish grin brings warmth and joy.
Your fur is softer than the dearest velvet
and when I pet you,
you make the most beautiful sound.

You are the best, the only one of you
and I love you.

Beatrix Kielhauser

An Anchor Books Anthology

Rottweiler, They Say . . .

They say . . . That you're evil
The devil's own dog -
I say a worshipper of the devil
I clearly am not

They say . . . That your eyes
Are piercing and cold -
I see only eyes
That are loving and bold

They say . . . You're a beast
With intent to do harm -
But your eyes have a gaze
That is gentle and calm

They say . . . That you're hard
Have they not stroked your head?
To not stroke your head
Must be something they've read

For your head is of velvet
So soft to the touch
Something which pridefully
I do very much

They say . . . When you speak
They wish to run a mile -
Can they not see it's been said
With a loving Rott smile?

They say . . . That you're evil -
But it is they who are evil
For blackening your name
And causing you pain

You look up at my face
And I see you ask 'Why?'
As I look deep into your eyes
All I can do is cry

For you were born with a curse
Maliciously given by mankind
A curse that would be
Far better left behind

A dog from the devil?
Or a dog from above?
The Rottweiler I love
Definitely a dog from the Lord up above

Amanda Hawes

Bosom Pals

Missey, a greyhound, with a fine, silky coat
And Reef, a cream Labrador, so cuddly to quote
They both enjoy freedom at Jessamine farm
And make sure the owners come to no harm

They welcome any callers with their loudest bark
Wagging their tails, they find newcomers a lark
But with a certain cautious air, warn them to beware
And make sure that all folk should take care

Missey takes off when let out of doors, soon gone
Reef patiently waits for her, for so long
And when she returns with another conquest
Reef wags his tail with a welcome, his best

He rolls on the floor, full of glee
Thankful no effort he was obliged to be
With all the excitement of Missey's return
They settle for a snooze until the meal time they yearn

The sneaky pair under the table steal
Whenever their host has prepared a meal
Guests sat down to enjoy the festive fare
Suddenly find their knees nudged with care

Any titbits are welcome for their shiny nose
They know no one can resist a plea from those
Such a nice pair of loveable dogs, do no wrong
They give so much pleasure, where happiness belongs

C King

Kins

Hello, it's Christmas morning
And I'm waiting patiently
To see what Father Christmas
Has left beneath the tree
My family are still in bed
But I've been up since three
So I just hope that Santa
Has not forgotten me
I've had a little sniff round
I can smell some kitty chocs
Thank goodness I'm a kitty
At least I won't get socks

Jean Mason

A Cat's Christmas

C heery, seasonal times ahead,
H ere, while I dream on my bed.
R eal fires warming me
I nside, just where I want to be.
S now may fall outside,
T urkey and treats where I abide!
M arzipan fish but not in my dish!
A candle burns cinnamon spice,
S ugared mice and all things nice.

T insel streamers for me to chase.
I cicles form and hang from space.
M agical parcels, each one a surprise!
E vergreen trees, golden memories.

Theresa M Carrier

The Chestnut Mare

June in bloom and meadows green
Were echoing days of spring,
As thistles swayed and breezes turned
A gentle cuckoo sang!

She stood so proud 'neath cobalt skies,
When Gary paid his visit . . .
Streamlined body - soulful eyes,
No child could e'er resist.

Walkers couldn't fail to miss,
The nod of her beckoning mane -
As sunset tenderly lavished a kiss
'Pon the hair of this chestnut queen.

Betwixt the hedges little hands
Would offer to her their greetings . . .
So coy was she to understand -
The motive of their meeting.

Cosseted with the fresh pickel hay,
A pat on her chestnut brow,
She welcomed the children that brightened her day
As she grazed with the sheep and cows.

When the lambs came out to play,
As cows were giving birth -
Rays of sunset ever displayed
The glints on her glossy girth.

Wendy Watkin

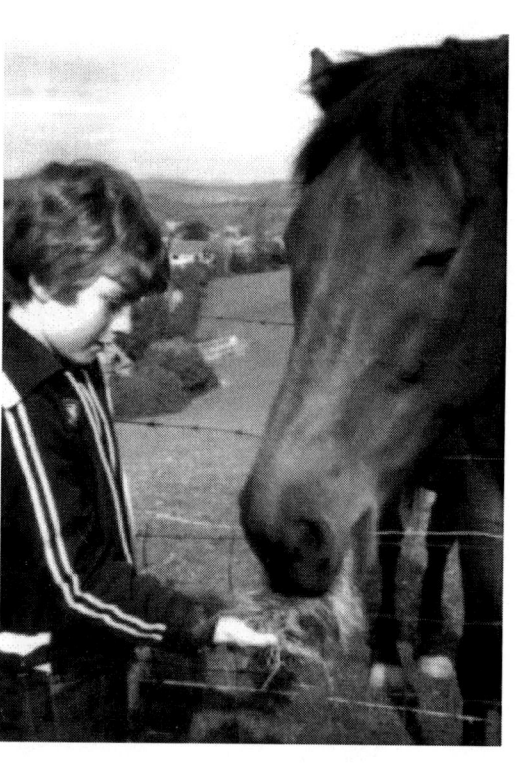

Tessa's Love

Her faithful brown eyes shed tears -
She had loved him for many years
Where is he? Where has he gone?
At night, when she's alone
We hear her crying and sighing;
For Tessa, there is no praying.
The eyes that shone so bright
Are dim now, for she's so sad,
Why leave her? She's not been bad,
Tess kisses Teddy, it's not the same,
The one she loves is Dad, that's his name,
Mother, too, seems different, why?
She too is sad, tries not to cry.
Once, Tess saw him in a strange place,
With lines of sorrow on his face;
She just couldn't understand,
But, she gently licked his shrivelled hand.
Dogs, they say, don't go above,
But Tessa's very special love
Will take her up to find her dad,
Who'll wait, no longer sad,
'Come, Tess,' he'll say. 'You were never bad.'

Sylvia Moulds

Benji

On her fifth birthday, my granddaughter said that she would like a pet
But Mummy is allergic to cats and dogs, so what sort could she get?
A rabbit would be rather nice so they bought a little black Dutch one
The hutch, straw and food were ready, and so was the garden run.
For a while he was happy, playing and jumping all around
Then one morning before school, he was nowhere to be found.
They hunted the garden, then Mum said, 'Shush,
I can see him hiding behind that big bush.'
They crept up slowly so he wouldn't take fright
Then Mum caught him quickly and held on tight.
After a gentle stroking he was safely locked away
And the run was repaired later that day.
They gave him some toys and a child's chair
Whatever the weather you can see him sitting there.
He likes it when the rain is pouring from the sky
He knows a cuddle in a towel will make him dry.
He really is delightful and so much fun
There couldn't be a nicer rabbit under the sun.

Lynne Walden

Tubbs In Spring

Spring brings in a bloom of flowers
After the spring showers
They see the light and start to bring in some delight
They are such a lovely sight
Daffodils yellow and white, bluebells too,
With tulips of all kinds of hue
And with them too the honey bee
To pollinate them all you see
Birds sing in the morning dew
And fill the air with a lovely tune
You try to catch them Tubbs and eat them too
There is plenty of spring left in you
You are like a star that shines
So bright in the sky at night
You sure are a real delight
You love me to hold you tight
Every day and every night
I can see clearly every day
How you love to run and play
So glad you came here to stay
You are in Heaven every night and day
You are my darling bud of May

Gordon Forbes

Norman And My Dog Charlie!

Come on Charlie, let's go for a walk,
You give me a bark, I wish you could talk,
You've been my friend for many years,
Shared my laughter and my tears,
You love to lie down at my side,
Gazing up at me with eyes open wide,
You love to be fussed, you're loyal to the end,
I have you around, you are more than a friend,
You have a rug at the side of the bed,
You curl in a ball, resting your head,
You're now growing old, your reactions are slow,
But as a friend and companion I want you to know,
You're the best!

Ivor Emlyn Percival

Mashie

My little Mashie is an English setter,
A very naughty puppy, but she'll get better.
When she's older and learns to be good,
It's very hard work with her destructive mood.
Bounding here! Nosing there!
Little Mashie gets *everywhere!*
Eating the flowers! Licking the slugs!
Paddling in the drinking bowl
And other tails she tugs!
Biting and *shrieking!* When her temper she loses!
Then falls asleep in any bed she chooses.
What a little madam my Mashie can be,
But what a little 'sweetie' when she kisses me.
She rolls her big brown eyes to Heaven above,
This bundle of energy, mischief and love.
I love little Mashie with all her naughty ways,
Because I know that one of these days
A grown up beautiful dog she will be,
As she walks through her life at the side of me.
With her silky fur and pretty face,
She will glide along with pride and grace.
Her sweet and friendly ways will shine,
And I'm so very glad that little Mashie is mine.

Maureen Roberts

A Cat's Eye View

In my mind I call you Daddy even though I know your name
I know how much you love me and I love you just the same.
You have loved me from the start like a young girl loves her dolly
From the moment of my birth in that old blue shopping trolley.
When you gently lifted us out, my mum and brothers too
That, Dad, is the moment when I fell in love with you.

I know my name is Echo, it was you that gave it me
I run to you when called down from my old oak tree.
I love it when you talk to me and when you sing a song
I join you in your songs of love, you can hear me purr along.

I wish that I could talk to you just to tell you how I feel
I would sing songs back to you to show our love is real
But Dad, you know I cannot talk, that's one thing I cannot do
But I see how much you love me as I have a cat's eye view.

Mark Strong

An Anchor Books Anthology

Milo

'Is he a rottweiler?' she asks
'He thinks he is,' I say.

And there he trots down the street
with bandy legs and clumsy feet.
Hair in desperate need of a comb
I'll try again when we get home.
He looks and barks at everyone
embarrassing! But to him it's fun.
He chases birds and rolls in dirt
at every tree he has a squirt.
He pulls and pulls, I yank him back
any dog he will attack.
The postman runs the fastest mile
Milo sits with half a smile.
He hides his bones in every corner
when Sister calls I have to warn her.
Gas man, milkman, neighbour too
have all had ankles bit right through.
He chews my slippers and all he can
and even barks at the ceiling fan.
He licks my hands, my feet, my face
after he's licked his private place!
He's been accused of looking strange
but not one single hair would I change.
Of all my time in every day
my favourite time is time to play.
He's my friend, my companion, my best mate too
I wouldn't even give him to you.

Christine Redmond

Not Likely

Our cheeky puss with the angelic face,
Hopped out from the chair with stealthily grace,
She slid thru the long grass by the large tree,
A baby bird is what she could see,
But daddy bird saw her and sounded the alarm,
The little birds vanished away from all harm.
The garden was silent; our puss was put out,
That she could catch one, there was some doubt.
Now her eyes close as she curls up to dream,
Of exciting chases and what might have been.

Barbara M Twort

Casey

(04.07.2000 - 29.08.2003)

Everyone that knows me knows the demons of my past,
Move on and upwards, I'm told the pain won't last.
But yesterday again it reared its ugly head,
As I cradled my dead cat in my arms on my bed.

Casey was only three, he didn't deserve to die,
But now he's playing with Rusty up in the sky.
My two beautiful boys, I lost you both this year,
Now losing Max as well is one of my fears.

Casey, I had to let you go, the angels came for you,
But at least you're up with Rusty, 'God', I miss you two.
I know you could hear me talking as the angels came,
And my life without you, darling, will never be the same.

They said you couldn't hear me but darling you opened your eyes,
And when you touched me with your paw I couldn't help but cry.
I was telling you, darling, that you were going home,
I knew all along that from Heaven you were just on loan.

Someone as beautiful and as pure as your soul,
Came into my life as a gift to make me whole.
Three years we had, so brief, yet filled with love,
And for that my darling Casey, I thank God up above.

We lay together last night as everyone was out,
It was the most moving feeling in my life I've ever felt.
I think I'd always been frightened of saying goodbye before,
But I had to share my last cuddle with you before closing the door.

You lay so warm and peaceful in my arms so tight,
I could have stayed there forever but we only had last night.
Today I sent you on a journey to a place that's filled with love,
And now I'll always have a special star shining on me from above.

Your eyes were bluer than the sky on a beautiful summer day,
And to forget you my darling there is no way.
I'm really hurting, Casey, and I feel I can't go on,
But I'll do it just for you, as I promised I'd be strong.

God bless my little angel, it was time for you to go,
I just wanted a few minutes to let you know
I love you Casey xxxx.

Angie Kesteven

Ambrose The Cat

I am a British smoke short hair cat called Ambrose,
I am black and like a lot of other cats I suppose,
'Smoke' means I look black when my roots are white,
And if so I am really quite a cute sight,
Long white whiskers decorate my little face,
By my pitch-black nose in just the right place,
My claws are sharp, as of course are my teeth,
My tail swishes above me and my paws beneath,
I like eating, sleeping and watching the world,
Sitting in the window, a tail around me, curled,
I always like to watch everyone I see walking by,
Some even wave at me and sometimes I say 'Hi!'
My keeper talks to me, I have no idea what is said,
Our chats are one-sided and pass over my head,
It makes no difference what my keeper will say,
As the only word I know is 'miaow' anyway!
When I am hungry, I swallow what I have chewed,
Then I am in the cat litter tray, recycling my food,
I always purr when I am content, like other cats,
When not snuggled up into a ball, asleep, perhaps.

Christopher Higgins

Jack

He stalks with cunning, guarded step
His evil eye stares on;
No spider is safe beneath his gaze,
His vicious claws and teeth dismays

He is the predator.

He wrecks the room
The china flies
The mats take off, as
Loud he cries;
The chase is on,
Some poor moth dies,
Nothing is safe once in his eyes.

It's four in the morning and I can't sleep
I lie in the dark alone.
I feel his foot upon the bed
He drops his face down to my head
He purrs, he nuzzles close to me
He makes me feel so cosy
He's soft and warm and he comforts me.
I love my ginger tabby.

Shirley Hillier

Jerry

He's like a mini tiger, prowling all around,
Stalking birds in the garden, creeping without a sound,
Purrs when happy, wags his tail if he's cross,
Taps the pet rabbits to show them who's boss,
When you go towards him and he runs away,
Peeps behind the furniture, it's a sign he wants to play,
If hungry and you're sitting down, he'll miaow till you're on your feet,
But sometimes it's a crafty plan to curl up on your seat,
He lazes in the sun but comes in when there's rain,
Minutes after brushing him, he'll roll in the dirt again,
He's a comfort and companion and means the world to us,
We wouldn't be without him, our ginger and white puss.

Ann Sykes

An Anchor Books Anthology

Otis

He's the smallest member in our family
But makes his mark as you will see
He knows the best places to sleep all day
Won't be disturbed till he's ready to play

Comes alive after it's dark
Then he's out in the street, the garden and park
You can't keep him in at night
He's one of the boys and he loves a good fight

He reappears in the sunlight
Scratched and scarred but quite alright
Now he's ready for another hard day
Sleeping in the sun, on the bed or window bay

Once he's asleep you can't wake him
But for the sound of the spoon in the Whiskers' tin
Then he's up in the kitchen like a shot
Wrapping himself round you as if tying a knot

Cupboard love, that's what we call it
But it's a love I could never forfeit
For it's the only kind he knows
So it will do, I suppose

He's getting older now, our cat
We've had him some years, I can tell you that
How much longer can he go on?
He'll outlive us all, I bet that one!

Penny Pritchard

Dillon And Mu

Mu's fast asleep on the fireside rug,
Dillon's stretched out too,
Between them both I realised,
Of the fire I had no view.

Dillon went out to the garden,
Mu followed close behind,
At last the warmth hit my toes,
Which really blew my mind.

What was this thing that sent out heat
To ease the cold and pain?
Before my toes had chance to guess,
They both came in again.

K Townsley

Wake Up! It's Sunday

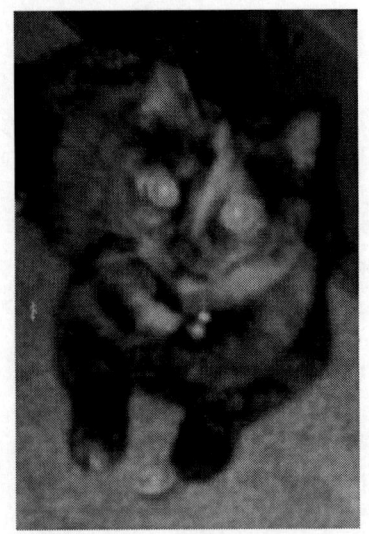

God called me to His service, that a Verger I must be.
The church will need unlocking with its ancient iron key.
I shall open up the tall porch gate and heavy wooden door,
That worshippers may come to pray and tread the hallowed floor.

On Sundays I must leave my bed, be up by six-fifteen,
My darling cat is there to help, she really is quite keen.
Just how she knows it's Sunday is a mystery to me,
No doubt a cat psychologist could tell me - for a fee!

Some folk trust the Holy Spirit, others need a loud alarm;
God gave *me* precious Lottie, soft and warm, and full of charm.
She pats me gently on the face, and purrs into my ear -
A pleasant form of wakening, she really is a dear.

Her attentions are persistent, very loving, full of care,
No chance of going back to sleep; to dream I wouldn't dare.
This state of things would seem ideal, except for one small flaw.
Sweet Lottie cannot tell the time - it's only half-past four.

Jill Richards

Easily Pleased

I swim around in my glass tank
So much to see! Who do I thank?
Oh look! A house with a little door!
I'd never noticed that before

Think I'll go clockwise this time round
So many wonders to be found
Oh look! A house with a little door!
I think I'll go in and explore

Anticlockwise now I go
Sometimes fast and sometimes slow
Oh look! A house with a little door!
I've never noticed that before

There's other fish, all colours bright
Some even glow when it's not light
Now something's tapping on the glass!
What's that? It's grub! Hey, this is class!

I'm full up now - I must have eaten
This lifestyle just cannot be beaten!
Oh look! A house with a little door!
I think I'll go in and explore . . .

Peter Elliott

Oh, For Dog's Sake!

My well-trained greyhound bitch named Sable
Will quietly sit beside the table
My breakfast she won't try to share
But fixes me with injured stare
Such great sad eyes imploring there
With guilty pangs I view my treat
But feel reluctant now to eat.

Gordon Paul Charkin

Harvey

Found as a stray, as you had decided to roam,
We took you in when you needed a home.
Your fur is so soft and coloured light brown,
You've bright hazel eyes and lop-ears hanging down.
We try to take very good care of you,
And bring you apples and carrots too!
With free run of the garden you have no care,
Nice fresh water in a bowl is there.
Your hutch is filled with sweet, fresh hay,
You sit under a bush to escape the heat of the day.
When we sit outside having a barbecue,
We laugh at the running, jumping games that you do.
We bring you in when the nights are cool,
And you watch TV with us as a rule.
It's funny seeing you watch the telly!
We bathe you clean when you get smelly.
You like to sit on the settee, all stretched out,
Or explore the bedrooms, hopping about.
You also love to jump up on a knee,
And nibble a cracker for your tea.
Our daughter makes 'plate picnics' for you as a treat,
You make grunting sounds as you run round our feet.
You stamp your back feet if you are cross with us,
And feel we are making too much of a fuss!
It's a bit of a nuisance that you eat our flowers,
And can sit doing nothing much for hours,
But we love you, Harvey, our rabbit dear,
We're so glad you are living here.

Patricia Summers

Little Wilfred

Little Wilfred,
What can you see?
Can you see birds
Resting in a tree?
Can you see people
Briskly walking by,
Or fluffy white clouds
Floating way up on high?

Little Wilfred,
What can you see,
Lying on the bed
In this room with me?
Curled up so peacefully,
Resting a weary head;
I'm glad you are with me
And not out there instead.

Geraldine Laker

Sheba Canine Queen

To know you was to love you.
Your brown eyes shone with love.
Those eyes, long lashed and doe-like.
Kind and gentle as a dove.

All you needed was kindness,
And without motive or guile,
Your love you gave freely.
We even taught you to smile.

I think of you constantly,
Tri-coloured; black, white and brown.
With a face so angelic,
Yet you could be such a clown.

You were well known, all about.
So well known in fact for miles.
If they didn't know your name,
They'd call you 'The dog that smiles'.

Sheba, you've left me alone.
I miss you and I still cry.
Missing your smile and your love
And asking, 'Why did you die?'

A E Roderick

An Anchor Books Anthology

Doggie For Sale

I took my Yorkie out for some Christmas fayre
And with us came my aunt who was in a wheelchair
A table in the restaurant we did book
The waiter gave us a funny look

So Toby had to go outside
When my aunt's wheelchair he had spied
We sat him in the wheelchair and said,
'You stay there 'til we've been fed.'

So the wheelchair is where he sat
With my husband's scarf and cap
To keep him warm and have a laugh
He looked so cute in Lou's chequered scarf

We thought he would wriggle his way out
But he thought he looked posh, there is no doubt
And there he sat quite happily
For passers-by to giggle and see

When we came out a note had been left
A lady who trained dogs had said,
'I think he looks cute in his little bed.'
And she pinned the note upon his head

This note we took and duly saved
For it congratulated us on the way he behaved
This story is true, I want you to know
About our little dog that we love so.

Dora-Jean

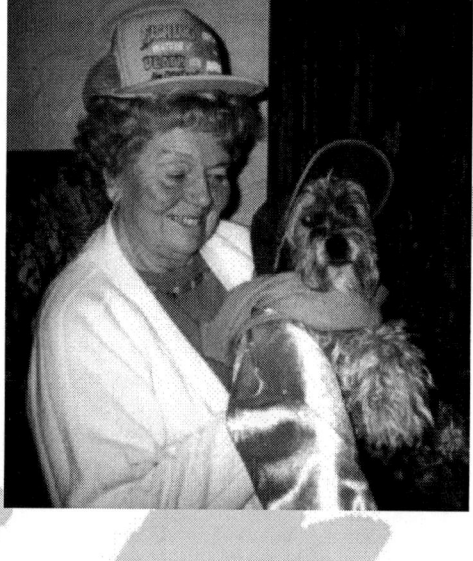

Morning Breaks

I am number one.
The day has just begun.
The cat thinks he is too
And lets me know
At three!
The cockerel is at four
And lets ev'rybody here
Hear that he is full of the joys,
As the bedsprings
Creak and groan.
My dog is the best.
Unlike all the rest,
Sleeps and sleeps
Well after five
With her ears
Shut tight!

Lyn Sandford

Ben

Life without Ben is like living in a void,
His scratting drove us mad, his hairs made us annoyed.
But there's nothing we wouldn't give,
To give our little dog another chance to live,
Benny, our shadow, our companion, our dearest friend,
How long before our broken hearts mend?

Jackie Heath

Timmy Tinker Boy

In my home there are lots of cats, in all there are seven
But there is one who is a real tinker out of them
It's the ginger tabby, Timmy Tinker Boy I call him
Always up to no good, he's the one into everything,
He is still only very small, although he is nearly four
Looks and acts like a kitten, don't think he will grow no more!
Can't leave clothes about like trousers, jackets or socks
As they end up with holes in them as he chews the lot
He will chew belts, zips, buckles on shoes, and buttons
My earrings, watch, necklace, whatever I have got on

I bought all the cats a toy mouse, so each could play
He ran off with his, started chewing it straight away,
Off came the ears, tail, all the fur, no more a mouse
Just all the bits from it scattered around the house
Couldn't find the inner part, looked for it the next day
He had only eaten it, as found it in the litter tray
Boxes he loves to chew, lots of cardboard everywhere
After he's made a mess, looks at me without a care
He might be a tinker boy when it comes to chewing
But when people visit, he's so nervous, he goes running

I wish he wouldn't chew, would play nicely with his toys
No, he won't ever change, will always be a tinker boy,
Another thing he likes to do is sit upon my back
He really is a strange, funny boy, my Timmy Tinker cat,
Giving me kisses, licks on hands, must love the taste
He makes me laugh, always putting a smile on my face
If he can't sit on me, he will go off and keep crying
As on my lap some of the other cats could be lying
Though he has chewed lots of clothes, which I had to bin
With his cute sweet kitten face, loving ways, I love him.

Linda Roberts

Buttons

A lovely lady in a black fur coat,
With enormous lemon drop eyes,
She waggles her tail to tease the boys,
Then, runs away to hide,
Sometimes she'll hide in a cupboard,
Or under a big armchair,
She'll even hide in an open drawer,
Or in the back of the car,
I run around calling her name,
Suddenly she appears,
Innocence written all over her face,
A gentle purr, a soft miaow,
Didn't you know I was here?

Wendy Dawson

Cocky Jocky

Cocky Jocky,
The cockatiel,
Never loses his appeal,
He talks away,
All day
With zeal,
His antics keep us all amused,
He flaps his wings,
He chirps,
He sings,
While all around us he runs rings,
And leaves us feeling all confused,
His incessant chatter,
'Jocky's a cheeky boy',
'What's the matter?'
He is as mad as a hatter,
And tries to bath in his drinking water,
He keeps us all going,
There's no slowing
Down with age,
Watch out, Jocky the cockatiel is on the rampage.

Alan Pow

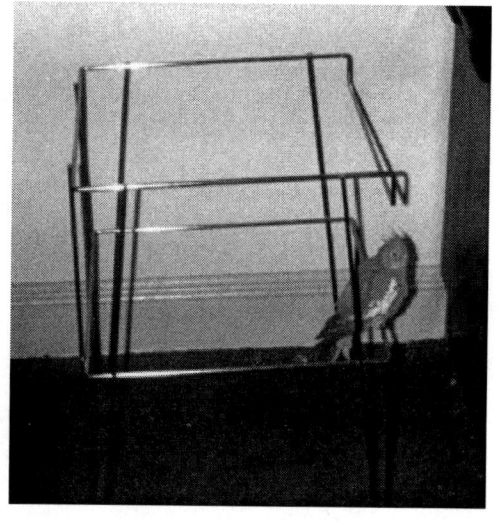

This Little Guinea Pig

This little guinea pig in the pet shop for sale,
A little twitching nose and short stubby tail.

This little guinea pig, black, brown and white,
Fur *so* soft, eyes *so* bright.

This little guinea pig, took him home with me,
We called him Speedy, he's so fast you see.

This little guinea pig, gave him to my son,
A cheeky little animal, a bundle of fun.

This little guinea pig, in the cage he went,
Running up and down, happy and content.

This little guinea pig, racing round and round,
Can you hear his feet, pitter-patter on the ground?

This little guinea pig, makes his bed of hay,
Curled up in a ball is where he likes to stay.

This little guinea pig, food he does seek,
When he hears you coming, he begins to squeak.

This little guinea pig, getting rather tubby,
Rolling in the dirt, looking *very* grubby.

This little guinea pig, we give him a bath,
Out of the sink he jumped, and we began to laugh.

This little guinea pig, out in his pen,
If you try to catch him, he goes inside again.

This little guinea pig, a picture of health,
Looking a little sad, all by himself.

This little guinea pig, I know we won't regret,
Returning to the pet shop, another one to get.

These little guinea pigs, snuggled down together,
Inside their cage, friends forever.

Leanne Thompson

An Anchor Books Anthology

Master

Other dogs are not so blessed,
Not chosen for one so adept
As my master, kind and true;
There is no friend as good as you.

You're strong and firm when I am bad;
You cuddle me when I look sad.
No other dog has been so blessed;
My dad, my friend, you are the best!

Grace Christian

Emma's Review Of Life

I'm having a review of life
And what I want to be,
A rather snooty dressage horse,
Perhaps that's not for me.

Maybe a top eventer,
Supersonic fit,
But then I'd have to work a lot,
I don't fancy that a bit!

Long distance horse might suit me
I'd be very good I bet,
Miles and miles of country lanes,
Then probably the vet!

I've got it, I will write a book,
It will be so very funny,
I will be a famous author,
And earn bags and bags of money.

And then it will be made a film,
I'll become a superstar,
I'll be in glossy magazines,
And worshipped from afar.

Oh well, it's good to have a dream
And I can dream all day,
But as for now it's back to lunch,
And munching on my hay.

Sue Walters

Ode To Daisy

A little white cat just appeared one bright day
She stood on her hind legs and wanted to play
Ad cried, 'It's Casper!' Her antics were crazy
She pawed at the insects and chewed at the daisies

One eye is yellow but the other eye blue
A freak of the genes like 'A Boy Named Sue'
She drank from the birdbath; she sprang with the grass
And when it was sunny she'd lay there and bask

This snowy-white cat is a joy to behold
With a thick furry coat she would never be cold
She played with the mayflies, she'd suddenly freeze
When she sensed baby birds, she hid under the trees

A mad game of pretence - like safari-style trip
Till a black cat appeared and then Daisy let rip
She confronted her peer on the top of the fence
The black cat retreated - a white danger it sensed

This strange cat meant business; he knew it was Daisy
Unlike the shy tabby (his other peer, Maisie)
We watched from a window as she stood her ground
'Til she leapt from the fence - an almighty bound

Our Daisy is special and a real kitten-cat
With intelligent feelings, unlike that black prat
We still called her 'Casper' (her real name is 'Daisy')
Her nickname is 'Odd-eye' although that sounds hazy

There's a twist to this tale (but forgive the slight pun)
For the little white freak is delightful and fun
Den's digging the garden; then layering with sand
With square slabs of concrete so where can she land?

The garden has changed since that day she appeared
Instead of couch grass, it's soft sand and it's weird
She sniffed every object to make sure it's our house
Then she ran, ears pinned back, away from my spouse

Now she plays with the sand where she used to chew grass
And when the sun's shining she'll stretch out to bask
We've grown a new flower and I know this sounds crazy
It's no longer Michaelmas. It's called Lazy Daisy.

Judy Studd

Soddoffpuss Gremlin

For many years poor Gremlin thought his name was Soddoffpuss
Because of the greeting he always got, when he came to any of us.
Of nature, sweet, to all but mice, birds, fish and creatures small.
He'd bring his victim to our bedroom door and we'd hear his plaintive call,
'Waahh, waahh - waahh. Waahh, waahh, waahh'. No rounded 'miaow, miaow, miaow'.
This would persist until someone hissed, 'Soddoffpuss, right now'.
If we weren't too tired we might get there in time to save what he'd brought in.
If we took too long, by daylight's dawn, there'd be only bits for the bin.
Take him down to the vet for injections, he'd purr all the time they were doing it,
But paint or concrete in the garden and Gremlin was sure to ruin it.
He'd carry in fish from the fishpond, but they weren't always ours, I would guess,
Cos behind the fence in dulcet tones, we would sometimes hear a clear 'Soddoffpuss'.
He would sleep with our dog of an evening, but when the moon rose over the hill,
He would flex his claws in soft little paws, and slink-sway out to kill.
He'd sit ever so still by the rabbit hutch in the garden over the way,
And suddenly, breaking the stillness, 'Soddoffpuss', we'd hear somebody say.
So he'd come back to us at his leisure, belly a-sway, wanting fuss,
He'd holler aloud, while his green eyes glowed, pleased to hear our welcoming, 'Soddoffpuss'.

K Titmus

My Dog

His two brown eyes
With hidden depths of love.
Begging me - the needle enters
Eyes shut.

Gladys Baillie

Zoro, My Horse

Zoro, my horse
is a symbol of force
with a shapely, big head
which should think instead of me

Zoro, my horse
likes the seashores
he gallops along
to the words of my song
he may think ahead instead of me

Zoro, my horse
takes its course
I ride him at times
to the rhythm of my rhymes
he lifts up his head to think
instead of me

Zoro, my horse
knows no remorse
he strides as bred
straight on ahead
does he think instead of me?

So I sit on his back
and lack the shapely, big head
that he has instead of me

Zoro, my horse
I love his force
the flicker from my brains
touches his reigns
and he moves ahead
with his shapely head
and myself . . .

Wila Yagel

An Anchor Books Anthology

Jodie

She appeared after the Christmas that my dad took ill,
When my world seemed to be fresh out of happy endings.
Last season's baby, now a homeless stray,
She slipped in through a gap in our thorn hedge,
Was soon absorbed in play, oblivious of the chill.
Chased withered leaves in winter beds,
A misplaced sunbeam under skies of grey.
We gave her food because she looked so thin
And called her Kitten as we didn't know her name.
My sister said, 'If snow comes we'll have to take her in.'
Out of the lowering, laden clouds the snow never came.

That spring the earth grudgingly gave birth to daffodils,
Forcing them painfully through the hard clay.
Carefree Kitten skipped among them every day.
My dad was worse, Easter brought little joy,
Merely reminding that death's a requisite of resurrection!
We weren't sure if the cat was a girl or a boy.
Probably male we thought, as it turned out we were wrong.
However, by that time we'd called her Jodie,
A name that we remembered from a song.

In the stifling summer night my dad lay dying.
My sister whispered softly, 'Come with me.'
Fearing the worst, I followed filled with dread,
Wondering what new horror I would see.
On the front doorstep Jodie was lying,
Proudly watching as her kittens played
Like flurries of snowflakes under starry skies;
Her gift of life to us when all seemed numb and dead.
Her face turned towards us, noting our surprise,
Deep love and trust seen clearly in her golden eyes.

Clare McAfee

My Letter To Benji

Dear Benji, you are just asleep
Free from pain and in peace
We loved you from a puppy for fifteen years
Excuse me while I dry my tears

You were my very best friend
We had such happy times together
My love for you will never end
It will last forever

A kind man saved you when you were a few weeks old
From drowning in the canal
I thank you for your life with us
It was more precious than gold

I have saved your collar, lead and dish
If only I could have one wish
To see you use them once again
I know it would heal all this pain

There were some days when I would feel low
You would nudge me with your nose and make me go
We knew each other so very well
How sad I feel now I could never tell

May Ward

Meeka

Meeka's the cat with attitude,
Confidence is what he exudes
To see him swagger down the street
With his oh so straight tail and his big white feet
You'd think him the king of all he surveys
But you'd be surprised that what he conveys
Is not what he feels or how he is,
He's just a big softy, a big furry kid
He needs his cuddles, lots of them,
He's happier with ladies than with men
He doesn't know why except that I feed him
And love and care and yes I need him
To run to the car each night I come home,
To play with the cord when I'm on the phone
To sleep on my bed and be there for me
And fly for no reason up the willow tree
I hope we'll be there for each other for years
For to lose him now would bring so many tears.

Marion Jones

An Anchor Books Anthology

Dear Deeley

Not another few agony letters to answer, Deeley thought to himself,
He was getting awfully bored trying to sort out the problems of his feline brothers,
'I suppose I best get on with it, as there's a mountain of mail to get through today,'
Deeley then took another drink of goat's milk and reached for his pen.

'Dear Deeley, I'm constantly being harassed by the standard poodles next door,
Every time I went into the garden to catch the sun and destroy the lavender bush,
They would start barking at me, it was so loud that it would shatter ceramic pots,
So my servant would usher me indoors until those dogs were out of sight.
What should I do?' Tiddles of Oxford.

'My advice for you is to climb onto the garden bench and place your paws on its nose,
Then tickle the nose. Now this sounds like a dangerous idea but believe me,
After about five minutes those standard poodles will be putty in your paws,
They should be your friends for life. Good luck!'

'Dear Deeley, I cannot stand those squirrels roaming around my garden,
They keep helping themselves to the food my servant puts down for me,
So I keep chasing them up the chestnut tree at the bottom of the garden,
One particular morning I got stuck up that tree and I was there for three days,
No one came to rescue me, not even the fire service with their extended ladder,
I was cold, frightened and extremely hungry for a bowl of cod and shrimp,
I cannot let them get away with that but I'm afraid of getting stuck up that tree forever.
What should I do?' Troy of Stratford-upon-Avon.

'My advice for you is not to worry about being stranded up that chestnut tree too much,
I receive hundreds of letters like this every week and I always provide the same advice,
The local owl population adore the company of the cat, so don't worry too much,
You shall automatically be welcomed into their social circle.
So good luck!'

I think I'll have a well-earned cat-nap now and answer another letter later,
I hope it's not raining, I wonder is there fresh food in the dish?
I wonder, has my servant put a saucer of creamy white milk down for me?
You see, they're not the only ones with the problems.

You can contact me on cat@log.

Ben E Corado

Twa Dugs

Dandie Dinmount lived there aboot
Sandy the Scottie was also hanging oot
Running free they jockeyed along
Nowhere to go, no place to belong
Their only home was running the streets
When winter came it was no great treat

But one day an old lady came their way
Put her hand down, patted them to say
'You're two lovely boys, I must confess
Come home with me and you'll progress'
A haven the dogs soon came to know
No longer drifting space with roots to sow

A loving person had passed one fine day
Changed their lives forever a place to stay
Barking happily a new life had begun
Chasing around in a garden was so much fun
A new mummy had taken them into her heart
No more need to wander only joy to impart

Breakfast ready to see them through the day
Food always on hand more time to play
Out for their walk after the early morning meal
Then back home the fireside a nice warm feel
Dandie and Sandy had found a new home
With love and affection, no more need to roam

Every day was so sunny and bright
Befriended with kindness a wonderful sight
A Florence Nightingale carrying a lamp
Passed their way when they were wet and damp
But now twa dugs were no longer astray
An angel had passed by on a midwinter day

Norman S Brittain

My Mischievous Friend

He can open doors and shut them too
He's cheeky, crafty and sly
He chases 'the cat' and also the birds
He's so naughty that you want to cry
But when he's played out at the end of the day
And he snuggles his head on my knee
I know that I'll give unconditional love
And I know that he also loves me

Marion Thacker

An Anchor Books Anthology

Gone But Not Forgotten

Many years have passed,
still to this day you're not forgotten.
Fond memories will remain with me for life,
and beyond that it shall go.

You watched over me when I was younger,
protected me from the world around.
You cuddled me with warmth,
all around, each day.

And as I keep on growing,
I will always remember,
what you showed me. And that was
that love comes in all shapes and forms.

You're gone but not forgotten.

Gillian McKinley

A Dog

Don't treat a dog like that
just because he will chase a cat
but doesn't bark when you want him to
a dog that really loves you.
All dogs are not the same,
and to him it's only a game,
he's playing the only way he knows
but don't have him running away from the blows
when he looks at you, don't you see the love in his eyes,
please don't make it fear that changes him,
for once the love has gone
he will never trust anyone

Maureen Morris

Mum's Moggies

She feeds us meat and munchies,
And all the things we like,
And if we need some more supplies,
She tears off to the shop on her bike.

She talks to us and fusses us,
We each have our own chair,
And we bring her pressies of mice and birds,
To show her that we care.

We've tore up and down the curtains,
Left messages on the floor,
And occasionally we have a mad half hour,
And get our bums kicked through the door.

We come in many shapes and sizes,
Our characters are different too,
Mum finds time for all of us,
And our arguments are few.

Sometimes we stalk the neighbour's dog,
Or plant stinkpods in her garden,
But if we purr and curl up on her lap,
We're usually let off with a pardon.

We try to keep the vermin down,
To prove just what we're worth,
And all sit and smile at tea time,
Cos we know we cost the earth.

But mum's day is special, she's our queen,
And we love her, all of us,
We are her loyal and furry subjects,
Each and every puss.

A Corfield

Toilet Training

The noise of the loo enticed my kitty to do,
The strangest of things, on peering right in,
She slipped straight in,
She slipped and slid and then stuck fast,
I knew she thought her time had come to pass,
I retrieved her tail and then her back legs,
With a splish and splosh her extraction was hailed,
With an extremely loud spluttering wail,
Needless to say now,
One flush of the loo and
She's history too!

Beverley Dales

An Anchor Books Anthology

My Gorgeous Guinea Pig

He is furry and white,
His eyes glow at night,
They are red and round,
Ollie makes lots of sound,
With an eek and a squeak,
He is so sweet.
He lives in a cage,
He is only two years of age.
I only have one,
But he is such great fun,
My gorgeous guinea pig Ollie.

Georgina Biggs

The Odyssey Of Joannie's 'Jack The Donkey'

My aunt Joan saved a poor mistreated donkey,
By buying him for ten quid from his keeper,
Near the Orsett hospital, she kept him in a field,
His bray was like a klaxon, but much deeper.

The hospital complained because the patients couldn't sleep,
So loud was poor old Jack's nocturnal braying,
And when the doctors told the nurses what they had to do,
The nurses couldn't hear what they were saying.

So then it was decided poor old Jack would have to move,
And Joannie's uncle lived not far away,
He had a nice big field where he would let old Jack reside,
And do just as he wanted, night and day.

So Joannie and a friend went out to transfer Jack one day,
From near Orsett hospital to his new and waiting home,
It was apparent right away that Jack wanted to play,
Which caused a few headaches for Auntie Joan.

Joan put a rope around Jack's neck to lead him down the road,
Then off went Jack, just like a bloody rocket,
While Joannie, at the other end, went soaring through the air,
And Jack ignored her fervent pleas to stop it.

Then all at once Jack changed his mind and skidded to a stop,
And for the hounds of hell would not have shifted,
Joan and her friend pushed from behind, but still he wouldn't move,
They thanked the Lord, Jack's tail never lifted!

Jack's odyssey had started in the afternoon at three,
When he arrived at last, the sky was dark,
He'll never be a famous mount like Shergar and the like,
But on Aunt Joannie, Jack sure left his mark!

Mick Nash

Sam

I bought a little baby, I named my baby Sam,
I loved my little pup as much as any mother can,
The second day I'd loved him, Sam, he got a cough,
I rang the vet, got my coat, and we were off,
They gave my Sam some tablets,
Three days passed, the cough had gone,
I was so very happy, telling everyone,
But then came Friday morning, my little Sam so sad,
I rang the vet and rushed him down, the news was very bad,
Sam was dangerously ill, and there was no magic pill,
I took my little bundle home, but the vet again I had to phone,
The vet, she met me at the door as I took my Sam once more,
As I laid him on the table for the vet to see,
My baby Sam was dying right in front of me,
She said, 'His heart's stopped beating.'
Little Sam was dead,
My knees felt like jelly with what she had said,
My niece brought Sam back home and we both dug his grave,
And he is in my garden, his sweet memory will never fade,
My Sam was only ten weeks old, I'd had him sixteen days,
And I loved him very, very much with his playful little ways.

Ellen Chambers

Selwyn

He surveys the scene through amber eyes.
Those deep dark pools of intelligence assess the mood.
Faithful shadow, trusted confidante.
A perennial pup, master of fun and frolic.
His glossy sheen of polished jet
Ploughs across mud and mire,
Crashes through the densest growth, to fetch or find.
(No pampered lapdog this.)
With nose honed to perfection,
To sate an all-consuming hunger,
And soft velvet jowels to conceal his tools,
He's a sneak thief and dustbin raider.
Or snoring hearth rug lover,
Where toasted paws twitch in reverie.

Diane Humphreys

An Anchor Books Anthology

Rocky The Snake

Rocky the snake ended
up my only friend. My
old friends came to
see my slithering pal
in his tank of glory.
They watched him
play in his water and
stick his tongue out at
them. They watched
him eat a live cricket
and they winced.
They decided then that
they didn't like me
anymore, just because
I had a pet called
Rocky the snake.

Catrina Lawrence

Friendship

My cat can't move so has never caught a mouse,
It can't miaow or make free of the house,
But sits on my pillow without any sound,
(Although when I need it it's always around).
No purr, no fur (because it's made of felt,
Which is *always* clean - unlike the usual pelt).
Its eyes shine brightly on top of my bed
But don't change expression or ever see red.
The tail's not erect. It cannot wave about.
Curls stiffly round its body without any doubt.
So why do I keep it? It doesn't do tricks,
Or amuse our family with cute antics.
Perhaps because it was given by a friend,
Now long dead, which is why these lines were penned.

M Carr

A River Of Tears

(Dedicated to my beloved Cally)

My little dog angel - I loved you so
That I wonder why you had to go
I know at the end you heard no sounds
But your love for me still knew no bounds
Now your wagging tail - soft eyes are stilled
And there's a hole in my life which can't be filled
I reach out my hand to caress your ears
And down my face runs a river of tears
My shadow companion and faithful pal
Now you'll never know how I loved you Cal
So I must sit here alone and cry
For my little dog angel in the sky

Irene Beattie

Teddy

Is he a cat or a big teddy bear?
He lies on my bed: I know he's always there.
But one thing is certain, a definite must,
He needs to be picked up and cuddled and fussed.

A very big pussy, white slippers on feet,
He doesn't go out much, but does love to eat.
Part chinchilla, part moggie, an unusual face,
With a look so bemused with the whole human race.

He loves everybody, each kitten and cat.
He even plays 'mother' and is good at that!
He never gets angry, no hiss and no spit.
Just a pat from his paw cools them down for a bit.

His eyes are pure gold and his character too.
My beautiful Teddy, so much I love you.
A nature so gentle, so precious and rare,
With the name he lives up to, my big Teddy Bear!

T B Chadwick

Whisper

Last week my son phoned up to say,
'Please do us a favour Mum,
We're off next week on holiday
But Whisper just can't come!'

'We'd better ask your dad,' I said,
'He'll have to take her walking,
And also see that she is fed.'
'Let me do the talking!'

Well Dad's agreed so Whisper's here,
And she's settled in a treat,
Dad reaches down to scratch her ear,
She dozes at his feet.

Three times a day he takes her out,
In every kind of weather,
When they return they're both worn out,
And fall asleep together.

And so it goes from day to day,
I feel a bit neglected.
Though she's quite happy here to stay,
It seems I've been rejected.

When she goes home we'll both feel sad,
And the house won't be the same,
'But still next holiday,' says Dad,
'We can have her back again.'

'I'm going home tomorrow
Back to Mum and Dad:
I want to thank you Grandad
For the lovely time I've had.'

Margaret Doherty

Joe

You came into our garden
Looking for a home
We named you Joe
No more you were alone

You took a time to trust us
Still you stole your food
Brought it home to show us
Your gypsy blood to prove

Gradually you settled
Never to roam again
Now you never leave us
You're happy once again

Sonia Riggs

Lewis

I have a dog called Lewis
He's big, red and white
He's such a loveable softie
But guards my house at night
With his big, droopy eyes
And such an ugly face
That's enough to scare
The human race
Yes people say he's ugly
But he's beautiful to me
He's supposed to look that way
He's a boxer dog you see
Named after Lennox Lewis
Born on boxing day too
So you see, my Lewis
Is boxer through and through
He has had lots of lady friends
To many puppies he's been dad
He's a big, happy fellow
Although always looks sad
He tends to know when I'm happy
Or if I'm ill or if I'm sad
He's there by my side always
My loveable lad
Lewis is almost five now
Boxers have a lifespan of nine
So for all of his lifetime
Lewis will be mine

Heather Dunn-Fox

An Anchor Books Anthology

Dixie

A ball of fluff with nose so black,
We knew this was the pup for us.
Eyes so bright, making no fuss,
This little one was what our lives did lack.

Into the house he crept, slowly that day,
A wriggle, a squirm, a small squeaky yap.
Curiosity filled him as on wobbly legs he did sway,
Small paws, warm tongue, he sat upon my lap.

Hoping to tire him we'd go for a walk,
Dixie would run and roll in muck!
Windows wide open, we did baulk!
Could we wear Dixie out? No such luck!

Dixie so full of fun, with sticky-up ears,
Would scamper off to seek some food.
Every day he'd allay my fears,
Then play with a friend he had wooed!

Tiring us out, always on the go,
Dixie in the garden would chase cats away.
He was the most adorable dog I did know,
Gave me the greatest of affection every day.

As Dixie grew older and less bold,
His walk faltered, eyes grew dim.
Now in Heaven, warm, not cold,
Dixie rests and I remember him.

J H Russell

Walking The Dog

No matter what the weather, my dog still wants his run
Trudging through the rain and mud to him is damn good fun
He does not seem to notice freezing fog and ice
And frolicking in gale force winds he thinks is very nice
A five mile hike that leaves me exhausted to the core
Is a quick stroll to my dog who looks eagerly for more
I throw his ball a hundred times, hoping he will flag
But no such luck for every time it's me who starts to lag
I stop to rest upon a seat some kind soul has donated
And all too soon I'm made aware more action is awaited
So I drag my aching body further on uphill
While my ever active dog runs on ahead until
He finds a stretch of water where he can swim and fetch
The stick that must be thrown by this poor knackered wretch
But then as I continue on my foot-sore weary slog
I know I wouldn't be without my faithful, loving dog.

Jenny Hitchen

Our Dog Basil

Delicate and dainty is our dog
Basil,
With his coat soft and grey,
Sure-footed on our walks every single day,
With his tiny feet and a fluffy tail,
He walks everywhere,
'Basil'
Has lots of love,
Joyce and I are given a very large share,
At home it's peace and paradise,
The birdsong sounds so very nice,
But when we're not feeling well,
'Basil's' by our side,
And if by chance I drive our car,
'Basil' jumps in too,
He sits upright in his seat,
And barks!
Where are we going to?
We head to where the Isis runs,
With people everywhere,
But to our call he always comes,
And at the ducks and swans he stairs.

The Warrior Poet - Eamon John Healy

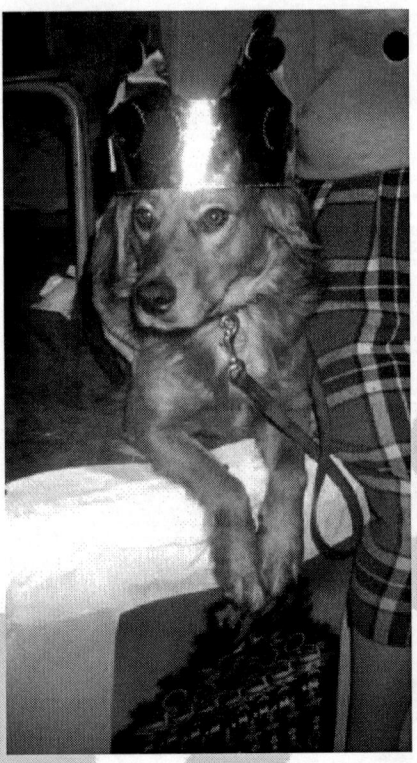

Brandy

A dog who loves music and children and travelling,
The perfect companion, at home and away,
If I play the piano, he sits there beside me,
Or under the stool he is happy to stay.

Out walking, the children all stop to admire him.
Our greeting at playgroup is always the same:
He obligingly stands, while seven small hands
Stroke him and pat him and call him by name.

The group's Christmas party's a wonderful time,
They send him an 'invite', they make him a hat
While I play the music, he watches the party games,
Then come the biscuits - he wouldn't miss that!

He's first in the car when I open the door,
The thought of a journey, a wonderful treat.
And on our arrival, my friends smile to see him -
The 'co-pilot', proudly upon the front seat!

Daphne Wilkinson

An Anchor Books Anthology

Sparky

In among the raised-bed plants,
Where thrift, her pale pink florets dance,
Where oils of thyme the air enhance,
There sleeps Sparky.

A foot or two above the ground,
What a vantage point she's found,
She surveys it all with regal frown,
There sits Sparky.

A matted nest of brown and green,
Marks the spot where she has been,
Her place of rest, her chance to dream,
There sleeps Sparky.

Eighteen out of twenty-four,
Knock how you will upon her door,
This is the feline's common law,
There sleeps Sparky.

Secure upon her man-made hill,
She always has much time to kill,
The hunt is on, the chase, the thrill,
There dreams Sparky.

A twitching whisker, restless flail,
Marks the progress of her tale,
To see it through she must prevail,
There dreams Sparky.

A furry plate of burnt sienna,
A British black, though fate could lend her,
Hue of pitch with which to blend her,
Our Miss Sparky.

The penguin picture is complete,
With white bow tie at neck replete,
Her two front legs like columns neat,
There sits Sparky.

Furry feline female form,
Silky source of queens unborn,
But just for now, it's still a yawn,
Sleep calls Sparky!

Graham K A Walker

Kitten Watching

Adora, Misty, Melody and little Tiffany
Four of the most beautiful kittens you've seen
All have their own characters, all very brave
Loving of course they are, sometimes they even sleep

Do they know their names? No, they don't
You have to go and pick them up, well, they are soft
Then they purr all innocence, 'It was not me Mum
I didn't chew her ear, it was one of the others.'

Feeding time, do I feed the cats first or the kittens?
It had better be the kittens, their claws are sharp
The others just look resigned, 'You'd better feed them
Then we can eat in peace and finish off theirs too.'

Trips to the vet's you bet, lots of them
Still the pleasure they give is wonderful
I sit all day just watching them
No, the work's not getting done, still it will be

Kitten watching.

Carole A Cleverdon

What Is It?

A white ball of fluff is all you can see
She has four legs, four feet and sixteen toes
Two big ears, a twitchy nose and lots of whiskers
And she can fit into the palm of your hand

She has razor-sharp teeth
And they love to chew
She lurks in the corners
Searching for things to scratch through

She has a pouch in her cheek
And she yawns up to half the size of her body
She knows no tricks
And her name is Sugar, she's afraid of cats

But I still love my pet . . . *hamster.*

Christopher Lesflores (13)

Guardian Angel

I kissed you goodbye on a summer's day, when all I could feel was our rain
Knowing I would never have the chance to hold my precious gift in my arms again.
I needed to take away your pain, so I placed it inside of me
Without words you told me you needed to be set free.
I no longer could watch you hurt, you handed me the lifeline to cut
It was the time for your journey to end, I gave you my heart to take with you as I lost my fragile friend.
I watched you take the steps to Heaven, your soul fly through the sun
A life together now over as our new life begun.
I know the peace that only love can bring. I've lost the shelter of my angel's wings
Can you still hear me? Do you feel the sadness my heart now sings?
Sometimes I can hold you in my dreams, I wish upon a wish you were still here
Then I feel you watching over me, I know now you're always near.
Your presence graces my earth with all the memories I still hold
Enhancing the miracle of birth in each thought, you're there like hidden gold.
I've lost my crutch but I have learned to stand on my own
You're inside me, always beside me, so I can never truly be alone.
I love you,
I will love you until the sun and the moon meet
I will love you until the stars no longer shine
I will love you yesterday, today and tomorrow
I will love you until the end of time.
I know that you are waiting for me at Heaven's gate
For the happiness to return that we had to forsake
For a time we loved and I know we'll still in a million years
And when we meet again in Heaven
My guardian angel can kiss away my tears.

Linda Ann McConnell

Wibbly And Wobbly

Wibbly, wobbly around the tank,
Why has my friend just sank?
Wobbly, wibbly upside down,
Wish I was with my girlfriend out on the town.

I'm just a boring goldfish wobbling around all day,
Eating red worms and nowhere to play,
Wibbly, wobbly from side to side,
No other place to swim except to hide.

Perhaps a couple of friends will do,
At last my owner has got me two.
I'll teach them to wobble just like me,
Then my owner can prepare my tea.

Maggie Hickinbotham

The Rhodesian Ridgeback

(Written in celebration of my first Ridgeback, Kinza Zimba Gypsy (Simba))

Throughout my life, I've loved all dogs
Although my tastes have ranged
From collies, setters, Dobermans,
Alsatians and Great Danes.
For often did I ponder
Just which breed I'd choose,
When old age claimed the faithful 'Heinz'
I'd loved for many years,
But on seeing my first Ridgeback,
All former doubts dispersed,
I cast aside all other breeds
And reached inside my purse.

I raised my pup with tenderness,
With patience and with love,
To help him grow into a dog
Which we could be proud of.
I'm pleased to say he has fulfilled
All of our simple needs,
A loving pet, a family dog,
Fine specimen of his breed.
Though he might never win at Crufts
And thereby make his fame,
To us he is a special dog;
We love him just the same.

When asked just why I chose this breed,
I try hard to explain,
How I admire their dignity,
Agility and brain.
Although it was their beauty
Which first appealed to me,
(That subtle blend of power,
And graceful symmetry)
I've come to love their loyalty,
Their sense of humour too,
Their gentle, stable temperaments,
Dependable and true.

And when others cast aspersions about our lovely breed,
I argue that the Ridgeback is superlative indeed.
I'm sure all Ridgeback owners would join me in one voice:
'Once you've owned a Ridgeback, there *is* no other choice!'

Sheila Brookes

An Anchor Books Anthology

The Great Escape

To be a pig is not much fun,
Especially when you're the only one.
Boris the boar was sick and tired
Of being stared at through the fence all wired.
He didn't want to do party tricks,
Rolling in mud or picking up sticks.
Boris had a brain you know,
He could do stuff and had places to go.
Then one day as luck would have it,
He became great friends with a friendly rabbit.
'Oh dig a hole for me to get through . . .
I'd like to be free just like you.'
'Okay pal,' the rabbit replied,
'But I'm not very big and we could be seen.'

So Boris and the rabbit did the digging at night,
Hoping this would be alright.
But while they were digging under the fence,
A fox caught wind of it and his body went tense.
He dropped down low, couldn't believe his luck,
A plump little rabbit and he'd only had duck.
He crept up close so he could see
Just how near he could get from behind his tree.

The rabbit dug as hard as he could,
But puffing and blowing, it was just no good.
The hole wasn't big enough for a pig to squeeze through,
The rabbit collapsed, no more could he do.
Oh it was so tempting to hungry fox,
To be so close to a tasty lunch box.
The rabbit was inside Boris' pen,
And the fox moved closer and began digging again.
The hole was much bigger than the rabbit had dug,
And the fox hadn't seen the pig's ugly mug.

'Oh wow!' cried Boris as he spied the large gap.
'No time now to take a nap.'
So with rabbit sitting on his back,
Boris heaved and pushed and squashed the fox flat.
'At last I'm free,' Boris the pig cried,
'I'm not waiting around to be fried.'
So the two good friends ran off together . . .
And as for the fox . . . well, he was under the weather!

Audrey Lucas

Memoirs Of Sweet Billie

There was my dog, to write about I must
To tell you she was soft to touch
She was my friend, a faithful friend
Always with me right to the end

Her name was Billie, Billie sweet
Everyone loved her when we did meet
So gentle, loving and giving
Billie got her name in Heaven

She was black and brown with hazel eyes
Floppy ears, coat so fine
She was sloppy and cuddly with a cute little snout
So Mona Lisa, eat your heart out

She followed me around from morning to night
A lost lamb but that was alright
When she was hungry she would pick up her dish
Feed me, feed me, that was her wish

Her favourite food was chocolate Smarties
She could eat them from morning to tea
Milk was a must because she drunk plenty
The milkman had to collect many empties

When we went for our walkabouts
Sometimes she'd get lost but you'd hear me shout,
'Billie, where are you? I give you ten.'
She knew ten seconds or something then

Only one problem could be found
She loved to chase bunnies on the ground
Then chasing them to their underground
She lost me deep in the wood deep down

Her punishment was to be led for a while
It was better than a smacking or getting me riled
Because if she got lost I would've missed Billie so mild
As it would take away my smiles

Her love for a ride in the car
She knew peep, peep and tat tar
Peep, peep meant car, tat tar meant walk
Where are we going? If only she could talk

So my story ends about sweet Billie
I'll put it into one, she was silly
She used to roll upright to rub her belly
So her nickname was 'Silly Billie'

Now she's gone to a great place in the sky
But her memories live on with tears in my eyes
Bluebill Wood, Billie Mountain to name but a few
Billie, sweet Billie, I do miss you

P Brewer

An Anchor Books Anthology

The Climber

Look at a cat climbing a tree
It is quite funny to see
When the bird it is after flies away
He stops his climb and seems to say,

'Was it really worth the try
For me to climb so very high
Only to lose what I came for
And see it chirping on the floor?'

So now the cat hurried down
To try and get something on the ground
No such luck in this task too
So what did the cat do?

Off indoors the cat went
Going through the cat-hole vent
Only then to get stuck fast
Then the bird chirped like a laugh.

Jean Bradbury

Little One

My little one where have you gone?
My sadness lingers on and on,
Last night I thought I heard you bark,
But it's not you and it breaks my heart.

The night I brought you home with me,
So small and gentle upon my knee,
Watching children playing in the park,
But you're not here and it breaks my heart.

The loving paws and wagging tail,
The welcome hello from snow and gales,
When I am alone and in the dark,
It's you I miss and it breaks my heart.

My little one your soul is free,
And I feel inside, once more we will be.
But until that day when I depart,
You sleep alone and it breaks my heart.

Fergus Condron

Jack

(In loving memory of my rescued Jack Russell dog. 1990 - 2003 adopted from the RSPCA 1995 - a crazy character!)

Oh Jack, I wish I had you back
But I would not like to see you suffer.
You could be so naughty, yet at other times so good!
A little dog with funny ways, sometimes misunderstood.

I'll remember you in the rustle of the leaves,
Feel you in the cool breeze.
Walk with your memory on sunlit days, like these.

Swallowing the lump in my throat,
I'll think of you and smile.
I won't let my heart fill with pain.
I know you'll wait for me, until the day we meet again.

N J Brocks

Miaow

(For Mum)

How I love the temperament of the domestic cat
Lazing in the sun and getting fat
The common moggy in regal attire
Cosy nights purring by the fire

Around the world they're renowned
Miaow, miaow, what a heavenly sound
Egyptian magic and witchcraft lore
Persecuted and friends in war

They have the elegance of the all-seeing eyes
Into the night you can hear their cries
Kitty litter a humble abode
They strut the catwalk with their own little code

This is to the cat as it unravels the wool
Eating the fish until it is full
Lapping the cream, the cat's whiskers
Painting the roof tiles, miaow little sisters

Richard Appleyard

An Anchor Books Anthology

The Welcome

Who is this weary warrior
Limping up our pathway?
Who but Pussy all bedraggled
With a paw the size of two!
After amorous adventures
Fighting for some beauteous queen,
Sure he's the most disgraceful-looking
Cat I've ever seen!
With his scratched-up ears and eyes and nose
He's the most piteous sight!
There's nothing I'm more certain of
Than that Puss lost the fight.
Though I call him names and scold him
For the lust that makes him roam,
In my heart I'm thrilled, rejoicing
That my cat found his way home.
What of it if he's dirtier
Than any alleycat?
What matters his appearance?
Won't I soon take care of that?
My prodigal is back! I'm sure
As angels do, I feel,
When repentant sinners turn to God
And bells in Heaven peal.
And shall the God of love not welcome
The sorriest wanderer that
Returns to Him repenting
As I welcome this cat?

V M Archer

Basil

Basil, you were once a kitten all those years ago,
Playing by the fire with your toys, you know.
Your best friend was Chloe, a fine cat she is,
You would sit and purr together, eat and sleep, what bliss.

Then you both got older, your friendship stayed the same,
You'd sit, sleep, play together, but there was much less game.
But we could tell you were happy, your glossy coats would shine,
You'd sit and purr by the fire, you were both just fine.

Then yet again you got older, we grew older too,
We then appreciated how much we all loved you.
You've always been such nice cats, never scratch or bite,
And no sitting on our heads when we slept all through the night.

You were a pleasure keeping, we'd never let you go,
And how much joy you gave us you will never know.
When you were sleeping or sitting by our sides,
Or when we put you in our prams and gave you little rides.

Then you were old ladies, you were still both friends,
You would stick together to the very end.
Chloe became poorly, the worst we feared for her,
But then she got well again, we thought you'd both last forever.

But we were wrong cause you got ill, you just went downhill,
We tried so hard to cure you but you were just too ill.
Then the time came, you had started to suffer, something had to be done,
So we had to let you go, we were all so sad and glum.

We couldn't keep you forever, how foolish we had been,
Maybe if we noticed sooner you could still be seen.
But we still love you even though you're gone,
And we know you're in Heaven 'cause it's where you belong.

Thank you Basil, we owe you 3 cheers,
And we will never forget those cherished years.

Gemma White (14)

An Anchor Books Anthology

The Blackfoot Tribe

The weather's bad, there has been rain,
The blackfoot tribe are here again.
Along the working surface, all over my nice clean floors,
Are marks of little footprints from garden-muddied paws.
The tribe don't like bad weather, they certainly hate the rain,
No sooner do they go out than they're back inside again!
To be houseproud is impossible with the blackfoot tribe about,
I cannot reprimand them, they'd ignore me I've no doubt.
Well I don't mind those footprints, it's very plain to see,
That I adore the culprits and they walk all over me.

J A Berisha

Adieu

He's getting too big for his paws
Thank heavens his feet not his claws
He skips me, outruns me, leaves me to pant
I feel such a fool as I stand there and rant
Just wait till I get you indoors
(You're getting too big for your paws)

He's getting too big for his feet
So often I'm knocked off my beat
He trips me, out-jumps me, he's king and I'm knave
I feel such a fool as I stand there and rave
That's it, you can beg for your meat
(You're getting too big for your feet)

He's getting too big for my heart
From the moment you get one it starts
He jumps you, he loves you, slobbers so glad
I feel such a fool for pretending I'm mad
But no way can my dog and we part
(He's getting too big for our hearts)

Too soon it was time that he went
This small gift of life we were sent
Despite the best efforts of man
He turned towards Heaven and ran
Now I know that God sits on His throne
And he's there with Him, gnawing a bone
Sat puzzling the tears that we cry
(Was Adieu that he barked . . . not goodbye)

M J Banasko

Goodbye Tig

Little black pup,
Just six weeks old,
One look at you,
My heart was sold.

You brought no baggage,
Just your trust,
There forever,
Good life, a must.

Plenty of time,
Of being together,
Running and walking,
You leaving me, never!

Twelve years passed,
I loved you true,
Now spend my days,
Missing you.

But must keep going,
Must reach the ridge,
So wait dear Tig,
At Rainbow Bridge.

Shirley Chapman

Morning Walk

Time for 'walkies', off we go,
Whether there's hail or rain or snow,
Glad to be out in the pure fresh air,
I'm richer than a millionaire.

I don't know what I should do,
Without your little furry face,
And the sight of your wagging tail,
As you busily run from place to place.

I love the sound of your eager bark,
I love the question in your eyes,
You speak to me so eloquently,
And what you say is no surprise.

Time for 'walkies', off we go,
No matter if the winds do blow,
I wonder if you'll ever know,
Just how much I love you so?

Rosanna J Freeman

An Anchor Books Anthology

Kit-E-Kat Cats

We are two hungry cats
Who like our food in jelly;
It is so very tasty
We've seen it on the telly.

We love this food
Upon our plate;
It is so very good
We're never home late.

When we eat our Kit-E-Kat
We are contented cats;
It fills up our tummy,
We find it very yummy.

Kit-E-Kat is wonderful
Kit-E-Kat is great;
We think that every cat
Should have some on their plate.

Linda Finch

My Dog Mickey

I used to look along the road as I cycled home each night,
It could be a dark sky or filled with sun so bright,
As I turned the corner I knew Mickey would be there,
His nose pressed to the window while standing on a chair,
It did not seem to matter if it was wet or fine, windy or falling rain,
There was the outline of my dog looking through the windowpane,
He seemed to know at six o'clock I would be on my way,
Coming home from working on the farm all day,
When I came into sight his tail would wag so fast,
He seemed to be saying, 'My master is coming home at last,'
I would go up the pathway and open up the wooden door,
All at once I was nearly knocked down on the kitchen floor,
It was so nice to know there was someone pleased to see,
A man coming home from work as tired as could be,
There was only one happy loving dog for me at that time of life,
He came next in my thoughts after my family and my wife,
I knew someday he must leave us, then came that awful day,
But I thank the Lord for the dog that loved me in that way.

Stan Gilbert

My Pet Duck

I had this beautiful large duck, her name was Daisy
When I took her to the pond I soon found out she was lazy
Then I admitted to my wife I was looking at total defeat
This large bird just did not like stone-cold water upon her feet

Then I took her to Slimbridge for the experts to find out why
Why my duck Daisy did not like swimming, she just wanted to stay dry
Then the clever experts said, 'My friend you have made a big mistake.'
They said this waterfowl was not a duck, they said he was a drake

Then I had to rename him Ben, he just loved to visit the local stable
Then one afternoon my duck Ben was missing, I found him on a poacher table
I sobbed bitterly about Ben's demise, his passing hit me so very hard
Then I found him swimming so beautifully in a pool of lard

This was the end of Ben the drake, he was so cut up and eaten
Then, I am so sad to say, Ben's fear of swimming was sadly beaten
His large snow-white feathers were the filling in a pillow-like sack
The pain was so great, I would give everything just to have Ben back

J F Grainger

An Anchor Books Anthology

A Feline Friend

He was promised to me before he was born, so I waited the allotted time
Strong enough to leave his mother before I could call him mine
Small and soft with fluffy black hair, I could hold him in my hand
He liked to curl up in my lap, I could not him reprimand

What should I name him? I was not sure, his character had not unfolded
But it wasn't too long before I found out my peaceful life suddenly exploded
So I gave him the name Periwinkle, it seemed to be just right
For my face with laughter would crinkle at the antics of this bundle of life

In the house we had a young baby, Periwinkle expected the same care
Instead of searching around for a mouse, when we tended to Baby, he was there
One day I found him in the baby's pram, fast asleep, side by side
Companions, they looked so sweet, Periwinkle I could not chide

He would climb upon the window sill, in a bowl we kept a spare dummy
He would run about with the thing in his mouth, he looked so very funny
Then the dummy he would drop on the floor, with his paws push it from side to side
Almost expecting it to run out of the door or scuttle away to hide

Periwinkle and the baby grew together, each with their own special charm
When Baby sat in a high chair, Periwinkle sat on the arm
He waited patiently for his time to eat, didn't mind the wait
But as soon as Baby was out of the chair, Periwinkle ate the food left on the plate

Then he got adventurous, beyond the garden would go
Exploring places far distant, places we did not know
One night he did not come home, we thought it was a pussy cat's way
But the next day he didn't appear, our hearts were filled with dismay

We later discovered he had been killed by a speeding car on a bend
Our sorrow could not be contained at the loss of this adorable, loved friend
We miss the pitter-patter of his feet on the kitchen floor, his
impatient scratching at the back door
Our house will never be the same without the little friend
who gave us his love and more.

R Curryer

Pussy Cat

Go cat. Go and get it now
Knock over the vases and give me a miaow
Sprinkle the carpet and scratch all the floor
Make a loud noise 'til she opens the door

Pull all her wool and make a real mess
Leave it untidy and she'll never guess
Lie on the bed and make out you're asleep
When she comes in, take a wee peep

See if she's angry or just simply mad
I am not naughty. I am real bad
I'll hide in the cupboard and snuggle up fast
Hoping quite soon that the moment will pass

And maybe time later when she has calmed down
I'll wander for food and I'll wander to town
Until she's cooled her mood, I'll keep out her way
And maybe tomorrow I'll find wool to play

All over the house I'll wind it around
When she's asleep and not making a sound
'Cause she'll never hear me. I'll make sure of that
After all, what am I? I'm only a cat.

V J Haynes

Looking For Fudgie

I searched for a pair of eyes
Once upon a time.
They had to be loving and they
Had to melt mine.

And there they were
One day behind glass,
Looking at me
Not daring to ask.

They said, 'Take me home
I'll be yours forever.
Just give me love
And a bed I'll treasure.'

How could I resist?
And what joy you've brought,
Your unconditional heart
Gave me all that I sought.

Sharon Grimer

An Anchor Books Anthology

Past Pets

Inky was as black as coal
Fluffy was white as snow
Adventure was Inky's goal
Fluffy was in the know

Inky liked to go out
Fluffy stuck close to the house
Inky had to be given a shout
Fluffy would play with a mouse

Inky let the kids
Ride on his back
He didn't mind the bids
He had a knack

Fluffy was a lot of fun
Had the kids on the run
His only intent
Was to be content

Inky was first to die
We all had a good cry
Fluffy was next to go
Left us all full of woe

Inky and Fluffy were our best friends
We all lived together until the end
Our memories remain alive
All the joys we felt inside

I wish they could have survived
To see the way we've grown and thrived
Alas, that cannot be
They're up in Heaven, roaming free

Pat Hunter

Telepathy

Watching Crufts obedience tests on TV
A thought suddenly occurred to me
When the presenter said, 'Dogs seem to know
Instinctively what's up and where to go.'

I wondered, *could this be telepathy?*
So I would try it out on Jack to see
While I was working, he was fast asleep
Stretched out on the floor, down by my feet

I thought before I go to watch TV
The dogs had better go for a quick wee
As I thought this, Jack got up from the floor
Shook himself, then walked over to the door!

Valerie Ovais

Scamp

One morning it was damp
A neighbour brought over
A little black dog called Scamp
He needed a home
He was all alone
My brother and I got down on our knees
And said to our parents, 'Please
Can we have Scamp? Please, please, please?'
Our mum looked at our faces
And with a grin
She gave in and said yes,
We were delighted
Our pup, Scamp,
Our loveable little tramp,
He grew up with us into a fine dog.
We loved him so much
He lived for years
A nice and friendly pet
When he died we cried and did not forget
We buried Scamp
With his little red collar he came in
God bless Scamp, our first dog
Our special friend right to the end.

Caroline Janney

Measure The Cat, Or Kittenish!

Playfully bent, sure looking sunny,
Not quite like a cuddly bunny,
But if only a pussy galore,
Even just for the folk-lore.

Cats' eyes are so earnest and serene,
No plain stuff, evenly pitched for screen,
Neither apt, with fur wraps,
Nor rapacious perhaps?

Often glamorous,
Never timorous,
Playful certainly,
Carefree, fancy free.

With vibrant glaring eyes,
Added to miaowing cries -
Causes sit-come onto picture,
Without deference to change on fixture.

Cats cautious curiosity on predatory acts,
Leads terror on mice, and birds - mere facts
Even crossing the road, without code -
So impervious to danger with seeing bode.

Then all to perceive in the dark,
No sound, compare that bark,
It is 'purr with fur',
But not the slightest murmur!

No alternative woollen ball
Finding string on the call,
Same as some lionised creature,
With plethora of moves, staying pure.

        . . . as a pussy cat!

N Lemel

A Dog's Life

They get up in the morning and I jump from my bed,
I look at them with big brown eyes, and to the door I'm led.
I know it's time for wee wees, but all I want is food,
I guess I'll have to wait a while as Mother's in a mood.
I spot a lamp post over the road, so I cock my leg,
When back at home for my food, I guess I'll have to beg.
Then I fetch the paper, and her slippers too,
That's just a few of the things a dog is supposed to do.
Now I'm off to bark at my empty dish,
If it was only full up, that's what I really wish.
She's walking down the stairs now, and in a better mood,
Thank God for that, I tell myself, now perhaps I'll get some food.

Mandy Jayne Moon

Starting Over

My lovely dog, she suddenly died
My eyes were swollen, I cried and cried
Then the phone went, a voice on the line
Saying, 'Could you please help? We've not got much time
For I have a pup in need of a home
Her owner was cruel and she has nowhere to go.'
So I agreed again to start
To help this pup and heal my heart
So I put out my arms and welcomed you here
I built up your trust, I helped chase the fear
And you soon felt secure and started to be
A normal puppy, happy, carefree
And full of mischief no matter where you went
You chewed my shoes, you pulled clothes off the line
You sneaked to my room and made it yours and mine
You barked at the postman, you chased the cat
You lay on the sofa, you chewed the mat
But the love you gave for all your mishaps
More than made up when you sat on my lap
And I'm so glad that I'd agree
To let you come here, you mean the world to me.

Monica McNamee

An Anchor Books Anthology

My Pet

(For our grandchildren)

I asked my grandad for a pet as my birthday treat,
My gift arrived in a cage, all I heard was a 'tweet'!
It resembled a baby chic, a tiny ball of fluff,
A budgerigar it was, it sounded rather rough,
He was very bashful and could hardly fly,
When I cupped him in my hand he did sit and sigh.

I gave him plenty of TLC and talked to him each day,
'Billy' was his new name, this he soon did say!
Turned out to be a handsome bird, colours of yellow and green,
When not amusing everyone, his feathers he would preen,
When I lay down on the floor, he swoops to play with me,
Cover up you cup or glass, he'll drink your 'pop' or 'tea'.

He's a real comical chap, when you put him on his bath,
Shouting to hear the echo, making us all laugh,
Turn on the radio, to pop music he does dance,
But if the soaps are on TV, to hear them you have no chance,
We put a cover over his cage to try and calm him do,
He peeps out from underneath and plays peek-a-boo!

Billy is now in his prime, his vocabulary is vast,
Name, address and phone number he has learnt so fast,
Nursery rhymes and bingo numbers, he recites them all,
Put toys on his cage, he'll throw off and watch them fall,
Try to ignore him to get your homework done,
He promptly takes the pen away, to him a game of fun.

He rises with the dawn chorus and chatters till late at night,
'Good morning, nice day,' he says, as soon as it is light,
He tells you not to swear, then *comments* on wet weather!
Sometimes he gets confused, and mixes his verses together,
A conversation you can have, and never will get bored,
Being such a 'little' fellow makes me wonder where it's stored.

Glenice Siddall

My Dear Faithful Friend

The bright brown eyes which gaze into mine
  Are filled with a love that is almost divine,
They read my thoughts e'en as they are born,
  And they uplift my spirit when I feel forlorn,
When I am unhappy she makes me feel glad,
  Nuzzles my hand when my heart's heavy and sad,
She shares sorrow with me - helps calm my fears,
  She has been my faithful companion for many years,
She asks me for nothing, yet gives me her all,
  Remaining steadfast forever, whate'er may befall,
And I know she'll be with me right to the end,
  My trusting and loving, dearest loyal friend
My dog is growing old now, but then so am I,
  We both know that soon we will say goodbye,
But in some afterlife, still together we'll be -
  She'll be there behind the door, waiting for me.

F R Smith

Spider

I watched the tiny spider carefully weave a web
The only weapon that it had, for sustenance and bed
This would be its little home, flies had best beware!
Weaved in and out so intricately; this had to be its lair.

Flies have wings, they could flutter anywhere they like
Spiders depend on their skill, and little time to fight
So they would weave so cautiously, a trap to catch a fly
It would have its food today, or know the reason why.

Flies would fly so teasingly everywhere they might
Spiders hiding beneath the leaves, secure until the night
They would weave their hidden web, to catch a careless fly
Flies might flutter on their way and narrowly pass by.

The spider waited patiently for the web to quiver
A sign to say the fly was caught, now to have its dinner
The moral of this story is - don't fly too near the web
Head for open spaces, for all too soon you're dead.

Nature often seems to me, very cruel at times
Survival of the fittest, I often call to mind
Yet even for the fittest, life still comes to a halt
When we're getting older it's then we get a jolt!

Joan Prentice

An Anchor Books Anthology

The Sheepdog's Day

Morning has come to this small glen
I'm a collie dog whose name is Ben
Sleepy, I wake from a cosy makeshift den
Off to work I go to round up the sheep into their pen.

Now as the day's ongoing we go to collect last year's marrows
Sitting in an old squeaky, rusty barrow
As we approached, sighted was a rabbit's burrow
Youngsters eating the marrows that were for sale tomorrow.

Over the dale is the farmer's daughter
She had manners that you could not falter
And walking out with a man called Walter
Looking so sweet, he comes out all of a swelter.

Playing his cherished music from the bassoon
Melts the heart and makes her swoon
Arms round each other, so much in love, wrapped in a cocoon
They kissed longingly by the bright light of the moon.

Sizzling on the family's barbecue are sausages and meat
My master standing over the meal beside the intensifying heat
Loving children running races with each other and being beat
All the fault of our next door's brother who is a cheat.

On the swing is Jim, he just loves being idle
Polishing up the hunting horse's bridle
On the lawn, friends also standing in a circle, talking by the middle
By now they all turned themselves and started to giggle.

I fell flat on my face by not seeing the chair's caster
Gone to the hospital and now in full plaster
Looking at me, I saw the people that love me full of affection
At the agony of this terrible poor affliction.

Thank goodness the close of the day is ahead
It's been too much excitement for this pure thoroughbred
Wouldn't you agree if you had a sore head
That this little collie dog needs his cosy bed?

Jan Ross

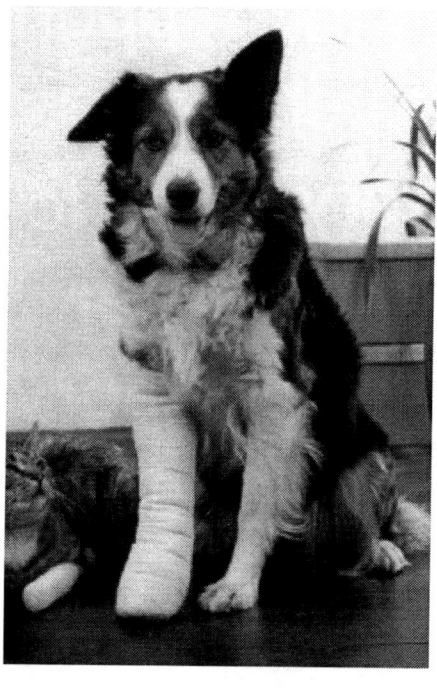

Bachelor Pad

When I went to bed
Sooty sat on my pillow
Purring happily,
And Spot lay at the bed-end
Snoring noisily
As I settled down to sleep
In contented, blissful ease.

But my sleep was brief!
While Sooty snuggled closer
And lay on my face,
Spot decided he could rest
In greater comfort
Lying like a ten-tonne weight
Heavily across my legs!

So next day I went
Into the local pet shop,
And hopefully bought
One large and one small basket
And some soft blankets,
So that my demanding pets
Might rest in their beds,
And leave me at peace in mine,
In our own bachelor pad!

Dan Pugh

A Loyal Pal

Your tail made smudges on the wall,
You often did not come when we would call,
You loved to scratch amongst the flowers,
Roll in the wet grass after stormy showers,
Sometimes you scratched on the floor,
There's a collar you never wore,
Your raggy doll is tattered and torn,
Old bones decay where they got buried,
Sticks now left that once you carried,
No bark of welcome for anyone,
But dear Tess, you were lots of fun,
The time came for you to depart,
You had a kind, loving heart,
In Heaven with other dogs you race,
Here on Earth, no one takes your place.

Margaret Upson

An Anchor Books Anthology

A Hunter's Greed

Deep in the jungle sleeps an elephant called Ader
She's just given birth to a son called Saber
Playing around with his mother, she feels frail
His dad, Reno, tells him off with a deafening wail
After waking up, Saber takes hold of his mother's tail
Then all three make their way onto the elephant's trail.

Walking through the night, then settling down to rest
By a waterhole right next to an old eagle's nest
They drink for a while and rest their tired, aching feet
Then all three snuggle up for a well-earned sleep
In the morning when they wake, it's time to eat, time to eat
Then a long, long bath to get out of the stifling heat.

Suddenly there's gunfire, Saber's parents are shot dead
Both of them lay silent, took bullets to the head
Saber, so scared, stands alone under a tree
He hears one of the killers shout, 'I'm sure there were three.'
He has no choice, the situation he has to address
And leaves his parents behind in a bloody mess.

After a few days, Saber died, his body got weak
Hunger killed him, he had no energy to eat
His folks were gunned down for their tusks, can you believe?
That Saber died alone in his sleep under a tree
In a couple of days all that was left was a carcass
Vultures ripped it apart to feed on the meat
Deep in the jungle lies the bones of Saber
The baby elephant
Whose parents were killed for a hunter's greed.

Stephen A Owen

Jack Russell Of The Rovers

I had a dog who, on a good day, would be worth millions to the FA,
Bobbing and weaving, trying to stall, my Jack Russell, Holly, was a wizard with a ball.

I could not get the football from her, I tried all I could.
Although her sense of direction was not very good.

She was so full of enthusiasm, bouncing, dribbling low.
Little legs running fast, dodging to and fro.

She would have been an asset to any team with her fast and furious feet.
She would not cost a team millions, just a daily tin of meat.

T A Napper

The Best of Animal Antics

369

Our Dog Kip

Kip was the name of our dog
To take him for a walk was a slog
He wouldn't come when you call
He wouldn't even fetch his ball
He didn't know the word heel
But we loved him still
If you didn't give him a chew
He would sit there and bark at you
Yes, he would growl and bark
But we knew he was having a lark
And when we gave him a bath
We always had a good laugh
Because he wasn't very fat
He would come out looking like a drowned rat
He hated cats
When he saw one it would drive him bats
He was a little terror
But to us he was a lovely fella.

Richard Trowbridge

Mitzi

A bundle of fur and eyes of blue
That was Mitzi when she was new
A loveable kitten, a joy to hold
Little Mitzi - 3 months old
Soon into a cat she grew
With bright green eyes instead of blue
So sleek of fur and haughty air
Her charisma beyond compare
Her haughty air belied the fact
That Mitzi was a friendly cat
She played with wool and balls of string
Very playful with anything
Mealtimes she was always cool
Showing she was no one's fool
Purring madly as if to say,
'I love you so much more today.'
Meal times over, face made clean
Then into a peaceful dream
Darling Mitzi, my dear friend
Always faithful to the end.

E Timmins

Beau Jeste

(Written for my daughter and her pony who came to her when she was 9 years old. She's now 21 and they are still the best of pals. No greater love than that of horse and master)

Beau so bold and handsome, but sometimes oh so bad
But how could I be cross with him, this precious gift from Dad?
We'd practise at our jumping, he seemed to know it all
He'd never stumble or refuse and he'd never let me fall
Some people did not like him, they thought him wild with spite
They didn't know that he'd been hurt, this horse I loved with all my might
The love I showered on him, at last gave back reward
He'd jump o'er old car tyres, and leap o'er old floorboards
We seemed to have a common bond, somehow we seemed to gel
With pride and joy I'd ride my boy, with love my heart would swell
He'd play me up, be naughty, but knew I'd understand
When given treats and polos he loved to lick my hand
But now my pal is older and just enjoys his time
No more shows or jumping, just grazing so sublime
Still sometimes he will run away and wait till I get near
Then gallop away as if to say, 'Chase me Mum, I'm here.'
But when he sees I've had enough and my patience wearing thin
He'll amble up and nudge me, then nibble me on my chin
He's always been my pal and friend, he's shared my tears and joy
And even though now we're both adults, he'll always be Mum's boy

A Tully

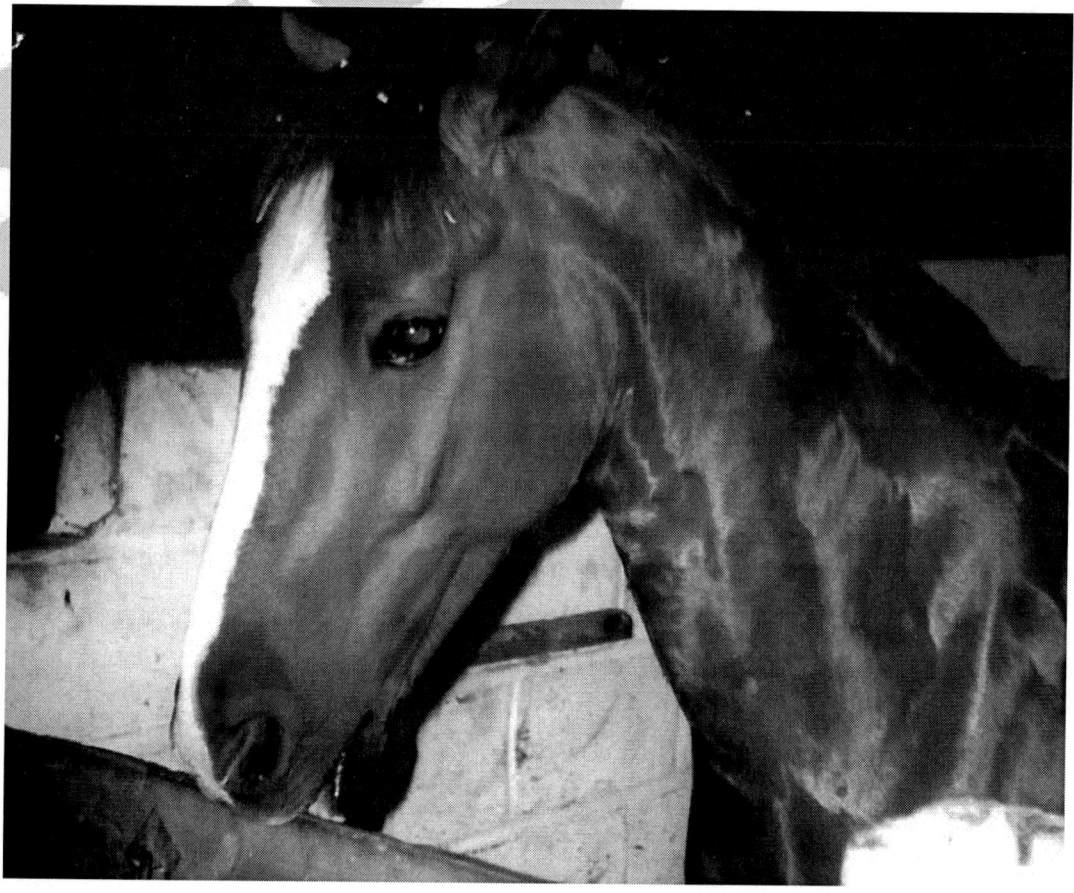

Worthwhile

A ball of fur, a waggly tail,
So many times we rant and rail.
Puddles to mop up, floors to be cleaned,
Muddy paws off the carpet is oft-times screamed.
Cushions we once had are now not there,
Only feathers and flock floating in the air.
Pieces of slippers strewn around,
In each corner buried bones are found.
Dogging our footsteps, under our feet,
Oh for the quietness of peace so sweet.
In love and war all is fair,
Losing the battle we resign in despair.
Head on one side, eyes cocked doggy style,
Two liquid brown eyes our hearts beguile.
Wee wet nose, lolling pink tongue,
Who can resist? Our swan song is sung.
One wet lick melts away all care,
After all, housework is always there.
With friendship and devotion we are repaid,
Right to the end his love never failed.

G Semmens

Beak

I've se'n the sunset stalking
O'er this fair Solway land,
For it paints the Firth as bleeding
Like a crimson haemorrhage on sand;

And in this twilight thus descending
Do the starlings murmur forth in shoals,
For the sparrow-hawk is sharking
'Neath the sun's weakening red coal;

Yet, enthron'd upon mine gable
Sits the Beak who's short a leg,
A seagull most familiar
Whose friendship I have fed;

Alas, his chorus is most inferior
Compar'd to the warbler's liquid note,
Yet his companionship is most faithful
At meal-times when he dotes;

So I'll watch this Cumbrian evening
Stretch forth its burnish'd hand,
Whilst the Firth as liquid diamonds
Bejewels the margins of the land.

M Dixon

An Anchor Books Anthology

Larry, Curly And Mo

Three little goldfish won at the fair,
Settled in a pond, had plenty of fresh air.
Tiny little bodies, good appetite,
Opened their mouths from morning 'til night.

At the bottom of our garden, a joy to see,
Happy and contented, lively and free.
Fed by all the family they started to grow,
Longer and longer - all in a row.

Then our family moved to a new pad,
Larry, Curly and Mo were sad.
Yet we couldn't leave them behind, oh no,
Part of our family - away we go.

They adjusted to the garden in a new home-made pond,
Delighted to swim in freedom, never uttered a sound.
Golden in colour, substantial in size,
Contented goldfish and certainly wise.

For fourteen years they swam together,
Grew bigger and stronger, didn't mind the weather.
In sleet and snow they survived each season,
Awaiting summertime, an incentive reason.

But sadly, one day, floating on top,
Larry, the biggest, did a belly-flop.
Lifeless was Curly, although huge in size,
Then Mo, a total of three, died before our eyes.

B Thomas

Puppy's Return

Well, our trip was great, Mum, we had a good time,
We walked and we swam, and the weather was fine.
We saw the red squirrels, I got used to those sheep,
After a long day's hiking I was soon fast asleep.

The hotel was just right and I made lots of friends,
Though sadly our break had to come to an end.
But when we got home, Mum, we had such a fright . . .
Had to rush to the vet in the dead of night!

How I'd caught kennel cough, Heaven knows,
After having those nasty drops up my nose!
But now I'm much better, my tail's found its wag,
Though I can't see my friend and it's such a drag!

J Munro

Two Strays Who Stayed

Forty years ago, Cindy strayed my way,
lost and all alone.
She's not pretty or furry, cuddly or cute,
but happily made this her home.

She pushes aside anything in her path
as she strolls around her domain.
She's proud and strong
but runs and hides if it begins to rain.

She's scaly and fast as tortoises go.
Her character is immense.
She can climb with great ease, up steps and down banks
and will try to dig under the fence.

Then came Sebastian, walking down the road.
He was another stray.
Escaping death as cars passed close,
he also came to stay.

Sebastian is timid, gentle and shy.
If tortoises can be cute then that's he.
Slowly eating cabbage, his favourite food,
and trusting of all he does see.

The two spend their summers on the grass,
lettuce, cabbage and fruit to eat.
They sunbathe and climb, sleep and dine
until winter frosts tell them to sleep.

Then into their boxes they go until spring,
sensibly sleeping in comfort and warmth.
Snug in their nests, dreaming of summers ahead
and lazing on the lawn.

Sue Tobin

An Anchor Books Anthology

What Is A Dog?

What is a dog? Just meat, skin and bone,
Damp more than dry, when you first get him home.
Gets under your feet, makes the mats fly -
He's here, he's there, then goes dashing by.
Leaves rubber ball lying right in your track -
You come along later - skid flat on your back.
He needs to be exercised, watered and fed,
Still wants that walk when it's my time for bed.
Everything now revolves around this pet,
There's brushing and combing and trips to the vet.
Bathing's a struggle, he's grown such a size,
Then I'm wetter than he is, oh help, was it wise?
When he nips at your arm, playing a bit rough -
You find yourself saying, 'Enough is enough.'

What is a dog? A loyal friend you will find,
Knows every thought that goes on in your mind.
He doesn't care if you are bald, thin or fat,
Loves and adores you in spite of all that.
He is your second shadow throughout the day long,
Still by your side when all others have gone.
Obedient and following your every whim -
No one will hurt you while you have him.
When night descends and the curtains are drawn,
And only the cats are still out on the lawn,
He will sigh and roll over - lay his head on your feet,
Closing brown eyes, tell you his pleasure's complete.
When he finally goes where all good dogs go,
And you miss him each moment for sadly you know,
Through field, wood or lane, he'll never again jog,
You will find yourself saying, 'Now *that* was a dog.'

Kathleen Stokes

The Instinct

He knew it would happen soon.
Today.
He felt it deep in those old bones.
An excitement, a trembling,
an instinct that he recognised.
It had been there almost from the moment he had slithered,
bewildered and startled,
into the outside world.
He knew the stillness.
He'd felt it, almost every one of his twenty-five years.
Here it was again,
running down into every drop of his Welsh blood.
Human eyes questioned the behaviour.
The pounding of the neat hooves,
embossing the same prints over and over.
Up and down the fences.
Then halting on the hill, nostrils flared,
chiselled head raised to greet the elements.
Then away again, snorting, a pawing of the ground,
tail raised and flowing like a myriad flying streamers.
Listen . . . not a sound now . . . not one bird singing.
Not one stirring from the tiniest creature.
Not one pirouette or gay ballet from fallen leaves.
Look! On the hill! He's there! Legs taught and spread.
Noble statue, save the lifting of long native mane,
eyes black . . . staring . . . bright . . . watching . . . waiting . . .
then it came,
the snow.

Anna Shannon

An Anchor Books Anthology

My Best Friend

Jack lays under the table
That's where he likes to lay
His old tail starts to wag
When I shout, 'Let's go out to play.'

He hears the rustle of the chain
And he rushes to the door
He sees the Bonios go in my pocket
But he has seen it all before

I open the door to take him out
And take him for his walk
I give him one of his Bonios
And he would thank me if he could talk

Jack, the best friend I have got
He will never let me down
He lays there sad and lonely
When I go into town

He soon bucks up when I get back
He is his old self once again
And his old tail starts to wag once more
When he sees me coming through that old street door

Bert Booley

Anchor Books Information

Anchor Books was set up in 1992 and has firmly established itself as the people's poetry imprint. It aims to publish poetry which is sincere, uncomplicated and a pleasure to read. Almost all of Anchor Books' material is traditional, rhyming poetry, which is suitable for all the family to read.

Anchor Books poets come from all kinds of backgrounds, and cover a wide age range. The subjects on which they write reflect everyday life. They tell stories, share anecdotes, marvel at the beauty of the world around us, and offer hope and inspiration in times of need.

The anthologies published by Anchor Books give these poets a welcome chance to see their poetry in print alongside the contributions of others.

Animal Antics - Your Poems About Pets Could Win You £1,000

Calling all pet lovers! Send us an animal poem accompanied with a photograph to be considered for a forthcoming animal antics collection.

Pets come in all shapes and sizes, but they all have one thing in common - with plenty of love and dedication they can truly become our faithful companions.

We are looking for animal poems to express your love for animals - whether dog, cat, horse or budgie! They could be poems about their antics, habits or why they mean so much to you.

So why not show your love for your pet - cute, cuddly, furry or feathery - by sending your pet poems and photos in for all to enjoy. (Please note photographs will be printed in black & white.)

Submission Guidelines

A maximum of 2 pet poems and of no more than 30 lines in length each, will be considered with a photograph of your pet. The address to send your animal poem(s) and photo(s) to is: Animal Antics, Forward Press Ltd, Remus House, Coltsfoot Drive, Peterborough PE2 9JX

Please remember to write your name and address on each piece of work and photo you send.

Alternatively, you can email your pet poem and photo to: inbox@forwardpress.co.uk (Please include your name and postal address.)